Chinese Trade

There's no question, compared to the advanced economies China's economic growth rates have been spectacular, but in most instances the economic analysts tend to forget that a large part of China's growth has been dictated by government industrial subsidies. How did China go from a bit player overnight to the largest exporter in the world in capital-intensive industries?

This book shows that government subsidies play a big part in China's success. Government subsidies include those to basic industries: energy (coal, electricity, natural gas and heavy oil), steel, glass, paper, auto parts, solar and more. A lot has been written about China's trade practices with the West, but none of this work addresses the real unsustainable dilemma. Much of the current literature discusses the problems but doesn't explain the root cause of China's lopsided trade practices with the West or explain in detail how China finances its government subsidies, with nothing written that explains that China's subsidized exports to the United States and European Union are basically self-funded by its enormous trade surplus with the West. A trade surplus represents a net inflow of domestic currency from foreign markets and is the opposite of a trade deficit, which would represent a net outflow. Moreover, this is the only book that describes China's current trade practices with the West as a zero sum game at the expense of the West.

This book provides two solutions to this endless quagmire: an increase in Western exports to China so that China and the West have more of an equal trade balance, or a very steep reduction of China's exports to the West.

Rich Marino is the former Senior Vice-President of Morgan Stanley, USA. After leaving Morgan Stanley, he completed an MSc (Research) in Economic History at the London School of Economics, UK, and he became an established economics author, publishing *Submerging Markets* (2013) and *The Future BRICS* (2015).

Routledge Studies in the Modern World Economy

For more information about this series, please visit https://www.routledge.com/Routledge-Studies-in-the-Modern-World-Economy/book-series/SE0432

Chinese Trade

Trade Deficits, State Subsidies and the Rise of China

Rich Marino

Routledge
Taylor & Francis Group

LONDON AND NEW YORK

First published 2019
by Routledge
2 Park Square, Milton Park, Abingdon, Oxon OX14 4RN

and by Routledge
52 Vanderbilt Avenue, New York, NY 10017

First issued in paperback 2020

Routledge is an imprint of the Taylor & Francis Group, an informa business

British Library Cataloguing-in-Publication Data
A catalogue record for this book is available from the British Library

Library of Congress Cataloging-in-Publication Data
Names: Marino, Rich, 1954- author.
Title: Chinese trade : trade deficits, state subsidies and the rise of China / Richard Marino.
Description: Abingdon, Oxon ; New York, NY : Routledge, 2019. | Series: Routledge studies in the modern world economy ; 178 | Includes bibliographical references and index.
Identifiers: LCCN 2018014079| ISBN 9781138488625 (hardback) | ISBN 9781351039826 (ebook)
Subjects: LCSH: China—Commercial policy. | China—Foreign economic relations. | China—Economic policy. | Subsidies—China. | Balance of trade—China.
Classification: LCC HF3836.5 .M37 2019 | DDC 382.0951—dc23
LC record available at https://lccn.loc.gov/2018014079

ISBN 13: 978-0-367-58783-3 (pbk)
ISBN 13: 978-1-138-48862-5 (hbk)

Typeset in Goudy
by Swales & Willis Ltd, Exeter, Devon, UK

Contents

Acknowledgements

Without question, no project can reach its final stage without the input and advice of others. In that regard, I would also like to thank all of the fine people at the Julis-Rabinowitz Center for Public Policy and Finance, the Woodrow Wilson School of Public and International Affairs at Princeton University where the bulk of the research for this book originated. More specifically, I would like to acknowledge and thank Dr. Cecilia Rouse, Dean of the Woodrow Wilson School, Dr. Atif Mian, Director of the Julis-Rabinowitz Center for Public Policy and Finance and Violeta Rosenthal, the Center's Assistant Director.

Part I

United States, the European Union and China

1   Introduction

This introductory discussion will first analyze China's current and forecasted growth rates and from there it will compare this data to the current and future growth rates of the United States (US) and the European Union (EU). According to the World Bank's *Global Economic Prospects* released June 2017 (pp. 4–11), China's GDP growth estimate for 2015 was 6.9 percent followed by its 2016 growth rate estimate of 6.7 percent. Moreover, the World Bank's report shows China's GDP projection for 2017 is 6.5 percent. Furthermore, the report breaks down countries either by region or income. Accordingly, the US and the EU are classified under "high income" nations.

By comparison, the United States GDP growth rate for 2015 was 2.6 percent followed by its 2016 US GDP growth estimate of a paltry 1.6 percent. Moreover, the US 2017 growth projection currently stands at 2.1 percent. In terms of the Eurozone, the Euro Area GDP growth rate for 2015 was 2.0 percent compared with a 2016 growth estimate of 1.8 percent followed by the Eurozone GDP growth projection for 2017 at 1.7 percent. For clarity purposes, the lapse time for the 2016 growth estimate percentage to become the "actual" growth percentage is 12 to 18 months from the end of the calendar year allowing for revisions (World Bank 2016, pp. 4–9).

The definition of GDP (Gross Domestic Product) is the total monetary value of all finished goods and services produced within a country's borders in a specific time period. Normally, GDP is calculated on an annual basis. It includes all of the private and public consumption, government outlays, investments and *exports minus imports* or GDP = C + G + I + (exports-imports) negative exports equal a trade deficit. After examining the above definition, an argument may surface that supports the statement that when the US and the EU import finished goods that result in trade deficits, they have inadvertently encountered a reduction in their national economies (*trade deficits = a reduction in GDP*).

According to the US Census Bureau in 2017, US exports to China amounted to roughly $117 billion and US imports from China in 2017 totaled approximately $462 billion giving China a trade surplus with the United States of around $345 billion. Moreover, according to the European Commission in 2017, the European Union's trade deficit with China has been increasing precipitously from around 55 billion euros in 2007 to approximately to 180 billion euros in 2017.

In support of the global economy, it should also be noted that one of the primary functions of corporate management is to enhance shareholder value of the corporation. In order to do that, these companies require new revenue streams and usually new revenue streams are the result of new markets. To that end, multinational corporations are constantly in search of new revenue streams irrespective of their home country's trade balance. Obviously, these data points as well as a whole host of others relative to China's trade surplus with the US and Europe will be discussed at great length in the succeeding chapters. It should also be noted that for the book's purposes the European Union (EU) and Europe are one and the same. However, the EU and the Eurozone are not the same.

The Eurozone is part of the EU and it represents 19 countries that use the euro as a common currency. The remaining nine countries in the EU use their respective sovereign currencies. It should also be noted that for the book's purposes the yuan (Y) and the renminbi (RMB) are one and the same.

During the Chinese president's trip to Europe in March 2014, he proposed a deep and comprehensive Free Trade Agreement (FTA). This was a significant departure from the external trade policy normally followed by the People's Republic of China. In the past, China had always favored trade agreements with emerging market economies in Asia or with countries in Africa or Latin America. At the time, Beijing's overture towards the EU had likely been triggered by the opening of negotiations on the more recent controversial Trans-Pacific Partnership (TPP), which was promoted aggressively by the Obama Administration, but one of the first actions by the new Trump Administration was to withdraw the United States from the TPP. Despite this, Beijing considers the TPP an impediment and a threat to its regional dominance. Moreover, it's very important to note that in 2014 the initial EU reactions to the Chinese Free Trade Agreement (FTA) proposal were only lukewarm at best.

In a concerted effort to evaluate President Xi's FTA proposal, in April 2016 the EU commissioned a study by the Centre for European Policy Studies entitled *Tomorrow's Silk Road: Assessing an EU-China Free Trade Agreement*:

> This study deals with three principal aspects: (1) the "why" of the FTA, (2) the "how" to incorporate a broad spectrum of trade policy areas usually found in "deep and comprehensive" FTAs and (3) the stylized "economic impact" based on a cutting-edge application of CGE modelling together with the newest GTAP database for such a demanding exercise.
>
> (Pelkmans and Francois et al. 2016)

Moreover, prior to the 2016 US-China Strategic and Economic Dialogue, the Obama Administration stated publicly that China's government was responsible for a massive breach of personnel records of as many as 22 million federal employees and contractors. In an effort to advance the already sarcastic discourse, then Vice President Joseph Biden made the case that:

any country that relies on unhealthy practices to undermine healthy competition with others ultimately limits itself because nations that use cyber technology as an economic weapon for theft of intellectual property are sacrificing tomorrow's long term gain for a short term gain today.

(US Department of the Treasury 2016)

For the most part, China was able to use its entry into the World Trade Organization (WTO) to gain EU market access without really having to reciprocate with EU companies. EU companies are still barred from many important government procurement contracts and they suffer a number of barriers to entry into China through national treatment protocols and other impediments, but more difficult than this is the unexpected fragmentation of the Chinese market (Kerry 2014). Due to the government's role in Chinese state-owned enterprises, the EU has denied China Market Economy Status (MES), which has evolved into a major sticking point between the two (EU trade-defense law). The EU makes the argument that China's state-owned enterprises are unfairly subsidized by the Chinese government and these state-owned companies have easy access to capital, which puts its EU competition at a distinct disadvantage.

In October 2016 the European Union established new trade rules in an effort to curb low-priced Chinese imports. This was the 18-month culmination of wrangling between the EU and Beijing over its EU-China trading relationship (dumping). Beginning in early 2016, the European Commission held public discussions generating in excess of 5,000 opinions on how to handle trade complaints against China. On October 3, 2016 the European Commission, member states and EU lawmakers held a joint news conference outlining their recommendations. In order to determine the imposition of import tariffs, the EU decided to treat all WTO members equally regardless of "market economy status" which China lacks.[1] Their joint resolution stated unequivocally that "dumping" occurs when export prices fall below domestic prices, but the EU may make an exception for cases of "significant market distortions" such as excessive state intervention, which will probably cover a number of Chinese companies.

Until this announcement, China had been treated as a special "non-market" case, which involved a very complex procedure of evaluating Chinese export prices in a third country like the US to determine if Chinese exports to the EU were artificially cheap:

> The European Commission, supported by the EU's 28 member states, believed the rules for China needed to be changed. This meant finding a balance between adhering to WTO rules and protecting EU companies threatened by dumping. "I am convinced we have met these two targets," said Bernard Lange, head of the EU Parliament's trade committee after the deal. Lange also hailed the new possibility of investigations into social and environmental dumping.
>
> (European Commission Press Release 2016)

Within the same time frame, the US Commerce Department also released a report that stated it had made its affirmative final determination that imported tires from China were sold in the United States at dumping margins ranging from 14.35 percent to 87.99 percent (US Department of Commerce 2016). Moreover, the Department concluded that the Chinese tire manufacturers and the Chinese tire exporters received Chinese government industrial subsidies ranging from 20.73 percent to 100.77 percent.

This latest round of tire dumping was brought to the attention of the US Department of Commerce by two US labor organizations: the United Steelworkers and the AFL-CIO. The Chinese Ministry of Commerce voiced strong opposition to such a decision and they're making the case that the entire investigation is against the rules of the World Trade Organization and United States laws. In terms of dollar value, the imported Chinese tires under investigation amounted to roughly $2.3 billion in 2015–2016.

On August 30, 2016 the US Commerce Department announced that it would set final dumping margins on imported light truck tires and imported passenger vehicle tires manufactured in China. This was the first time the Commerce Department had showed signs that it may impose punitive duties on these types of products. The final determination rests with the US International Trade Commission (ITC). If the ITC rules that the dispute is affirmative, then the punitive duties will take effect, but if the ITC issues a negative ruling, the entire investigations will be terminated. February 23, 2017 is the date scheduled for the Commission's final ruling. On February 22, 2017 the US International Trade Commission (USITC) made its final determination in its anti-dumping and countervailing duty investigation. In terms of imported passenger and light truck tires from China, the Commission found that the US tire industry was not materially injured by the imports of these tires.

Moreover, the Chinese Ministry of Commerce has repeatedly urged the United States to abide by its commitment against trade protectionism and work together with China and other members of the international community to maintain a free, open and just international trade environment (*China Daily* 2015). Since China's entry into the WTO on December 11, 2001, it has been named primary respondent in various and assorted trade violations against the United States 33 times and as a third-party respondent in a plethora of trade violations 121 times (Blanchard and Lawder 2016).

However, in October 2016, an announcement by the World Trade Organization claimed that China had won the majority of US complaints against China. The Chinese government took the position that the specific methods used by the US to determine anti-dumping duties on Chinese products were unacceptable. China initiated the counter-complaint in response to US 2013 complaints of China dumping. Basically, the Chinese government challenged Washington's way of accessing "dumping" or exporting Chinese products at unfair prices into the US and for the most part, China won the case. More specifically, "the panel found fault with the US practices of determining dumping margins in certain cases of 'targeting dumping', in which foreign firms cut prices on goods aimed at specific US regions, customer groups or time periods" (US International Trade Commission 2017).

From 2016 to 2017, China initiated export restrictions on raw materials like rare earths, which were identified as a major trade obstacle. China arbitrarily imposed a number of export restrictions on specific raw materials (rare earths): export quotas, export duties and additional requirements that would limit access to these raw materials for companies outside of China. The EU took the position that these measures significantly distorted the market and favored Chinese industry. Moreover, the EU filed a complaint with the WTO making the argument that these restrictions were in violation of the general WTO rules. On August 7, 2014, the Appellate Body of the World Trade Organization confirmed that China's export duties and quotas were not consistent with its original obligations under China's Accession Protocol and General Agreement on Tariffs and Trade (GATT). The WTO Body has requested that China rearrange its export regime so that it conforms to its WTO obligations (European Commission 2015).

At the time of writing, there are 26 separate EU investigations taking place for Chinese trade violations that occurred over the past 12 months. For the most part these investigations are by either the European Commission or the Council of European Union. The investigations are for trade violations on various products that range from aspartame, molybdenum wires, and silicon to sodium cyclamate, and so on. Technically, these are the preliminary investigations and when they're concluded and if they're affirmative, they are then filed as a complaint with the WTO and it usually takes anywhere from three to six months for the WTO to reach a decision.

The general consensus about the reliability of China's economic data can be exaggerated. The degree of unreliability would probably be less controversial if China were compared to other emerging markets (developing countries). According to the Federal Reserve Bank of St. Louis:

> the World Bank, which classifies China as a middle-income country, ranks low – and middle-income countries with populations greater than 1 million by a statistical capacity score, reflecting the country's ability to produce and disseminate high-quality aggregate data. The statistical capacity score aggregates 25 individual variables that measure aspects of a country's statistical methodology, source data, periodicity and timeliness. In the past, China's score has been at or below the median (38th percentile of low and medium-income countries scored in 2004 and 52nd percentile in 2015). However in the 2016 rankings, China earned a score of 83.3 out of a 100, putting it in the 83rd percentile.
>
> (Federal Reserve Bank of St. Louis 2017)

China's score is actually on the upper end of the distributive statistical capacity when compared with data from its statistical peer group. China's overall score improvement is the result of better methodology, which improved timeliness and reliable periodicity of data releases. Clearly, this is the result of China's determination to improve its statistical data releases in conjunction with the International Monetary Fund's Special Data Dissemination Standard. This standard in particular evaluates a nation's data dissemination based on the necessary criteria required by the international capital markets.

In June 2017, the bilateral summit between the European Union and China and its related events took place on June 1 and June 2, 2017 in Brussels. The overall summit was hosted by the President of the European Council, Donald Tusk and the President of the European Commission, Jean-Claude Juncker accompanied by the High Representative for Foreign Affairs and Security Policy, Federica Mogherini and the Commissioner for Trade, Cecilia Malmström. Moreover, China was represented by the Premier of the People's Republic of China, Li Keqiang, State Councillor, Yang Jiechi and the Minister of Foreign Affairs, Wang Yi. At the end of the meeting, the leaders adopted a joint summit statement and a separate statement on climate change and clean energy.

This was the first summit since the adoption of the new EU Strategy on China 2016, and it sets out how both sides can take advantage of their cooperation to promote long-term benefits for EU and Chinese citizens. It also stresses the need for reciprocal benefits and a level playing field between China and the EU.

The first item on the formal agenda covered the subject of EU-China bilateral relations with a focus specifically on trade and investment including the beginning negotiations towards the proposed Comprehensive Investment Agreement. Connectivity was also a pivotal part of the agenda. Leaders from both prioritized progress on the EU-China connectivity platform. The aim was to coordinate efforts on transport policies and to identify projects of common interest between the EU and China based on transparency and an even playing field. In terms of Geographical Indicators (GI), the leaders instructed their negotiators to accelerate work so as to complete negotiations by the end of 2017. To that end, an agreement was also expected to come out of the summit on the publication of the designated GI names pursuant to both sides soon after the meeting.

The summit's leaders also addressed the impact on EU industry pertaining to China's overcapacity in its steel industry and other sectors. Furthermore, the summit also provided a platform for the EU to reiterate its commitment to the promotion of human rights and the rule of law as an integral part of the EU's engagement with China. The summit also provided an opportunity to evaluate preparations for the upcoming EU-China Year of Tourism (2018). The meeting also addressed the common activities of "oceans governance" along with the agreed cooperation in this field beginning with the launch of the EU-China "Blue Year" (2017).

The second part of the agenda focused on global, international and regional issues. This included climate change and clean energy in particular relative to the implementation of the Paris Agreement. The leaders also addressed cooperation in the multilateral areas of migration, refugees, the G20 and the 2030 Agenda for Sustainable Development. Additionally, security and defense cooperation was evaluated with a focus on peacekeeping cooperation in Africa along with enhanced cooperation on counterterrorism. Finally, the working lunch was dedicated to the foreign and security policies of the EU and China. Along those lines, the two sides discussed at length the recent developments found in Syria, Libya, Ukraine, the Democratic People's Republic of Korea and the South China Sea.

Furthermore, since April 2009, the United States and China have engaged in an annual security and economic dialogue aptly named the US-China Strategic and Economic Dialogue. In April 2017, the Trump Administration renamed the annual US-China Strategic and Economic Dialogue the US-China Comprehensive Economic Dialogue. On July 19, 2017 at the completion of the newly named economic summit Co-Chairs Secretary Steven Mnuchin and Secretary Wilbur Ross released the following statement through the US Office of Public Affairs (2017):

> We thank Vice Premier Wang and the Chinese delegation for making the journey to Washington for this first session of the US-China Comprehensive Economic Dialogue. We also extend our gratitude to Secretary Perdue, Ambassador Lighthizer, Ambassador Branstad, Chair Yellen and Director Cohn for their participation in these meetings.
>
> China acknowledged our shared objective to reduce the trade deficit, which both sides will work to achieve.
>
> Since the Presidential Summit, the first 100 days made progress on important issues including credit ratings, bond clearing, electronic payments, commercial banking and liquefied natural gas. Also this is the first time since 2003 that the Chinese have allowed for imports of American beef.
>
> The principles of balance, fairness and reciprocity on matters of trade will continue to guide the American position so we can give American workers and businesses an opportunity to compete on a level playing field. We look to achieving the important goals set forth by President Trump this past April in Mar-a-Lago.

The research for this book also uncovered a return to a strong sense of nationalism among some of the more controversial EU countries. In France, right-wing ultra-nationalists back the referendum called for by Greece's socialist government. The reason behind this is the National Front Party in France headed up by Marine Le Pen. Apparently, Le Pen wants to use the Greek referendum as a model to call a French referendum vote to determine if France should exit the EU. She's adamant that France should leave the EU to regain its French birthright (Rubin 2015). With that said, the National Front is a splinter party in France, but that should not be taken lightly. They have a big voice and if things work in their favor, more and more people may listen to them.

For the most part, economic nationalism is on the rise in Western Europe. Consequently, this has set the stage for academics to analyze in its entirety the trends associated with this phenomenon and the trend that constantly takes center stage is economic globalization. In a new working paper, Italo Colantone and Piero Stanig from Bocconi University examined the relationship between electoral outcomes and the impact of economic globalization in 14 European countries between 1988 and 2007. The countries analyzed by Colantone and Stanig (2016) were Austria, Belgium, Finland, France, Greece, Ireland, Italy, Netherlands, Norway, Portugal, Spain, Sweden, Switzerland and the United Kingdom. With the exception of Switzerland and Norway, all are currently members of the EU. They analyzed the relationship between a very dissatisfied European relative to the never-ending surge of Chinese imports and his or her individual voting behavior. Their research showed that a strong backlash against Chinese imports by individuals resulted in a corresponding increase in nationalist political parties. Furthermore, they found that areas with greater exposure to international trade mainly imports from China saw a much larger increase in support for nationalism and the radical right than areas with less trade exposure.

Along the same lines in November 2016, MIT economists David Autor et al. (2016) argued that areas of the United States hit the hardest by trade imbalances and trade tremors were more likely to shift their votes away from centrist politicians to politicians that were far more extreme either to the left or the right. Their research analyzed the elections between 2002 and 2016, but it became readily apparent that in the 2016 US presidential election trade had become an enormous issue prompting the rise of Donald Trump and Bernie Sanders. It was during the primary campaigns that Hillary Clinton a centrist Democrat withdrew her support for the Trans-Pacific Partnership (TPP). At the end of the study, their thesis argued that in the absence of appropriate redistribution policies for those deeply affected by international trade, globalization may not be sustainable in the long term.

On January 7, 2016 German Chancellor Angela Merkel had a private meeting with Prime Minister David Cameron of the UK in his office in London. The primary reason for the meeting was to discuss the upcoming G7 summit, but the conversation also included Cameron's proposal to limit migration in the EU (Wintour 2016). Cameron, leader of Britain's Conservative Party, was constantly distracted by some members of his own party and the UK Independence Party (UKIP) who wanted the United Kingdom out of the EU. Coincidentally, on June 23, 2016, the citizens of the United Kingdom voted to leave the EU: Brexit. After the election, Cameron stepped down, but the new Prime Minister Theresa May is holding firm on Brexit and she's committed to follow the people's will. Apparently, when it came to the UK's position in the EU, many Britons were just not sure. They were not sure if being part of the EU really benefited them directly. Many of them were very concerned about migration from the poorer EU countries and the effects this had on the UK National Health Service (NHS) and the migrants' EU home residency tuition status at UK universities.

Throughout history, Europe has always had a keen sense of nationalism from its romantic nationalism of the 19th century beginning with the Congress of Vienna, the independence of Greece, the independence of Belgium, the unification of Germany and the unification of Italy resulting in the triumph of nationalities to the totalitarian governments of Germany, Italy and Spain in the 20th century. Repeatedly in terms of language, ethnicity and religion, the European people have always defined themselves and divided themselves on the basis of a strong, unwavering sense of nationalism and commitment to their respective homelands. A distrust of anyone or any organization outside the realm of the individual homeland was not unusual.

According to some EU academics, Greece may be the exit catalyst in the Eurozone for Italy, Portugal and Spain. These three countries face very similar debt problems while at the same time each of these three are seeing skyrocketing growth in national resentment against global lenders and international banks in general. Instant online communications are also becoming a mixed blessing. Radical elements like ISIS use the same system as a recruiting tool creating yet another reason for people to begin looking inward and shut the rest of the world out. Governments exist to protect their citizens from external influences that affect their economy, culture and physical security. It's only natural that the more aggressive outside influences become, the more people cling to their national identity.

Nationalism can also serve the state well if it can stay on the offensive. This is exactly what took place in Russia. With Putin taking Crimea and attacking the Ukraine, he had the support of the Russian people on a nationalistic basis so sanctions coming from the West were secondary to Russian citizens. Nationalism plays a big part in the mind of the average Russian.

China, on the other hand, has embraced capitalism, but not freedom. Moreover, because of China's very aggressive participation in the global economy, its international economic reach spans the entire globe. Consequently, over the past two decades, China has been able to raise the standard of living for millions of Chinese people in an effort to create a much bigger middle class. With that said and in spite of living under an authoritarian dictatorship, the Chinese people give the Chinese Communist Party 100 percent of the credit for their economic advancements and the increase in their standard of living.

In the past, statesmen like Henry Kissinger (2012) openly claimed that China doesn't believe in the balance of power and its position on that subject will never change. Much of China's behavior is justified by its history. China's history is replete with examples of its condescending attitude toward its neighbors, which the Chinese authorities view as weak and insignificant. More to the point, a parade was scheduled in late 2016 in Beijing to celebrate the 70th anniversary of Japan's surrender in World War II. The parade will evoke Chinese nationalism even more and at the same time, it will underscore China's historical hatred of Japan.

As for the United States and nationalism, America has always had a love affair with nationalism. However, in America, for the most part nationalism becomes interchanged with patriotism and the two are pretty much inseparable. Deplorably for the last two decades, the US has experienced a dwindling middle class coupled with gross income inequality and this dilemma is very worrisome. On average, the American people really don't say much and it's almost un-American to complain, but this horrific, debilitating trend will have to be reversed.

In the US, between 1979 and 2013 the top 1 percent's income grew 138 percent, yet the bottom 90 percent's wage grew at 15 percent. Moreover, the US middle class had $17,867 less income in 2007 because of the growth of income inequality since 1979 based on household income of the broad middle class from 1979–2013 (Piketty 2014, pp. 39–72). Unfortunately, the US has more income inequality than any of the other advanced economies. The two groups that lead the pack are the titans of Wall Street and the billionaires of Silicon Valley, but unfortunately their staggering wealth does nothing for America's middle class and the capital-intensive industries that employ the middle class have reduced their labor force considerably over the past four decades. For example, in 1974, the US steel industry employed over 520,000 workers. In 1990, that number had dropped to just over 210,000. Today the US steel industry employs roughly 150,000 steel workers. Moreover, from 1948–1973, US productivity was up 96.7 percent and hourly compensation was up a whopping 91.3 percent and from 1973–2013 productivity was up a respectable 74.4 percent, but hourly compensation was up a paltry 9.2 percent. That's a total increase of 9.2 percent in hourly compensation adjusted for inflation over a 40-year period.

On the surface, there seems to be a dichotomy underway between a country's citizens negatively affected by globalization and a country's corporate community who benefits significantly by the inordinate profits earned from its capital flows across continents. Globalization has created a competition between earned income from work and earned income from capital and that's nothing new, but in a more globalized economy if jobs are lost or wages become stagnant due to globalization, earned income from work is at a disadvantage. In a pure domestic economy, once technology and industry reach their highest level of development, earned income from capital is at a disadvantage.

The outline of the book

The book will be divided into five parts with two chapters in the first part, three chapters in the second part, four chapters in the third part, four chapters in the fourth part and one chapter in the fifth part. Obviously, Chapter 1 is the "Introduction" followed by Chapter 2, which is a very important chapter. It's entitled Nixon and Kissinger and it draws out the history of the thawing of relations between the United States and China. It begins with Henry Kissinger's secret trip to China in June 1971 and how that trip set the stage for President Nixon's week-long visit to China in February 1972.

Part II begins with Chapter 3. This deals with China's evolution into the world markets, which includes China's economic reforms from 1978 to 1990. Chapter 4 examines China from 1990 onwards. Chapter 5 analyzes China's infamous currency manipulation.

Part III starts with Chapter 6 which discusses in detail US foreign direct investment (FDI) in China. Along the same lines, Chapter 7 analyzes EU foreign direct investment in China. Chapter 8 examines China's foreign direct investment in the United States and that's followed by Chapter 9, which analyzes China's foreign direct investment in the European Union.

Part IV begins with Chapter 10. This chapter examines US trade policies and trade balances with China in the 1990s. In that light, Chapter 11 discusses

European Union trade policies and trade balances with China in the 1990s. Chapters 12 and 13 do in-depth analyses of US and EU trade policies and trade balances with China from 2000 onwards.

And Chapter 14 is the "Conclusion." This chapter will summarize the book's thesis. It will encapsulate the previously mentioned details pointed out in the preceding chapters and it will prove unequivocally that the West is exporting their national economy.

Notes

1 In EU trade-defense law (anti-dumping and anti-subsidies), there is a provision for different treatment between those exporting countries which are considered to have status of being market economy and those which are not. If a country is not granted market economy status it's easier to construct normal value of imported goods.
2 The Department of Commerce (Commerce) announced its affirmative preliminary determination in the antidumping duty (AD) investigation of imports of truck and bus tires from the People's Republic of China (China).

References

Autor, David, David Dorn, Gordon Hanson and Kaveh Majlesi, "Importing Political Polarization? The Electoral Consequences of Rising Trade Exposure," MIT Department of Economics and NBER, December, 2016.

Blanchard, Ben and David Lawder, "China Launches WTO Complaint Against US, EU Over Dumping Rules," Reuters, December 12, 2016, available at www.reuters.com/article/us-china-trade-wto/china-launches-wto-complaint-against-u-s-eu-over-dumping-rules-idUSKBN14112M.

Brown, Kerry, *The Diplomat*, in conversation, April 24, 2014.

China Daily.com, "US Sets Final Dumping Margins on Chinese Tires," June 13, 2015, available at www.chinadaily.com.cn/business/motoring/2015-06/13/content_20992799.htm.

Colantone, Italo and Piero Stanig, "Global Competition and BREXIT," *Baffi Carefin Center Research Paper Series*, No. 2016–44, September 28, 2016.

Council of the European Union, EU-China Summit, June 1–2, 2017, Brussels.

Directorate-General for Trade, European Commission, European Union, *Trade in Goods with China*, April 10, 2015.

EU-China Summit, Brussels, June 29, 2015.

European Commission, "China Trade," June 29, 2015.

European Commission, Press Release, October 3, 2016.

Federal Reserve Bank of St. Louis, "China's Economic Data: An Accurate Reflection or Just Smoke and Mirrors?" Second Quarter 2017.

Kissinger, Henry, *On China*, New York, NY: Penguin Books, 2012.

Pelkmans, Jacques and Joseph Francois, et al., *Tomorrow's Silk Road: Assessing an EU-China Free Trade Agreement*, Centre for European Policy Studies, April, 2016.

Piketty, Thomas, *Capital in the Twenty-First Century*. Translated by Arthur Goldhammer. Cambridge, MA and London, UK: The Belknap Press of Harvard University Press, 2014.

Rubin, Alissa J., "National Front Gets a Boost in French Regional Elections," *New York Times*, Europe, 7 December 7, 2015.

US Census Bureau, Data Accumulation Division, *International Trade*, March 11, 2017.

US Department of Commerce, Fact Sheet "Commerce Preliminarily Finds Dumping of Imports of Truck and Bus Tires from the People's Republic of China," August 29, 2016.[2]

US Department of the Treasury, "US-China Strategic and Economic Dialogue," 2016, available at www.treasury.gov/initiatives/Pages/china.aspx.

US International Trade Commission, "Truck and Bus Tires from China Do Not Injure US Industry," February 22, 2017.

US Office of Public Affairs, "Statement from Secretary Ross and Secretary Mnuchin," Wednesday, July 19, 2017, 6:35 PM.

Wintour, Patrick, "Cameron to meet Merkel for talks on refugee crisis and UK EU membership," *The Guardian*, October 5, 2016.

World Bank, *Global Economic Prospects: Divergences and Risks*, pp. 107–114, (June) Washington, DC, 2016.

2　Nixon and Kissinger

Unlike his predecessor, President Richard M. Nixon longed to be known for his expertise in foreign policy. This is a very important chapter that explains what historians refer to as triangular diplomacy: US, USSR and China. In June 1971, Secretary of State Henry Kissinger traveled secretly to China and it was that particular trip that paved the way for Nixon's week-long visit in February 1972. For the first time in over two decades, the world saw a China and the United States as two sovereign nations highlighting a significant shift in the Cold War balance. Nixon's week-long visit later became known as "the week that changed the world".

In 2002, The National Security Archive and the George Washington University's Cold War Group of the Elliott School of International Affairs published a collection of declassified US documents that detailed explicit communications that led up to the China-American rapprochement entitled: *The Beijing-Washington Back-Channel and Henry Kissinger's Secret Trip to China, September 1970–July 1971*. The documents were categorized sequentially by William Burr, Editor and published in the National Security Archive Electronic Briefing Book (2002).

As far back as 1969 and the beginning of his presidency, Nixon always had a keen interest in changing relations with China, but the earlier efforts to make contact with China were unsuccessful. These efforts were not done directly. They were all done through third and fourth parties. For example, an October 1970 meeting with Kissinger and Yahya Khan, the ruler of Pakistan showed potential for expediting the necessary contacts because Pakistan served as a conduit for earlier China-American communication. Nixon's interest in creating a dialogue with China wasn't necessarily altruistic; it was a political strategy that included the elimination of a nuclear threat, but also took advantage of the adversarial Sino-Soviet relationship and opened yet another front in the Cold War between the United States and the USSR.

With that said, in early 1970, Nixon and Kissinger struggled intensely in their efforts to discover how to create a new policy with China; one that would be acceptable to Congress and the American people, but needless to say, the 1970 US invasion of Cambodia more than exacerbated the entire process. At the same time, Kissinger was also trying to explore other conduits into Beijing.

One in particular involved his old friend Jean Sainteny who at the time was making inroads into China's embassy in Paris.

Sainteny was a French military officer, politician and diplomat with a reputation as an "honest broker" and a skilled negotiator. His vast experience with Indochina dated back to the late 1920s when he was a banker and a financial executive. His father-in-law was Albert Sarraut the French prime minister. He used his family's connections to create friendships with diplomats and politicians all over the world. He became acquainted with Kissinger in the 1960s. In December 1970, the Pakistani connection through Sainteny produced an important message from Zhou Enlai, the first Premier of the People's Republic of China and a close ally of Mao Zedong. The communiqué quickly generated a White House response; the memo was written by a Kissinger NSC staffer named W.R. Smyser to Kissinger. Please see Figures 2.1 and 2.2.

By April 1971, Kissinger received a belated reply from Zhou Enlai prompting the following two important memos (Figure 2.3).

The obvious interest by the Chinese government, mainly Mao Zedong and Zhou Enlai, in the possibility of a visit by President Nixon set the stage for Kissinger's secret trip to China in July 1971. In spite of their very divergent political ideologies, this marked the beginning of US-China efforts to engage in discussions about issues that had divided them for well over 20 years.

The National Security Archives documentations summarize and detail the efforts by Nixon and Kissinger, which ultimately produced Kissinger's secret trip to Beijing July 9–11, 1971. Kissinger flew to Beijing from Pakistan. His clandestine meetings there resulted in a mutual agreement that President Nixon would in fact visit China in February 1972. A closer look at the archive documentation also shows that the Taiwan issue was an essential part of Nixon's upcoming trip to China, and for the establishment of diplomatic relations between the US and China in general. The success or failure of Kissinger's trip depended on the US position on Taiwan. The Chinese officials had to be assured that a Two Chinas or a One China, One Taiwan solution was not in the offing. In his meeting with Zhou Enlai on July 9, Kissinger did not use Zhou's description that Taiwan was part of China, but later he basically agreed with it when he claimed that the US was not advocating a Two Chinas or a One China, One Taiwan solution.

On that note, Zhou reasserted his "optimism about a Sino-American rapprochement: the prospect for a solution and the establishment of diplomatic relations between our two countries is hopeful". Later in his 1979 memoir, Kissinger erroneously wrote that "Taiwan was mentioned only briefly during the first session."[1] However, some nine pages or roughly 20 percent of the 46-page record of the first meeting between Kissinger and Zhou on July 19, 1971 in Peking (Beijing) were about Taiwan. Kissinger disavowed Taiwan's independence and made the case that two-thirds of US forces would be withdrawn immediately after the end of the Vietnam War. The idea of abandoning Taiwan as part of a China-American rapprochement remained a sore point among the conservatives in the Republican Party during the 1970s. Kissinger's hope that the Taiwan

MEMORANDUM

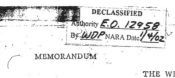

THE WHITE HOUSE

WASHINGTON

ACTION

SECRET/SENSITIVE/EYES ONLY

November 7, 1970

MEMORANDUM FOR HENRY A. KISSINGER

FROM: W. R. Smyser

SUBJECT: Letter from Your Friend in Paris, and Other Chinese
Miscellania

I have received a note for you from your friend Jean in Paris
(Tab A). The translation reads:

"Dear Henry:

"I have not forgotten our conversation of the 27th of
September at my home and I can confirm to you that
which I told you about the Chinese Ambassador in France.
He is indeed a former general, having participated in the
Long March and remained on good terms with Mao. The
fact that he is one of the two only ambassadors who are
members of the central committee proves that he must be
listened to in Peking. The only other Ambassador who is
also a member of the central committee is in Albania.

"Recalled to China at the moment of the Cultural Revolution, Hoang Chen, after two years away, appears to have
come back to Paris with his position solidified (consolide').

"I confirm that I have good relations with him and that it
would doubtless be possible for me to speak to him along
the lines we envisaged in our conversation. I await your
word.

Faithfully yours,
J."

I cannot suggest a reply to this since I do not know the state of play
of all our Chinese efforts. But I note that he appears to have taken
a long time to obtain rather basic information and that he does not

SECRET/SENSITIVE/EYES ONLY

Figure 2.1

Source: National Security Archives

refer to the interpreter problem he cited in our conversation. So I do not really know what to make of it. Maybe Jean first checked with his government. In any case, I stand ready to transmit a reply on my personal stationery.

The French Delegate in Hanoi has told Ambassador Godley that the Chinese Ambassador there has several times recently spoken of the possibility of China being admitted to the UN. He finds this remarkable because until the last two or three months the Chinese gave every appearance of having little or no interest in being admitted to the UN.

An official of the French Embassy here, M. Bujon, told me yesterday that he thought the Chinese were indeed interested in getting into the UN (which he also probably got from their man in Hanoi). He thought that their chances were pretty good, even this year. He cited Canada and Italy and said that Peru, Bolivia, Chile, Singapore and others would also support China's admission as well as vote against us on the "important question" issue.

Attachment

Figure 2.1 (continued)

DELIVERED BY HILALY
6·15   27 APRIL 71   TAB 19

RECORD OF A DISCUSSION WITH MR HENRY KISSINGER
ON THE WHITE HOUSE ON 16TH DECEMBER 1970.

I was summoned to the White House by Mr Kissinger
this morning at 11 a. m. He told me that in reply to the message
sent by Premier Chou en-Lai through our President which I
conveyed to him on the 9th December, President Nixon would like
to send a fresh message to President Yahya for passing it on to
the Chinese Prime Minister (he presumed this would be through
the Chinese Ambassador in Pakistan). He then gave me an unsigned
note in an envelope. When I asked him what it contained he said
that in response to Chou en Lai's suggestion that a special
representative of President Nixon would be welcome in Peking
to discuss the question of Taiwan, President Nixon wished to
inform Premier Chou en Lai that the U. S. Government was prepared
to attend a preliminary meeting at an early date in a location
convenient to both sides to discuss what the arrangements could
or should be made for sending a U. S. delegation to Peking for
high level discussions. In reply to questions from me, Mr
Kissinger said that the preliminary meeting could take place in
Rawalpindi if General Yahya's government would not be embarrassed
in any way by it. From the U. S. side the representatives could
be, Ambassador Murphy or Mr Dewey or Ambassador David Bruce.
Or it could also be himself. (He could arrange to pay a visit to
Vietnam and under that cover, arrange a halt in Pakistan for
the purpose of meeting the Chinese representative. It would
depend on what kind of official the Chinese would send to Pakistan
for this purpose).

Mr Kissinger added that if a U. S. delegation ultimately
went to Peking, the discussions would not be confined to the

Figure 2.2

Source: National Security Archives

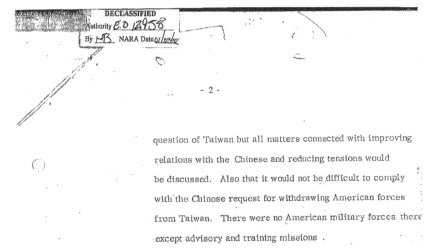

question of Taiwan but all matters connected with improving
relations with the Chinese and reducing tensions would
be discussed. Also that it would not be difficult to comply
with the Chinese request for withdrawing American forces
from Taiwan. There were no American military forces there
except advisory and training missions .

Figure 2.2 (continued)

issue would gradually fade away by uniting China with its wayward province was
foolhardy at best.

The following excerpts (transcripts) were taken from the Nixon Presidential
Library where Nixon is in conversation with top national security advisors about
his upcoming visit to China:

656-10 Excerpt 1 (1:24)

January 26, 1972

Richard Nixon (RN), Bernard Biesheuvel (BB), Alexander Haig (AH), and
William Middendorf (WM)

RN: Uh, we do believe that by starting the long process of some sort of
     contact, there will—I will say, obviously, it will not come to recognition
     on our part—

BB: No

RN: —because it cannot, since we still recognize Taiwan and will continue
     to honor our treaty commitments. They know this will not come out.
     What may come out of it will be, uh, however, uh, uh, some method
     of communication in the future, uh, some contact in the future, uh,
     perhaps reducing the chance in the immediate future of a confronta-
     tion between the United States and the PRC in Asia, such as we
     had in Korea and such as we had indirectly in Vietnam. And looking
     further in the future, uh, when they become a super power, a nuclear
     super power, uh, we, uh, can discuss differences and, and not inevi-
     tably have a clash. Now, also, no one can look at Asia, uh, and take

750 million Chinese out of it and say you can have any policy in the Pacific that will succeed in preventing war without having the Chinese a part of it. It's just as cold blooded as that.

DECLASSIFIED
Authority E.O 12958
By MB NARA Date 01/03/02

TAB 42

THE WHITE HOUSE
WASHINGTON

TOP SECRET   April 27, 1971

Major General Vernon A . Walters
Senior U.S. Military Attache
American Embassy
Paris, France
APO New York 09777

Dear Vernon:

Mr. David McManis of Dr. Kissinger's staff will deliver to you, together with this letter, two documents. The first (at Tab A) is a letter from Dr. Kissinger to Mr. Jean Sainteny and asks him to assist us in a sensitive matter which you will, in turn, explain to him when you deliver the letter. You should, therefore, contact Sainteny, show Henry's letter to him and ask him to arrange a private meeting between you and the Ambassador to France of the Peoples Republic of China or with some other appropriate Senior Chinese Communist representative in Paris. In the meantime, Dr. Kissinger will alert Sainteny by telephone. It is important that Mr. Sainteny merely read Henry's letter to him and that you reclaim it after he has read its contents. Hopefully, Sainteny will then arrange a private meeting between you and a designated representative of the Chinese.

The second document (at Tab B) is a note which you should subsequently deliver to the designated representative of the Peoples Republic. The contents of this note should, under no circumstances, be divulged to Mr. Sainteny and you should merely tell Sainteny that you have been instructed to deliver a note, without further explanation of its nature or content.

In sum, we visualize the scenario as follows:

    --   You are to contact Mr. Sainteny who will have been alerted by Henry.

    --   Allow him to read Henry's letter to him, being sure to reclaim the letter at the end of the meeting and being sure not to

TOP SECRET

Figure 2.3

Source: National Security Archives

divulge the content of the second note which is destined for the
Chinese representative. At this meeting, flesh out Henry's letter
by telling Sainteny that we hope he can arrange a private and secure
meeting alone between you and an appropriate representative of the
Peoples Republic assigned to France.

--   Mr. Sainteny, in turn, will arrange an appropriate
secure rendezvous between you and the Chinese representative.
At this private meeting, you would then deliver the note at Tab B.

Please keep us posted on the scenario as it unfolds.

                              Best regards,

                              Alexander M. Haig, Jr.
                              Brigadier General, U.S. Army
                              Deputy Assistant to the President
                                for National Security Affairs

Enclosures

TOP SECRET

Figure 2.3 (continued)

15

Λ

*N ever delivered.
because it
crossed
with Pak.
note*

Dear Jean:

Once again, the President and I would like to impose on
your invaluable good offices to assist us in a matter of
the greatest sensitivity. The bearer of this message,
Major General Vernon Walters (our Defense Attache in
Paris), will explain to you our specific need for your
intercession. The project is one requiring the kind of
skill and delicacy which have characterized your earlier
efforts in our behalf and no one, other than the President,
myself and General Walters is aware of it. Therefore,
it is important that after talking to General Walters you
inform no one of the nature of your conversation with
him, with the exception of President Pompidou.

Both the President and I hope you will find it possible to
help. It would increase our already large debt of grati-
tude to you.

Warm regards,

Henry A. Kissinger

Mr. Jean Sainteny
204, Rue de Rivoli,
Paris, France

Figure 2.3 (continued)

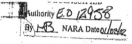
In the light of recent events, it seems important to have a reliable channel for communication between our two Governments.

If the Government of the People's Republic of China desires talks that are strictly confidential, the President is ready to establish such a channel directly to him for matters of the most extreme sensitivity. Its purpose would be to bring about an improvement in US-Chinese relations fully recognizing differences in ideology. On the United States side, such a channel would be known only to the President and his Assistant for National Security Affairs, and would not be revealed to any other foreign country.

If you are interested in pursuing this proposal, initial contact should be made with the bearer of this communication, Major General Vernon A. Walters, the U.S. Defense Attache in Paris. Dr. Henry Kissinger, the President's Assistant for National Security Affairs, would be prepared to come to Paris for direct talks on US-Chinese relations with whomever might be designated by the People's Republic of China to explore the subject further.

Figure 2.3 (continued)

656-10 Excerpt 2 (1:02)

January 26, 1972

Richard Nixon (RN), Bernard Biesheuvel (BB), Alexander Haig (AH), and J William Fulbright (JF)

RN: We will discuss a lot of things. We will discuss their role in the Pacific and our role in the Pacific. We will disagree on a lot of things. But the most important thing about that visit is that it occurs, and that the Chinese and the United States will have begun a process of, shall we say, getting to know each other. Now, this is not said in any sense of sentimentality. There are many people who-who have looked at the China visit and interpreted it exactly the wrong way. Uh, they say "oh, this is great-the-now the United States and China, really never had any differences—

BB: Uh-huh.

RN: —everything's going to be settled." It's not that. Uh, no one in this world knows how great the gulf is between their philosophy and ours, their interests and ours. Uh, but also no one in the world, I think, knows better than I do, how imperative it is to see that great nations that have enormous differences, uh, where you've got the nuclear thing hanging in the balance, have got to find ways to, you know, get along.

92-1 Excerpt 1 (1:42)

February 29, 1972

Richard Nixon (RN), Allen Ellender (AE), Michael Mansfield (MM), J William Fulbright (JF), Henry Kissinger (HK), et al.

RN: Looking in the future, of course, speaks in terms of our common interests and, uh, normalization of relations of relations, uh, and, uh, our common interests in, uh, starting to build this long process of, of, of better relations between two countries.

Now, let me get down to some cold turkey. Uh, what brought us together? Uh, some rather naive, uh, reporters have indicated that uh, observers, have indicated that what brought us together is that, uh, well mainly, both China and the United States, the People's Republic of China and the United States realized that we really didn't have a, uh, that really despite our philosophies we really weren't all that far apart, and that if we'd just to know each other better-that, uh, everything would be a lot better with each other. Not true at all. Getting to know each other better will reduce the possibility of miscalculation and that we have established, because we do have an understanding. And I know they, and they know me. And I hope that would be true of whoever happens to be sitting in this office in the future. This means that there will be talking and rather than having that, that, uh, inevitable road, uh, of suspicion and miscalculation, which could lead to war. A miscalculation which, incidentally, led to their intervention in Korea, which might have been avoided had there been this kind of contact at that time.

92-1 Excerpt 2 (1:35)

February 29, 1972

Richard Nixon (RN), Allen Ellender (AE), Michael Mansfield (MM), J William Fulbright (JF), Henry Kissinger (HK), et al.

RN: It was not our common beliefs which brought us together. But, frankly, our common interests and our common hopes. What are those common interests? One is the interests that both of us have in maintaining our integrity and our independence. And second is the hope that each of us has to try to build a structure of peace in the Pacific, and going beyond that, in the world. And, uh, and on that point that means that despite a total gulf, a gulf that will continue to exist as long as they're communist, and as long as we're basically a free country, a total gulf in beliefs that people of different faiths, of different beliefs, have got to find a way to live together in this world. And, to, in the case of the People's Republic of China and the United States of America, the most powerful nation in the world, and the most populous nation in the world, if we, uh, do not find a way to, uh, despite our differences to have discussions, we are on a collision course years ahead, which would be very, very serious. If we do find a way to have discussions as we have stated in this instance, there is a better chance that we will not have that collision course years ahead.

National Security Archives documentations are only part of the story. Notwithstanding the simple fact that Chinese archive sources are technically unavailable. In recent years a growing body of scholarship in China and the US underscores Chinese language sources that show the Chinese government was equally excited about the establishment of a new relationship between China and the United States. A few years ago, Chen Jian's book, *Mao's China and the Cold War* (2010) shows the internal deliberations that took place in Beijing in the late 1960s and early 1970s. The University of Virginia historian writes in fascinating detail about the appointment of four marshals in 1969 by Mao who were instructed to closely monitor world politics especially US-Soviet, Sino-Soviet and Sino-American relations.

In order to gain leverage with Moscow two of the marshals, Chen Yi and Ye Jianying, encouraged Mao to play "the card of the United States". According to the two marshals, this should alleviate any possible confrontations with the

USSR. At the end of the Cold War, top US officials would sometimes recommend playing the China card, but it is not unusual for an American policymaker to understand that the US may also be the target of other national card games.

As expected, this game of cat and mouse triangular diplomacy evoked concern in the USSR. Nixon's hopes included a détente with the Soviet Union. Consequently, in May 1972, Nixon made a significant trip to Moscow to engage in much needed dialogue about a nuclear arms agreement. The outcome of this visit was the Strategic Arms Limitations Talks (SALT I). The USSR and the US agreed to limit the number of intercontinental ballistic missiles that each country would build. The agreement also included a provision to prevent further development of anti-ballistic missile systems.

Moreover, Nixon and his Soviet counterpart, Leonid Brezhnev agreed to a trade deal. This deal in particular involved American wheat sold to the Soviet Union. Simultaneously, the two nations agreed to a joint space exploration venture known as the Apollo-Soyuz. Without a doubt, Nixon may have been the only president to reach this kind of an agreement with the Soviet Union and China without overwhelming backlash from members of his own party in Congress. It would do us all well to remember that at that time anti-communism was raging in the United States. Congress as well as the American people would view any attempts to make peace with either China or the USSR with great suspicion, but Nixon's lifelong anti-communist credentials along with his reputation with Congress as a staunch red-baiter earlier in his political career set the stage for his success in this endeavor.

Consequently, Nixon's overtures to both the Soviet Union and China were for the most part accepted by his colleagues in Congress and the American public in general. The Cold War continued to rear its ugly head all over the globe, but in these two particular incidents Kissinger and Nixon created at least a bit of a thaw.

*Declassified copy of the original transcript of the initial meeting between President Richard Nixon and Chairman Mao Zedong in Beijing begins on the following page (National Security Archive, Washington DC).

Mao Zedong meets Richard Nixon, February 21, 1972

Declassified transcript of the Beijing meeting between China's leader and President Nixon took place in Chairman Mao's living quarters.

Meeting attendees: Richard Nixon; Mao Zedong (Mao Tse-tung in the transcript); Zhou Enlai (Chou En-lai); Wang Hairong (Wang Hai-jung); Tang Wensheng (Tang Wen-sheng); Henry Kissinger; and Winston Lord as the notetaker.

February 21, 1972

MEMORANDUM OF CONVERSATION

PARTICIPANTS:

Chairman Mao Tse-tung

Prime Minister Chou En-lai

Wang Hai-jung, Deputy Chief of Protocol of the Foreign Ministry

Tang Wen-sheng, Interpreter

President Nixon

Henry A. Kissinger, Assistant to the President for National Security Affairs

Winston Lord, National Security Council Staff (Notetaker)

DATE AND TIME: Monday, February 21, 1972, 2:50–3:55 p.m.

PLACE: Chairman Mao's Residence, Peking

(There were opening greetings during which the Chairman welcomed President Nixon, and the President expressed his great pleasure at meeting the Chairman.)

President Nixon:	You read a great deal. The Prime Minister said that you read more than he does.
Chairman Mao:	Yesterday in the airplane you put forward a very difficult problem for us. You said that what it is required to talk about are philosophic problems.
President Nixon:	I said that because I have read the Chairman's poems and speeches, and I know he was a professional philosopher. (Chinese laugh.)
Chairman Mao:	(looking at Dr. Kissinger) He is a doctor of philosophy?
President Nixon:	He is a doctor of brains.
Chairman Mao:	What about asking him to be the main speaker today?
President Nixon:	He is an expert in philosophy.
Dr. Kissinger:	I used to assign the Chairman's collective writings to my classes at Harvard.
Chairman Mao:	Those writings of mine aren't anything. There is nothing instructive in what I wrote.
	(Looking toward the photographers) Now they are trying to interrupt our meeting, our order here.
President Nixon:	The Chairman's writings moved a nation and have changed the world.
Chairman Mao:	I haven't been able to change it. I've only been able to change a few places in the vicinity of Peking.
	Our common old friend, Generalissimo Chiang Kai-shek, doesn't approve of this. He calls us communist bandits. He recently issued a speech. Have you seen it?
President Nixon:	Chiang Kai-shek calls the Chairman a bandit. What does the Chairman call Chiang Kai-shek?
Prime Minister Chou:	Generally speaking we call them Chiang Kai-shek's clique. In the newspapers, sometimes we call him a

	bandit; we are also called bandits in turn. Anyway, we abuse each other.
Chairman Mao:	Actually, the history of our friendship with him is much longer than the history of your friendship with him.
President Nixon:	Yes, I know.
Chairman Mao:	We two must not monopolize the whole show. It won't do if we don't let Dr. Kissinger have a say. You have been famous about your trips to China.
Dr. Kissinger:	It was the President who set the direction and worked out the plan.
President Nixon:	He is a very wise assistant to say it that way. (Mao and Chou laugh.)
Chairman Mao:	He is praising you, saying you are clever in doing so.
President Nixon:	He doesn't look like a secret agent. He is the only man in captivity who could go to Paris 12 times and Peking once and no one knew it, except possibly a couple of pretty girls. (Chou laughs.)
Dr. Kissinger:	They didn't know it; I used it as a cover.
Chairman Mao:	In Paris?
President Nixon:	Anyone who uses pretty girls as a cover must be the greatest diplomat of all time.
Chairman Mao:	So your girls are very often made use of?
President Nixon:	His girls, not mine. It would get me into great trouble if I used girls as a cover.
Prime Minister Chou:	(laughs) Especially during elections. (Kissinger laughs.) Dr. Kissinger doesn't run for President because he wasn't born a citizen of the United States.
Dr. Kissinger:	Miss Tang is eligible to be President of the United States.
President Nixon:	She would be the first woman President. There's our candidate.
Chairman Mao:	It would be very dangerous if you have such a candidate. But let us speak the truth. As for the Democratic Party, if they come into office again, we cannot avoid contacting them.
President Nixon:	We understand. We will hope that we don't give you that problem.
Chairman Mao:	Those questions are not questions to be discussed in my place. They should be discussed with the Premier. I discuss the philosophical questions. That is to say, I voted for you during your election. There is an American here called Mr. Frank Coe, and he wrote an article precisely at the time when your country was in havoc, during your last electoral campaign.

	He said you were going to be elected President. I appreciated that article very much. But now he is against the visit.
President Nixon:	When the President says he voted for me, he voted for the lesser of two evils.
Chairman Mao:	I like rightists. People say you are rightists, that the Republican Party is to the right, that Prime Minister Heath is also to the right.
President Nixon:	And General de Gaulle.
Chairman Mao:	de Gaulle is a different question. They also say the Christian Democratic Party of West Germany is also to the right. I am comparatively happy when these people on the right come into power.
President Nixon:	I think the important thing to note is that in America, at least at this time, those on the right can do what those on the left talk about.
Dr. Kissinger:	There is another point, Mr. President. Those on the left are pro-Soviet and would not encourage a move toward the People's Republic, and in fact criticize you on those grounds.
Chairman Mao:	Exactly that. Some are opposing you. In our country also there is a reactionary group which is opposed to our contact with you. The result was that they got on an airplane and fled abroad.
Prime Minister Chou:	Maybe you know this.
Chairman Mao:	Throughout the whole world, the US intelligence reports are comparatively accurate. The next was Japan. As for the Soviet Union, they finally went to dig out the corpses, but they didn't say anything about it.
Prime Minister Chou:	In Outer Mongolia.
President Nixon:	We had similar problems recently in the crisis on India-Pakistan. The American left criticized me very heavily for failing to side with India. This was for two reasons: they were pro-Indian and they were pro-Soviet.
	I thought it was important to look at the bigger issue. We could not let a country, no matter how big, gobble up its neighbor. It cost – I don't say this with sorrow because it was right – it cost me politically, but I think history will record that it was the right thing to do.
Chairman Mao:	As a suggestion, may I suggest that you do a little less briefing? (The President points at Dr. Kissinger and Chou laughs.) Do you think it is good if you

	brief others on what we talk about, our philosophic discussions here?
President Nixon:	The Chairman can be sure that whatever we discuss, or whatever I and the Prime Minister discuss, nothing goes beyond the room. That is the only way to have conversations at the highest level.
Chairman Mao:	That's good.
President Nixon:	For example, I hope to talk with the Prime Minister and later with the Chairman about issues like Taiwan, Vietnam and Korea. I also want to talk about – and this is very sensitive – the future of Japan, the future of the subcontinent, and what India's role will be; and on the broader world scene, the future of US-Soviet relations. Because only if we see the whole picture of the world and the great forces that move the world will we be able to make the right decisions about the immediate and urgent problems that always completely dominate our vision.
Chairman Mao:	All those troublesome problems I don't want to get into very much. I think your topic is better – philosophic questions.
President Nixon:	For example, Mr. Chairman, it is interesting to note that most nations would approve of this meeting, but the Soviets disapprove, the Japanese have doubts which they express, and the Indians disapprove. So we must examine why, and determine how our policies should develop to deal with the whole world, as well as the immediate problems such as Korea, Vietnam, and of course, Taiwan.
Chairman Mao:	Yes, I agree.
President Nixon:	We, for example, must ask ourselves – again in the confines of this room – why the Soviets have more forces on the border facing you than on the border facing Western Europe. We must ask ourselves, what is the future of Japan? Is it better – here I know we have disagreements – is it better for Japan to be neutral, totally defenseless, or it is [sic] better for a time for Japan to have some relations with the United States? The point being – I am talking now in the realm of philosophy – in international relations there are no good choices. One thing is sure – we can leave no vacuums, because they can be filled. The Prime Minister, for example, has pointed out that the United States reaches out its hands and that the Soviet Union reaches out its hands. The question is

which danger the People's Republic faces, whether it is the danger of American aggression or Soviet aggression. There are hard questions, but we have to discuss them.

Chairman Mao: At the present time, the question of aggression from the United States or aggression from China is relatively small; that is, it could be said that this is not a major issue, because the present situation is one in which a state of war does not exist between our two countries. You want to withdraw some of your troops back on your soil; ours do not go abroad.

Therefore, the situation between our two countries is strange because during the past 22 years our ideas have never met in talks. Now the time is less than ten months since we began playing table tennis; if one counts the time since you put forward your suggestion at Warsaw it is less than two years. Our side also is bureaucratic in dealing with matters. For example, you wanted some exchange of persons of a personal level, things like that; also trade. But rather than deciding that we stuck with our stand that without settling major issues there is nothing to do with smaller issues. I myself persisted in that position. Later on, I saw you were right, and we played table tennis. The Prime Minister said this was also after President Nixon came to office.

The former President of Pakistan introduced President Nixon to us. At that time, our Ambassador to Pakistan refused to agree on our having a contact with you. He said it should be compared whether President Johnson or President Nixon would be better. But President Yahya said the two men cannot be compared, that these two men are incomparable. He said that one was like a gangster – he meant President Johnson. I don't know how he got that impression. We on our side were not very happy with that president either. We were not very happy with your former presidents, beginning from Truman through Johnson. We were not very happy with these presidents, Truman and Johnson. In between there were eight years of a Republican president. During that period probably you hadn't thought things out either.

Prime Minister Chou: The main thing was John Foster Dulles' policy.
Chairman Mao: He (Chou) also discussed this with Dr. Kissinger before.

President Nixon:	But they (gesturing towards Prime Minister Chou and Dr. Kissinger) shook hands. (Chou laughs.)
Chairman Mao:	Do you have anything to say, Doctor?
Dr. Kissinger:	Mr. Chairman, the world situation has also changed dramatically during that period. We've had to learn a great deal. We thought all socialist/communist states were the same phenomenon. We didn't understand until the President came into office the different nature of revolution in China and the way revolution had developed in other socialist states.
President Nixon:	Mr. Chairman, I am aware of the fact that over a period of years my position with regard to the People's Republic was one that the Chairman and Prime Minister totally disagreed with. What brings us together is a recognition of a new situation in the world and a recognition on our part that what is important is not a nation's internal political philosophy. What is important is its policy toward the rest of the world and toward us. That is why – this point I think can be said to be honest – we have differences. The Prime Minister and Dr. Kissinger discussed these differences.
	It also should be said – looking at the two great powers, the United States and China – we know China doesn't threaten the territory of the United States; I think you know the United States has no territorial designs on China. We know China doesn't want to dominate the United States. We believe you too realize the United States doesn't want to dominate the world. Also – maybe you don't believe this, but I do – neither China nor the United States, both great nations, want to dominate the world. Because our attitudes are the same on these two issues, we don't threaten each other's territories.
	Therefore, we can find common ground, despite our differences, to build a world structure in which both can be safe to develop in our own way on our own roads. That cannot be said about some other nations in the world.
Chairman Mao:	Neither do we threaten Japan or South Korea.
President Nixon:	Nor any country. Nor do we.
Chairman Mao:	(Checking the time with Chou) Do you think we have covered enough today?
President Nixon:	Yes. I would like to say as we finish, Mr. Chairman, we know you and the Prime Minister have taken

great risks in inviting us here. For us also it was a difficult decision. But having read some of the Chairman's statements, I know he is one who sees when an opportunity comes, that you must seize the hour and seize the day.

I would also like to say in a personal sense – and this to you Mr. Prime Minister – you do not know me. Since you do not know me, you shouldn't trust me. You will find I never say something I cannot do. And I always will do more than I can say. On this basis I want to have frank talks with the Chairman and, of course, with the Prime Minister.

Chairman Mao: (Pointing to Dr. Kissinger) "Seize the hour and seize the day." I think that, generally speaking, people like me sound a lot of big cannons. (Chou laughs) That is, things like "the whole world should unite and defeat imperialism, revisionism, and all reactionaries, and establish socialism."

President Nixon: Like me. And bandits.

Chairman Mao: But perhaps you as an individual may not be among those to be overthrown. They say that he (Dr. Kissinger) is also among those not to be overthrown personally. And if all of you are overthrown we wouldn't have any more friends left.

President Nixon: Mr. Chairman, the Chairman's life is well-known to all of us. He came from a very poor family to the top of the most populous nation in the world, a great nation.

My background is not so well known. I also came from a very poor family, and to the top of a very great nation. History has brought us together. The question is whether we, with different philosophies, but both with feet on the ground, and having come from the people, can make a breakthrough that will serve not just China and America, but the whole world in the years ahead. And that is why we are here.

Chairman Mao: Your book, *The Six Crises*, is not a bad book.

President Nixon: He (Mao) reads too much.

Chairman Mao: Too little. I don't know much about the United States. I must ask you to send some teachers here, mainly teachers of history and geography.

President Nixon: That's good, the best.

Chairman Mao: That's what I said to Mr. Edgar Snow, the correspondent who passed away a few days ago.

President Nixon: That was very sad.

Chairman Mao: Yes, indeed.

It is alright to talk well and also alright if there are no agreements because what use is there if we stand in deadlock? Why is it that we must be able to reach results? People will say . . . if we fail the first time, then people will talk why are we not able to succeed the first time? The only reason would be that we have taken the wrong road. What will they say if we succeed the second time?

(There were then some closing pleasantries. The Chairman said he was not well. President Nixon responded that he looked good. The Chairman said that appearances were deceiving. After handshakes and more pictures, Prime Minister Chou then escorted the President out of the residence.)

Note

1 Henry Kissinger's memoir of the first Nixon administration, *White House Years*, (Boston: Little Brown, 1979) remains an important primary source on the rapprochement, but it stands corrected by declassified material as well as important secondary sources, p. 749.

References

Burr, William, ed., The National Security Archive and the George Washington University's Cold War Group of the Elliott School of International Affairs, *The Beijing-Washington Back-Channel and Henry Kissinger's Secret Trip to China, September 1970–July 1971, National Security Archive Electronic Briefing Book No. 66*, February 27, 2002, Washington, DC.

Chen, Jian, *Mao's China and the Cold War*, Chapel Hill, NC: University of North Carolina Press, 2010.

Kissinger, Henry, *White House Years*, Boston: Little Brown, 1979.

National Security Archive, Washington DC, Declassified copy of the original transcript of the initial meeting between President Richard Nixon and Chairman Mao Zedong in Beijing, February 21, 1972.

Part II

Spectacular growth and the Chinese economy

3   China reforms from 1978 to 1990

In the 16th century, the Chinese economy was among the most sophisticated and productive in the world, and Chinese citizens probably enjoyed a much higher standard of living than the rest of its global counterparts. Founded by the invading Manchus, the Qing (Ch'ing) Dynasty (1644–1912) continued on with this envious coexistent lifestyle. In fact, some contemporary Chinese scholars call this time period "unparalleled in history" because all aspects of Chinese culture flourished: "China was considered a prosperous state with abundant natural resources, a huge but basically contented population, and a royal house of great prestige at home and abroad". However, in terms of China's population, by the late 18th century, the Chinese state began to sow the seeds of its own destruction, particularly in its expanding, unyielding population growth. With a population of around 100 million through much of its history, under the peaceful Qing (Ch'ing), the population doubled from 150 million in 1650 to 300 million by 1800, and reached 450 million by the late 19th century. At that point, there was no longer any land in China's southern and central provinces available for migration: the introduction of New World (American) crops through trade – especially sweet potatoes, peanuts, and tobacco, which required different growing conditions than rice and wheat – had already claimed previously unusable land (Asia for Educators, Columbia University 2009).

With only 10 percent of the land fertile, the typical Chinese farmer had an average of only three acres under cultivation and unfortunately there were many who were trying to survive with only one acre:

> The right of equal inheritance among sons (versus primogeniture as practiced in Japan) only hastened the fragmentation of land holdings. To compound these problems, the state's political control was diminishing. The size of the bureaucracy remained the same while the population grew. By the 19th century, district magistrates at the lowest level of the Chinese bureaucracy were responsible for the welfare, control, and taxation of an average of 250,000 people. This left control and responsibility for government increasingly in the hands of local leaders whose allegiances were to their localities and families, rather than to the state.
>
> (Asia for Educators, Columbia University 2009)

China's economic history is rife with spurts and starts. Some economic historians even make the case that China's economy began to disintegrate in the middle of the 17th century at the fall of the Ming Dynasty and other economic historians claim that its economic decline began as early as the 16th century.

Under the leadership of Mao Zedong between 1949 and 1976, the Chinese Communist Party (CCP) implemented any number of socialist economic policies and platforms. In the early 1950s, industrial central planning with an emphasis on heavy industry was introduced. Heavy industry was an emphasis that was part of the Soviet's original five-year plan immediately after the Bolshevik Revolution. Consequently, the first Chinese five-year plan was patterned after the Soviet's first five-year plan and of course, included in the first Chinese five-year plan was the collectivization of agriculture.

In the 1960s and 1970s following the collapse of the Great Leap Forward and the political split between China and the USSR, China's economic policies fluctuated between the more conventional socialist policies put forth by party leaders like Deng Xiaoping and Liu Shao-chi and the more radical ultra-left social and economic policies initiated by Mao Zedong. This impasse was obviously deeply criticized by Mao who claimed that his opponents were taking the capitalist high ground and for that part, he succeeded in overpowering their proposed policies until his death in 1976. One of the early signs of progress made by Deng Xiaoping took place in 1977 when the Chinese government announced that China's universities would be reopened and university entrance examinations would resume. The Chinese university system was one of the casualties of Mao's Cultural Revolution formerly the Great Proletarian Revolution which began in 1966, and although Mao called for an end in 1969, the Revolution still had lingered remnants until 1976. China's Cultural Revolution is the subject of a completely different book, but it should be noted that Mao's Cultural Revolution was his way of keeping the 1948 Chinese Communist Revolution alive.

In December 1978, under the leadership of Deng Xiaoping and other reformists in the Communist Party of China (CPC), the People's Republic of China embarked on a policy of economic reform. At the Third Plenum in December 1978 the famous four-character policy, *gaige kaifang* was initiated (Huenemann 2013). In general, this became the complete reformation of China's economic system. It involved not only economic and social reforms, but also it was the first time since the 1948 revolution that the law allowed for the opening of the Chinese economy to the outside world. Moreover, on January 1, 1979 the United States and the People's Republic of China (PRC) established full diplomatic relations.

Since the Third Plenum and into the 21st century, there's been a great deal of disagreement within the Chinese Communist Party, but there's no question the reforms have succeeded as originally intended beginning with the de-collectivization of agriculture, the dismantling of the Soviet style central planning in industry especially heavy industry and the positive impact of a more open Chinese economy. Since 1978, these reforms have had a dramatic effect on the Chinese economy in general which in turn has raised the standard of living

Table 3.1 China 1952 to 1978 income and production

	1952	1978	*Annual Rate of Growth Percent*
National income (NDMP) billion renminbi	58.9	301	6.5
Total value of industry production-renminbi	34.9	406.7	9.9
Heavy industry production-billion renminbi	12.4	231.4	11.9
Light industry production-billion renminbi	22.5	173.3	8.2
Total value agricultural production-billion renminbi	46.1	156.7	4.8
Amount of food grain production-unprocessed million tons	163.9	304.8	2.4
Population-yearly average million persons	574.8	962.6	2
Per capita food grain output-unprocessed, kg	285.1	316.6	0.4
Per capita national income renminbi	104	315	4.4

Source: Author with data from the National Bureau of Statistics

for millions of the Chinese people. The aforementioned disagreements within the CCP are based more on sentimentality and reverence for Mao Zedong and less on economic reality.

Table 3.1 shows China's overall national economy between 1952 and 1978, when its national income increased by a factor of more than five, representing an annualized growth rate of 6.6 percent. Industrial production in that same time period increased by more than a factor of 11 giving China's industrial production an annual growth rate of 9.9 percent. Heavy industry production between 1952 and 1978 increased by almost a factor of 20 representing an annualized growth rate of 11.9 percent. Light industry production in that same time frame increased by a factor of eight or an annualized growth rate of 8.2 percent.

The total value of agricultural production between 1952 and 1978 grew from 46.1 billion yuan in 1952 to 128.9 billion yuan in 1978 representing an increase of 278 percent or approximately 4.0 percent per year. Moreover, the amount of unprocessed grain production grew from 163.9 million tons in 1952 to 304.8 million tons in 1978 – a percentage increase of roughly 100 percent or 2.4 percent annually. On the other hand, in 1952 China's population was 574.8 million people, but in 1978 China's population had grown to 962.6 million people. Consequently, in the 26 years from 1952 to 1978 China's population had almost doubled and that statistic in itself was very troubling for the Chinese authorities. The per capita national income in China between 1952 and 1978 grew at an annual rate of roughly 4.4 percent. Unfortunately, the inflation data in that time frame is unreliable so it's virtually impossible to make any kind of a value judgment between nominal and real on that particular statistic.

Clearly, 1978 was a turning point in China's economic and social history. We can also credit China's economic reforms in 1978 with the mind-boggling, spectacular economic growth rates of the Chinese economy from 1978 onwards. The economic reforms that began in 1978 involved a two-part effort. Obviously, the first part originated in the late 1970s and ended in the early 1980s. The first part was probably the most arduous because it involved the de-collectivization of agriculture, and for a country with a mostly agricultural economy, this can be a monumental task. Consecutively, the Chinese government slowly allowed foreign direct investment and at the same time, the government also granted permission for some entrepreneurs to start businesses, but this was a process that required government authorization on a piecemeal basis. It should also be noted that most industry in the first part of China's economic transformation remained state owned.

The second part of China's economic transformation occurred between the 1980s and the 1990s (Naughton et al. 2008). In that time frame, the Chinese authorities allowed for the privatization of industry and the government also began to open up its industrial base to foreign contractors, but there were very stringent guidelines that foreign contractors had to follow. For the most part, foreign contractors had to manufacture their industrial output in China using Chinese employees. Protectionist policies were slowly abated and probably the biggest advance for the overall Chinese economy was the methodic, slow removal of price controls on a product-by-product basis. However in the 1990s, some state-owned monopolies were still in place in some sectors, e.g. banking and petroleum. Towards the end of the 1970s due to a massive increase in China's population, food supplies and production became so deficient that the Chinese authorities were warning its citizens that their country was about to repeat the Disaster of 1959 where famines killed millions of Chinese during the Great Leap Forward. During the de-collectivization of agriculture, the Chinese authorities emphasized the Household Responsibility System. This system divided the land dedicated to communes into private plots thereby creating an economic base away from the masses and into individual families. The structure was very much like the typical tenant farmer in the United States. The farmer keeps the overage income generated from the land after paying a percentage of the income to the state.

This move in particular increased China's agriculture production dramatically which in turn increased the living standards for millions and millions of Chinese farmers, but equally important it stimulated and revitalized a rural industry that just a few years earlier was described as deficient and for the most part decimated. This particular approach has been described by academics as the Bottom-Up Approach as opposed to the Top-Down Approach of the perestroika found in the old USSR. Later, the Bottom-Up Approach became an important component of China's successful agricultural economic transformation.

In an effort to increase urban productivity, similar economic reforms relative to a dual-price system were introduced. State-owned enterprises were allowed to sell any production above the plan minimum. Commodities were also sold at both plan and market prices, which allowed the Chinese to avoid the shortages all too often found in the Maoist era. Moreover in the 1980s, the creation of the Industrial Responsibility System facilitated the advancement of the state-owned enterprise by allowing individuals or groups to manage the enterprise by contract. Private businesses were also allowed to operate and over time they were responsible for a greater percentage of industrial output. At this point in

China's economic history, for the first time since the Kuomintang era this country had opened its doors to foreign investment. In order to facilitate this effort, the Chinese authorities created a list of economic zones for foreign investment. Although these so-called zones were supposed to be less regulated by bureaucrats, they were in fact heavily regulated. However, at the end of the day, these designated regions became the catalyst for national economic growth.

Early in the 1980s, Deng Xiaoping's economic policies continued to emphasize less regulatory controls on private enterprise, which resulted in less government intervention along with some small-scale privatization of state-owned enterprises. The decentralization of government control was an important turning point that gave the provincial leaders the leeway to independently experiment with different methods to increase economic growth in an effort to privatize state-owned enterprises relative to their specific province. There's usually some opposition to most progressive movements. In this case it was an effort led by Chen Yun, Elder of the Chinese Communist Party, to prevent major reforms, which would have affected the financial interests of certain special interest groups affiliated with the centralized government bureaucracy. At the time, there was an upsurge in inflation combined with the ongoing corruption, which contributed in part to the Tiananmen Square protests. Afterward, the conservative element who was vehemently against the political and economic transformations blamed the unrest on a more liberal attitude on behalf of the centralized government. Consequently, some key reformers were ousted and the conservative backlash threatened to reverse many of Deng's reforms, but he reaffirmed these and he continued with China's political and economic transformations as well as reopening the Shanghai Stock Exchange, which was closed by Mao Zedong some 40 years earlier. Overall, the economy grew robustly during that time period, but the economic problems centered on inflation and the heavy losses stemming from the inefficient state-sector resulted in an inordinate drain on China's overall general economy. In terms of the success of China's economic reforms, there have historically been a number of theories put forth by scholars on that subject, but all of these theories are predicated on understanding what it means for a nation to go from a planned economy to a socialist market economy. China had to overcome its decades' old anti-market propaganda. And that was a not an easy mindset to overcome; hence the backlash from the elder conservatives. For many of them, communism was their capitalism and a socialist market economy meant that their accountability was challenged. A corrupt system builds on more corruption until the economic system reaches the point of no return where everyone and everything involved in a corrupt economic system will eventually come to a grinding halt. If a widget maker's pay is the same no matter how many widgets he makes, his incentive is to make as few as possible.

The concept behind China's socialist market economy was to create an increase in productivity to counter a work ethic that had been under significant erosion for decades, but in order for that to happen, the workforce has to be incentivized. An increase in productivity resulted in an increase in wages for millions of Chinese families, which in turn resulted in an improvement to their living standards. In terms of theories to explain China's successful economic reforms, one very interesting theory is that decentralization of state authority energized the economy. That gave the local leaders the leeway to experiment with various ways to privatize the state sector. It's also clear that Deng was not the originator of many of the reforms, but at the end of the day, he gave approval to them. Another theory deals with the internal incentives within the Chinese government. Officials presiding over areas of high economic growth were more likely to be promoted. Scholars have also noted that local and provincial governments wanted to lure investment and along those lines, they would compete to reduce regulations and barriers to investment in order to boost economic growth and their own careers.

Even though this chapter addresses China's economic transformation from 1978 to 1990, for transparency purposes it would be useful to evaluate these economic reforms against the backdrop of China's Gross Domestic Product (GDP) growth from 1952 to 2015. For all intents and purposes, 1952 was really the first year of economic normalcy for China's new revolutionary government. Moreover, 2015 was selected because that's 25 years beyond the 1990 time frame. The 25-year time frame is required in order to establish economic growth momentum. Table 3.2 shows that from 1952 to 1960 China's economic growth edged up by a factor of 2.14 and from 1970 to 1980 China's GDP growth grew by a factor of 2.0. From 1978 (the start of economic reforms) to 1990, China's GDP growth grew by a staggering factor of 5.14. In that time frame, China's economic growth starts to take hold in a rather impressive fashion compared to the flat line beginning in 1952 some 38 years beforehand. From 1990 to 2015, China's economic growth is nothing less than a straight up arc (Rawski et al. 2008).

Table 3.2 People's Republic of China's nominal gross domestic product 1952–2015

	GDP renminbi billion at current prices	GDP per person Renminbi	Real annual GDP growth rate Percentage
1952	67.9	119	
1960	145.7	218	–0.3
1970	225.3	275	19.4
1978	365	382	11.7
1980	455.2	464	7.9
1990	1,877.4	1,654	3.9
2000	9,977.6	7,902	8.4
2008	31,675.2	23,912	9.6
2010	40,890.3	30,567	10.6
2011	48,412.3	36,018	9.5
2012	53,412.3	39,544	7.7
2013	58,880.9	43,320	7.7
2014	63,613.9	46,629	7.3
2015	67,770.0	N/A	6.9

Source: Author with data from the National Bureau of Statistics

It took time for China's new economic reforms to come to fruition, but when they did, the multiplier effect really took hold. The economy gained momentum and it built on itself. A production increase created more goods and services, which in turn created a comparable increase in total wages and that gave the worker more money to purchase an increase in goods and services.

The collapse of the Soviet Union and for that matter the Soviet Bloc's centrally planned economies in 1989 gave the Chinese government more reason for even more economic reform through different economic conduits in order to avert a similar fate. Moreover, China wanted to avoid anything remotely close to the market capitalism experiment that took place under Boris Yeltsin in the old Soviet Union in 1989 and 1990. That was a disaster and it was capitalism at its very worst. Shock Therapy Capitalism created Russian oligarchs and rampant corruption. Today, Russia's industrial base almost doesn't exist and technically it's an energy economy like Saudi Arabia only with six times more people: a country of 150 million people inextricably linked to one commodity and one commodity price. Russia's exports are almost 100 percent hydrocarbon or hydrocarbon related products. According to the Russian government, Russia's energy sector amounts to roughly 30 percent of the Russian economy, but according to the Carnegie Endowment for International Peace (Stronsky and Sokolsky 2017) that number is closer to 67–70 percent.

Not unlike the economies of Eastern Europe, China's transition from a planned economy to a socialist market economy underwent a similar transformation, but without the major economic shocks that plagued the Eastern Bloc. Although some of the components of China's economic reform have already been discussed, a closer look is still required in order to put the reforms in their proper perspective; otherwise this effort will create a thesis with far too many loose ends.

In terms of economic reforms, China's agriculture at the time was by far the most important and to that end, the Chinese farmers deserve most of the credit. In the past, a Chinese farmer would not get the extra reward for extra work because all members of his standardized 40-member team would share in the additional output. The commune system was replaced by a redistribution of China's agricultural land to individual households to farm separately. Moreover, each farming household received additional rewards after delivering a fixed amount of output to the central team for delivery to the government procurement agencies resulting in the creation of the (aforementioned) Household Responsibility System.

Privatizing certain state-owned enterprises was a very involved process that required methodical step-by-step procedures. The first step required more autonomy away from the central planning system. Each enterprise needed more autonomy in production, marketing and investment decisions as opposed to the dictates of a central planning system not the least bit familiar with the enterprise, its production, marketing or investments. This experiment began in the Sichuan Province in 1978 with six pilot enterprises and by the end of June 1980, 6,600 industrial enterprises producing roughly half of the total output of the state-owned enterprises had followed suit.

The creation of financial independence became the second step in the privatization of these enterprises. Each enterprise was allowed to keep the profits after paying taxes to the state as opposed to a system where the government was the recipient of all revenues. A decision by the Central Committee of the Communist Party in 1984 and later in 1987 involved the creation of a responsibility system similar to the Household Responsibility System in agriculture. In 1984, the enterprise was allowed to keep the remaining profits after paying a fixed amount to the parent enterprise.

In 1987, the Chinese authorities created the Contract Responsibility System for the industrial enterprise system, which meant that each state enterprise was allowed to keep the remaining profits after paying a fixed tax to the appropriate government jurisdiction. Those funds in turn are supposed to be distributed to the staff and workers with a percentage set aside for capital investment. On the surface most of this was very appealing to the economic officials who designed it, but in reality, the results were less impressive. First, the fixed tax portion of the Contract Responsibility System wasn't really fixed at all; it was more of a graduating tax depending on profitability. If profits increased, the tax levy increased. Moreover, managers at that time were woefully underpaid so the additional income couldn't really become too much of an incentive for the manager; a high salary for a manger was socially and ideologically unacceptable. On the other hand, when profits increased, the workers were usually paid with in-kind additional compensation, e.g. durable goods: TV sets, radios, refrigerators and so on. A third component to China's economic reforms post 1978 was the establishment of an open-door policy. After 30 years of a closed-door policy, in 1978 China created a system that encouraged foreign direct investment (FDI) and foreign trade. In 1978, the total value of foreign trade (imports and exports) amounted to roughly 7 percent of GDP, but by 1987 that number had reached 25 percent. Moreover, trading companies in cooperation with domestic industrial enterprises manufacturing export products were created specifically to decentralize trading activities.

Furthermore, special treatment was given to exporters and enterprises engaged in the manufacture of export products and services. In terms of foreign exchange, these firms were allowed to keep part of the foreign exchange earned by them and they were also offered special loans for either short-term financing for foreign exchange or long-term capital expansion providing the borrowed funds were used specifically to manufacture products for export or to finance the export process.

In 1981, several coastal provinces including Guangdong and Fujian were designated export-processing centers by the Chinese authorities. Foreign investors were encouraged to set up manufacturing operations there. These manufacturing facilities could either be 100 percent foreign owned or they could also be a joint venture with a Chinese company. A very important note should be interjected here: the Chinese government levies no import duty on imports that are to be used in the manufacture of exports. The underlying premise in this effort among other benefits was to utilize Chinese labor and at the same time use the capital and technological knowledge of foreign corporations. It's very clear that the actual formation of China's open-door policy was underscored by its voracious appetite for exports, and understandably so. Exports involve foreign exchange and if China can export more than it imports from any one country, that country's trade deficit with China results in excess cash flow for China.

Foreign investment was the second part of China's open-door policy. In 1982, the Shenzhen economic zone bordering Hong Kong was set aside by the Chinese authorities as a manufacturing area for foreign investors. Shenzhen was ideal for foreign investors to establish factories. The area was perfect for foreign corporations. It was abundant with inexpensive skilled labor and these companies could pay their employees market determined wage rates, which were much different than the wage rates in other parts of China. They also received special tax breaks. In less than a decade Shenzhen went from a piece of abandoned farmland to a bustling, modern city. Direct foreign investment can take any of three forms: cooperative enterprises, joint ventures, and 100 percent foreign owned enterprises. Moreover in 1982, the citizens of China could only enter Shenzhen with special permission; this was because of the vast differences in economic opportunities compared to the rest of China. Later, economic zones and special areas were created in other parts of China in order to facilitate foreign investors. Although China encourages foreign investment, the government's inability to fully understand the benefits aligned with free trade and free capital flows create constraints, which are normally not part of a free market economy. The Chinese government views the market economy as nothing more than a useful tool in the promotion of China's economic development and modernization, but that's where China's notion of a market economy stops. The government takes the position that it's the responsibility of the Chinese government to regulate market forces. The government will encourage specific sectors of foreign investment if that investment will directly enhance economic development and it will discourage and even prohibit other sectors of foreign investment. The Chinese government will encourage foreign investment to facilitate new technologies in agriculture; to enhance energy production; to upgrade transportation and any process that will make it easier to access essential raw materials. The government welcomes foreign investment in facilities that will enhance the process of renewing resources or new technologies that reduce environmental pollution. China also encourages foreign investment for upgrading technology for traditional industries and increased technology for labor-intense industries. Anything else is either not welcome or prohibited. A potential foreign investor should realize the regulated barriers involved with foreign direct investment in China; the legal procedures are extremely complicated and daunting. To begin with, the Chinese government structure at the local and national levels involves many government bureaus and officials and each of them has jurisdiction over a proposed investment project. Consequently, a foreign investor needs approval from all of them in order for the project to proceed. Most foreign investors are not familiar with China's way of conducting business.

The Decision of the Central Committee on Economic Reform in 1984 included China's price system as well as the three previously mentioned economic reform components: agriculture, state-owned enterprises and its open-door policy. What began as good progression towards a free market price system soon became more of a complex complicated pricing system that involves two tiers. Originally, the main objective was to decontrol the administratively determined prices gradually and allow prices to be determined by market forces. However, the administered prices cannot be decontrolled immediately. First, there is the problem of equity. To allow prices of basic consumer goods to increase would affect the welfare of consumers who were subsidized. A compromise solution was to introduce a two-tier price system.

In China's two-tier price system, one set of prices remained the same as before (no change), but market forces determine the second price system for the exact same product. According to the Decision of the Central Committee, state-owned enterprises may buy specific amounts of inputs and sell fixed amounts of outputs at the administered prices as before. Moreover, each SOE can buy additional inputs and sell above quota outputs at market-determined prices. China's approach in this instance was to establish an incentive price system where an enterprise will economize on its inputs and at the same time, maximize its output for profit. There seems to be a certain amount of inconsistency in the research available whether the enterprise should maximize output or increase output, but if the profit-side of the equation is based on output, common sense makes the case that the enterprise should maximize its production. In this system, if market demand increased for certain outputs greater than the amount of inputs centrally allocated by the government, prices will increase and the producer could increase production by paying for inputs at market prices.

This system also forces the producer to economize on the use of inputs purchased at market prices in order to satisfy demand and increase output production. An enterprise that receives given quantities of inputs at less than market prices is no different than an enterprise that receives a government subsidy. On the other hand, if an enterprise sells a given quantity of output at a below market price, that's the equivalent of paying a lump-sum tax. According to China's calculations in this instance, either a fixed government subsidy or a lump-sum tax has no effect on the optimal input and output decisions of the firm.

Given that enterprises continued to produce, the two-tier price system of the 1980s was an economically efficient, but excessively complicated price system. A single market price system would have been much simpler. The demand for the output would be satisfied and the producer could create output (production) directly proportional to demand and inventory requirements at the lowest possible price. China's two-tier price system carried over to its housing market. In the early 1980s, rent for housing supplied by employers to their employees was extremely low, not much more than several yuan per month for an apartment and that included practically all of China's urban housing at that time. Urban rents increased very gradually until the turn of the 21st century and at that point, most of urban housing was privatized. Simultaneously, there was also a two-tier price system taking place in the construction and sale of urban apartments by public, private and foreign developers. These developers were allowed to build apartments to be sold at market prices for those who could afford them. Most urban workers lived in the apartments assigned to them by their employers and the rents were gradually increased, but only as wages increased. When housing privatization took place, these workers were allowed to purchase their apartments at below market price and with a subsidy in the form of very low mortgage rates. The fifth component found in China's economic reforms of 1978 included non-state sectors. In addition to state enterprises, there are three other types of enterprises in China: collective, individual and overseas-funded. It should also be noted that the overseas-funded enterprise was part of China's open-door policy. Collective enterprises are basically urban or rural collectives. This included previous state-owned retail stores or small state-owned factories. In order to establish incentive, these business units were transferred to collective ownership in an attempt to make them more efficient and more profitable. It's important to note that new collective and industrial enterprises were established in urban areas.

Individual enterprises were established in townships and villages in rural areas with the support of local governments. After the successful transformation of agriculture, this became the logical next step in China's economic transformation in general. In terms of foreign-owned enterprises, these businesses were usually much larger in size and scope. For the most part, these are usually an extension of multinational corporations, but as was previously mentioned, the enterprise has to provide a technology or know-how unknown to China and the facility has to employ Chinese citizens.

All of the information provided so far in this book applies to Mainland China only. Special Administrative Regions of China, e.g. Hong Kong and Macau are more like separate countries; although they're governed by the government in Beijing on matters of foreign affairs and national defense, they are for the most part independent territories. As of this writing, China recognizes two Special Administrative Regions (SARs): Hong Kong and Macau. Beijing has publicly claimed that should Taiwan want to return to Chinese rule, it too would take the form of a SAR. The whole concept of a special administrative region was developed in response to the return of its former colonies Hong Kong and Macau to Chinese rule. Both Hong Kong and Macau enjoyed a very high level of independence. Moreover, both of them enjoyed the benefits of capitalist economies and the rule of law especially Hong Kong. In that light, their residents were very unsure about the impending communist rule. The SAR infrastructure was the result of very deliberate and distinct discussions and agreements between the Chinese government and Great Britain prior to the handover of Hong Kong to the Chinese government at midnight on July 1, 1997. Included in the 1984 Decision of the Central Committee was an effort to modernize China's banking and financial sector. Prior to the economic reforms, the People's Bank was basically a deposit bank with branches scattered throughout China to accept deposits from the Chinese public. In addition to accepting deposits, the Bank's other functions were to issue currency and extend loans to state-owned enterprises in accordance with the needs and specifications of the central planning authority. The principals of the Bank had no authority in the decision-making process regarding these loans. Technically, commercial banks did not exist. At least, they did not exist in the sense that they could originate loans to enterprises on the basis of profitability. In 1983, the People's Bank was nominally transferred into a central bank. And from that point forward, China created specialized banks: the Industrial and Commercial Bank of China, Agricultural Bank of China and the People's Construction Bank of China. These banks were given some autonomy in terms of loan origination in the early 1980s very similar to the independence of the state-owned industrial enterprises to make decisions about production. The creation of China's central banks resulted in a rapid increase in the money supply. The increased money supply was in response to the loan origination taking place in the specialized banks. All total in 1984, China's money supply increased by roughly 50 percent which in turn increased its inflation rate to a staggering 8.8 percent according to the overall retail price index in 1985 (Allen et al. 2008). In addition to the banking system, in 1981 the government established the China International Trust and Investment Corporation (CITIC) in an effort to attract foreign capital. This set off the creation of a whole host of investment trusts by China's various government provinces. In addition to the reopening of the Shanghai Stock Exchange in 1990, a new stock exchange was also established in Shenzhen. Moreover in 1990, pensions were provided under the creation of China's new social security system and at that point, pension funds became an important source for saving and investment. At the same time, domestic insurance businesses were allowed to reopen after 20 years and for the first time foreign insurance companies were allowed to operate in China. Included in China's economic reforms was its economic and social infrastructure. After the Communist Revolution, all of China's schools were brought under government control. Higher education was modeled on the USSR system and technical training became a major emphasis. After the Cultural Revolution, the education system returned to normal and it was making reasonable progress. On the whole, Chinese students are very eager to learn especially in math and science. From 1985 onwards, the Ministry of Education or the State Education Commission sponsored various and assorted educational programs in conjunction with foreign educational institutions in a concerted effort to improve education in China. Much of the success in higher education in China can be attributable to China's ongoing commitment to invite foreign scholars and professionals to teach for either one or two academic terms. Moreover, China's higher education emphasized textbooks written in English and so it became incumbent on its students to learn English. Universities like Harvard, Princeton and New York University have established campuses in China for both foreign and Chinese students. Since the 1990s, private education in China has flourished. For the most part, China has reversed its stance on higher education away from the Soviet-style universities that emphasizes specialized and technical education to a more liberal and broad-based education system obtainable from more comprehensive universities. Overall, China realized that its economy is a global powerhouse and in order to retain that momentum China's education system had to become a global market place for ideas. In terms of the rule of law in China, since the 1980s China has made a very serious effort to modernize its legal system. Since that time, the

Ministry of Education has made any number of impressive improvements in a legal education in China. Moreover, the People's Congress has enacted a number of laws in order to facilitate the function of a market economy. Specific examples are the Commercial Bank Law and the Central Bank Law. These are bankruptcy laws. The People's Congress also enacted other laws governing foreign trade and investment and acceptable corporate behavior. All of this contributed to additional legal reforms in the late 1990s, but the changes made to the Chinese legal system up to 1990 showed the participants in the global economy that China had taken the first steps to establish a rule of law that protects not only Chinese business interests, but also the business interests of all its global participants.

References

Allen, Franklin et al., "China's Financial System: Past Present and Future," in Loren Brandt and Thomas G. Rawski (eds), *China's Great Transformation*, Cambridge: Cambridge University Press, 2008.

Asia for Educators, Columbia University, 2009, available at http://afe.easia.columbia.edu.

Brandt, Loren and Thomas G. Rawski, *China's Great Transformation*, Cambridge: Cambridge University Press, 2008.

Dahlman, Carl J. and Jean-Eric Aubert, *China and the Knowledge Economy; Seizing the 21st Century*, WBI Development Studies, World Bank Publications, January 30, 2008.

Huenemann, Ralph W., "Economic Reforms, 1978–Present," *Chinese Studies*, 2013, pp. 1–10.

Naughton, Barry et al. 2008, "A Political Economy of China's Economic Transition in China's Great Transformation," in Loren Brandt and Thomas G. Rawski, *China's Great Transformation*, Cambridge: Cambridge University Press, 2008.

Rawski, Thomas G. et al., "China's Industrial Development," in Loren Brandt, and Thomas G. Rawski, *China's Great Transformation*, Cambridge: Cambridge University Press, 2008.

Shirk, Susan L., *The Political Logic of Economic Reform in China*, Berkeley and Los Angeles: University of California Press, 1993.

Smith, Adam 1776, *Wealth of Nations*, William Strahan & Thomas Cadell.

Stronsky, Paul and Richard Sokolsky, "The Return of Global Russia," Carnegie Endowment for International Peace, December 14, 2017, available at https://carnegie endowment.org/2017/12/14/return-of-global-russia-analytical-framework-pub-75003.

4 China from 1990 forward

Since the economic reforms of 1978, China's shift from a centrally planned economy to a market socialist economy has paid off handsomely for the bulk of the Chinese people: the consequence of rapid economic growth and social development. Until recent times, on average GDP growth was roughly 10 percent per year, the fastest economic expansion by a major economy in history (World Bank 2016, 1–2). This effort lifted more than 800 million people out of poverty. Moreover, China reached its Millennium Development Goals by 2015 and at the same time, it made a major contribution to the achievement of the MDGs globally. With its population greater than 1.3 billion people, China will continue to play an important role on the global economic stage. On the other hand, China still remains a developing country (emerging market economy) with a per capita income much smaller than the advanced economies and its market reforms have barely touched the surface for a great many of its poor. Unfortunately, due to its very large rural population, China's poverty reduction does not correlate with its economic growth (Angang 2005, 1–5).

> Until 2020, the central government is expected to target poverty alleviation in the provinces of Guizhou, Sichuan Yunnan and Gansu where it is needed. For the effective allocation of resources, the use of big data is handy and would discourage local officials from fudging figures to meet targets.
>
> (Angang 2017, 1)

According to the World Bank, between 1980 and 1990, the poverty in China's overall population went from 542 million down to 375 million representing 167 million Chinese taken out of poverty. However since the 1990s, China has slowed its pace of poverty reduction. In that same time period China has maintained a very high growth rate, but there are indications that the poverty reduction in the rural areas has slowed. The annual reduction within the poverty population in the rural areas has only decreased by 8 million annually. Obviously, the research was disappointing to say the least, but most of the academics who have written on China's correlation between economic growth and a decrease in poverty reduction are not detailed enough in their reasoning to satisfy the interest of the world academic community.

Between the economic reforms of 1978 and 1990, hundreds of millions of Chinese rose above the poverty line, but in the following years the earlier advances in the percentages of poverty reduction were not matched. This phenomenon has more to do with the reduction of China's rural population and job retraining within urban manufacturing. In October of each year, China celebrates Poverty Alleviation Day. It's a day filled with forums and fundraisers. Basically, it's designed to rally efforts to fight deprivation. And thanks to China's very rapid and large economic expansion, it alleviates a great deal of poverty.

Rapid economic growth in China has brought on many challenges mainly high income inequality, urbanization that's unable to keep up with residents' basic living requirements, challenges to a clean environment and external imbalance relative to its ongoing foreign criticism on trade. One factor rarely talked about within the context of China's staggering economic growth is its aging population. An aging population exacerbates its internal migration of labor.

There's no question that very significant economic and political adjustments are in order if China expects its inordinate growth rate to continue at its current pace. Economic history shows that transitioning from a middle-income economy to a high-income economy is much more cumbersome than transitioning from a low-income economy to a middle-income economy. That's not to say that China is a middle-income economy by Western standards, but nonetheless its gains have been spectacularly unbelievable and when compared to its economic peer group – the emerging market economies mainly the BRICS countries (Brazil, Russia, India, China and South Africa) – it would be a middle-income economy in no uncertain terms.

As of writing, China's growth is beginning to fall back a bit, but what's even more worrisome from an economist's point of view is its debt to growth ratio. Right now in the Chinese economy, it takes $6 to $8 dollars of debt to increase its growth by $1 dollar as opposed to the United States and the European Union where it takes only $3 of debt to increase growth by $1 dollar. These problems are addressed and analyzed in China's 12th Five-Year Plan (2011–2015) and the most recently approved 13th Five-Year Plan. In terms of Chinese debt and Chinese growth, Shenzhen is a very important place to begin this analysis. In less than a generation, Shenzhen has gone from backwater farm ground to an important financial hub in less than a generation. Shenzhen is an excellent example of China's ever-changing economic and financial landscape. However, within the past 24 months, the city has faced unaccustomed uncertainty. The financial markets have lost ground and the ongoing increase in rising corporate costs has forced some well-known corporations to relocate elsewhere in China. These are issues that must be addressed by the Chinese financial authorities in order for China in general to achieve a secure future in terms of sustained and sustainable development. Financial tremors have shaken most of China's metropolitan areas and the word rebalancing are heard over and over again (Lipton 2016, 1–3).

Economists point out repeatedly that the term "rebalancing" can have inordinate connotations and it may not be that easy to implement. Rebalancing requires a new range of actions and that by no way means taking the necessary actions to facilitate the new, but it's imperative and equally important that necessary actions are put in place in order to downsize in a smooth transition the entities that are outdated or overbuilt. And all of this has to be done in a timely fashion otherwise the situations worsen with time and the problems will seem insurmountable. According to a recent conference by the Chinese Economist Society (CES) in conjunction with the IMF, rebalancing has become a priority that is of critical importance in terms of China's economic future relative to the global economy. The ramifications of China's rebalancing on the global economy are a foregone conclusion. Over the past 20 years, the world economic community has learned firsthand especially in the major economies that disruptions in one country's economy can create worldwide economic reverberations.

In terms of reverberations a case in point was in 2015 when the world financial markets took a sudden downturn overnight following the instability in the Chinese markets. Moreover, earlier in 2018 when the price of crude oil plummeted below $30 dollars per barrel, the world financial markets went into utter chaos. Normally, low oil prices are good for the economy: the consumer has more money to spend on consumer discretionary products, but in this case and in light of the 2008 banking meltdown, the financial markets were more concerned with the amount of energy debt owed to the world's banks.

On the surface, China's economic growth remains strong by any measure except China itself over the previous 25 years. So it's important to maintain a solid sense of perspective, but there are some disturbing indicators. One in particular stands out, China's current account surplus is currently running somewhere between 2–3 percent of GDP down dramatically from its high in 2007 of around 10 percent of GDP. Moreover, the contribution of net exports which was the key driver of China's phenomenal growth in the not too distant past is hovering around zero.

In 2015, one very interesting statistic stood out which showed capital inflows to China have slowed dramatically, but the effective exchange rate has inexplicitly remained, for the most part, stable. Ironically, this was underscored by the IMF's decision in 2015 to include the renminbi (RMB) in its basket of currencies to show that the RMB's portion of the Special Drawing Rights (SDR) was based on China's determination that the RMB is a freely usable currency. Simultaneously, China's effort to domestically rebalance its economy has been mixed, but with that said, there's been moderate progress transforming the economy from investment to consumption.

These are growth impediments that most Western capitalist economies dealt with years ago, but in China's situation with its market socialist economy; this is an unexplained nuance. China's overall debt profile has basically three elements: government debt, household debt and corporate debt. China's overall debt is roughly 225 percent of GDP of that amount 40 percent is government debt and roughly 40 percent is household debt. Both are not particularly high by international standards, but China's corporate debt is approximately 145 percent of GDP and that number is very high by any measure. According to the IMF, state-owned enterprises contribute a 22 percent share of China's overall economic output, but state-owned enterprises account for roughly 55 percent of corporate debt and then to add additional exacerbation, China's state-owned enterprises are far less profitable than their private counterparts (Lipton 2016, 3). This kind of an economic environment is counterproductive. A combination of deteriorating earnings and increasing indebtedness is an economic challenge to say the least. That kind of a hurdle makes it very difficult for the enterprise to pay its suppliers and service its debt. The IMF claims that the Chinese banks are inadvertently creating more and more nonperforming loans or NPLS. The past year's credit boom is just extending the problem. Unfortunately, there are too many state-owned enterprises that have liquidity issues (Lipton 2016, 3). According to the IMF's latest "Global Stability Report" (2018), the potential losses for China's banks relative to their corporate loan portfolios are equal to 7 percent of that country's GDP. Moreover, the Report further states that this is a conservative estimate based on certain bad-loan recovery assumptions and the estimate does not include its shadow banking latent exposures.

Corporate debt difficulties are nothing new for a great many nations and it seems to be more prevalent in the countries that are transitioning from an emerging market economy to an advanced economy. The transition itself involves a different economic mindset on the part of government authorities in terms of regulation. Moreover, the IMF stresses three broad remedies: 1) act quickly and effectively to contain the problem; corporate debt problems today can become systemic problems tomorrow which can lead to recessive economic growth and/or a banking crisis; 2) the regulators need to deal directly with both the creditors and the debtors; it's not good enough to just move bad bank loans off the banks' balance sheets in an effort to recapitalize the banks; history shows that leaves the banks undercapitalized and the debtor enterprises usually go out of business; the authorities need to fix them both; 3) it's not enough to fix the problems, but the authorities need to put governance mechanisms in place to assure the taxpayer that these problems are behind them; otherwise the effort becomes just another temporary solution. As of this writing, there's deep concern that a third China "bubble" is about to pop. The first was China's property bubble burst and that was followed by China's stock market bubble in the summer of 2015 and now talk among Western financial centers focuses on a Chinese credit bubble, mainly consisting of corporate bonds. China's corporate bonds have literally exploded over the past 24 months due to the avalanche of bond buyers in the West where in some countries short-term bond yields are negative. Western buyers want yield and a five-year Chinese corporate bond yields roughly 5 percent. China's ten-year government bond yields close to 3 percent compared to the West, which averages around 2.5 percent depending on the country.

The Chinese financial scenario pretty much went like this: as Chinese stocks tumbled last summer investors moved money from the China stock markets into the credit markets especially corporate bonds. This was great for China's debt heavy corporations. Demand for their bonds was so intense that they could keep running on easy credit. The issuance of China's corporate bonds increased 21 percent from 2014 to 2016 and the alarming statistic is that by the end of 2015 their

Table 4.1 China's local government bonds expect dramatic growth

Chinese yuan (CNY) trillion (TN)							
25							22.3 TN
20					17.5 TN	19.8 TN	
15				14.7 TN			
10			8.5 TN				
5							
	2.3 TN	4.4 TN					
0							
	2014	2015	2016f	2017f	2018f	2019f	2020f

Source: Author with data from the Ministry of Finance

total equaled 21.6 percent of China's GDP compared to 18.4 percent in 2014. Simultaneously, the Chinese government triggered a move onto an important project where it converted local government debt from its infrastructure into a real municipal bond market. In March 2016, the government allowed the conversion of $160 billion of local government debt into local government bonds (LGB).

The concern for most bond analysts is that China's supply of debt instruments has increased dramatically, but the demand for Chinese bonds is waning especially among foreign investors. In July of 2015, China's government eased restriction into its marketplace, but the result was negligible at best. Faster and easier access to bond markets would normally translate into more foreign investor demand for bonds, but recent capital flow data indicates a diminishing interest. At that point, Moody's put China's government bonds on negative credit watch in March of 2016 to make matters worse. Moreover, earlier in 2016, the Chinese government announced that it would allow investors to use margin loans in its stock markets again. If the margin loans conform to industry standard, that should have very little effect in China's overall economic situation. In the short term, margin equity purchases could help increase equity prices overall. It's doubtful that the Chinese investor would move money out of the bond market and into equity markets. For one thing, the price multiples on Chinese equities are too rich at this time and for another, the yields in China's bond market favor the investor providing the so-called oncoming bond bubble is circumvented. In June of 2016, the Chinese authorities issued a press release through Reuters News Service that corporate debt issuance dropped in the previous month. This was the first time there had been a reduction in corporate bond issuance in nearly six years resulting in downward pressure on Chinese bond yields, but according to a number of bond analysts the situation remains tenuous due to a rash of high profile defaults (Taplin 2016, 1). The Chinese bond markets have become skittish over the direction of the

Chinese government relative to a change in government policy due to the high levels of corporate debt. The reduction in corporate bond issuance in May 2016 was the central focus of data released from China's central bank. Interestingly enough, those figures were more detailed than the monetary data released the day before. The May 2016 gross non-financial corporate bond issuance amounted to 550.5 billion yuan ($83.56 billion) representing a decline of 22.7 percent from the previous month. Simultaneously, net corporate bond issuance was negative 39.7 billion yuan down from 209.6 billion yuan ($31.82 billion) in April.

In April of 2016, China's onshore bond market underwent a major correction due to press releases from China's central bank that the bank intended slow over-capacity in some of China's legacy industries. This news combined with several defaults affected investor confidence in state-owned debt. Historically, investors have always purchased state-owned debt instruments with the assumption that these bonds had implicit government protection. That same April, $15 billion of corporate bond issuance was canceled or at the very least, delayed by Chinese firms due to an increasing spike in yields during the month. AA-rated one-year commercial paper jumped 60 basis points at the beginning to the middle of April 2016 before finally leveling off at the end of the month in conjunction with a series of capital infusions by China's central bank. The dramatic decrease in corporate bond issuance became the catalyst for yield stabilization.

The growth of the M2 money supply also slowed markedly in May 2016 and the anemic growth that took place in that month compared to the very weak money supply growth of June 2015. Of course, all of this helped ignite fears that rapid tight credit was the result of record loan and corporate bond issuance numbers recorded in the first quarter of 2016. The reduction in the debt issuance numbers may not allow for the ongoing municipal debt swap for local government bonds (LGBs) which allowed cities to refinance more expensive corporate debt.

At the time of writing, yields on China's corporate debt appear to have stabilized a bit, but as previously mentioned, the stabilization of yields probably had more to do with the dramatic reduction of corporate debt issuance than China's corporate balance sheets. Nonetheless, as of June 17, 2017, five-year AA rated bond yields ticked down one basis point on the week to 4.63 percent compared to an average 1.13 percent in the West. Moreover, yields on equally rated one-year commercial paper were up one basis point to 3.88 percent compared to the West's 90-day commercial paper with an average yield of 0.60 percent.

Economic history suggests that in Asia rapid economic growth, rising living standards and large capital inflows equal easy credit. In the 1980s prior to China's rapid economic growth, a number of Southeast Asian countries mainly Indonesia, Malaysia and Thailand as well as South Korea in East Asia made phenomenal success in terms of economic development until the problems associated with access to easy credit resulted in major consequences for much of Southeast Asia and South Korea.

In response, many Southeast Asian countries thought the answer was fixed exchange rates, which were supposed to minimize risk for domestic and foreign investors. So, local banks borrowed offshore capital at very low short-term rates and then they would make loans to corporate manufacturers and developers for a longer period of time at very substantial premiums.

The biggest problem facing long-term corporate debtors is slowing economic growth. Profits start to deteriorate, but the debt payments remain the same and after a while the corporate debt level becomes overwhelming. Decreasing profits meant that Korean, Indonesian and Thai corporations had a very difficult time making their debt payments. Plus the fact that most corporate debt obligations at that time in the above-mentioned Asian nations were denominated in US dollars, which exacerbates an already exacerbating situation.

In order to keep these struggling corporations afloat in South Korea, Thailand and Malaysia, the banks made the decision to loan them more money. The last thing these corporations needed was more debt; what was needed was more growth. Needless to say, the result was a huge increase in corporate nonperforming loans, which added more economic stress to economies that had already lost their momentum, but at the end of the day, the nonperforming loans took their toll on the financial sectors in South Korea, Thailand and Malaysia. Consequently, a great many of these banks were already insolvent before the 1997 run on the Thai baht. In terms of Thailand, one-third of its nonperforming loans were real estate mortgages and another one-third was in the manufacturing sector, which by the mid-1990s was rife with overcapacity. Today China faces a similar dilemma.

Transparency was nowhere to be found prior to the 1997 Asian crisis otherwise investors and policymakers wouldn't have been caught off guard. Moreover, the financial sector's lack of transparency and disclosure created a sense of mistrust among investors combined with the governments' efforts to defend their currencies and downplay any possible problems did much more harm than good. Moreover, the relationships between the respective governments and the various businesses were mind boggling. This was out and out concealment and it exemplifies the real dire nature of the situation as Asia stumbled into 1997.

In July of that year with its foreign currency reserves nearly exhausted Thailand turned to the International Monetary Fund (IMF). Unfortunately, South Korea was following the very same path and the Asian panic began to spread to countries with the same economic summary: Indonesia, Malaysia and the Philippines. Though Japan was far more advanced than any of its other Asian counterparts, worries were starting to take hold about the health of the Japanese banking system.

At that time, the main concern in the case of the Japanese banking system was the massive increase in corporate nonperforming loans. Prior to the 1997 crisis, the Japanese banks for years had propped up some firms in the Japanese corporate sector with highflying loans, but unfortunately these same companies had been earmarked by the IMF as "zombie" corporations some years earlier. Regrettably when the Asian economic slowdown peaked in 1997, these so-called "zombie" companies declined into corporate comas.

In general, the Asian financial crisis was economically very severe resulting in the bankruptcy of any number of corporations and pushing most of the economies in the region into a recession. It even took its toll on the overthrow of the

Suharto government in Indonesia. However, the Asian crisis did put the governments of Southeast Asia and South Korea into an untenable position of having to implement structural reforms and increase higher levels of foreign exchange reserves. Since the 1997–1998 disaster, South Korea and the other Southeast Asian countries have strictly monitored their structural reforms as well as their foreign exchange reserves and to date their efforts have been successful.

The 1997 Asian crisis is now fodder in the form of déjà vu in China's current economic situation: a slowdown of economic growth, a massive increase in corporate debt and voluminous industrial overcapacity. Moreover, many of China's legacy industries, e.g. steel manufacturing, shipbuilding and mining have become antiquated and inefficient and to make matters even worse the very same industries have enormous corporate debt which makes rebuilding even more difficult. China's negative demographics and environment include an aging population, repulsive pollution and climate change. China's most pressing quandary is obviously its corporate debt and this is the direct result of its 2008 decision to pump billions of dollars into its economy while at the same time, encouraging its banks to make more and more corporate loans in a concerted effort to stave off the impact stemming from the global financial crisis. In the interim it worked at least on the surface. While the rest of the global economy was shrinking in economic size and scope, China was putting up some very impressive growth numbers, but growth underscored by the addition of enormous corporate debt to fund domestic projects is unsustainable and quite frankly unrealistic.

Moreover, according to Goldman Sachs, China's total debt picture went from 130 percent of GDP in 2008 to 235 percent in 2015. Goldman's Asian analysts claim that at this pace, by 2020, China's total debt position will increase to 344 percent of GDP (Editorial Board 2016, 1). China's economic problems are just part of its overall problem scenario. Like Southeast Asia and South Korea in 1997, the Chinese government and more specifically China's central bank is suffering from an erosion of confidence due to its inability to control its country's economic direction.

Nowhere is this more apparent than in its foreign exchange reserves which fell from $3.9 trillion in June of 2015 to roughly $3.1 trillion in August of 2017, which represents a roughly 20 percent drop in its foreign exchange reserves. For a country that uses its exports to create a trade surplus with all of its trading partners, this is detrimental in terms of free cash flow. There's no doubt that the Chinese authorities are under extreme pressure to rectify the current situation. The 1997 Asian crisis gave impetus to the Chinese buildup of foreign exchange reserves. The Chinese government sought to create an insurance policy against running out of cash. Their situation is critical, but it's certainly not fatal. However, if the current drop in foreign exchange reserves continues at this pace year over year, China's economic future will be increasingly uncertain. As previously mentioned in the Introduction, on June 6–7, 2016, Beijing hosted the US-China Strategic and Economic Dialogue. This is an annual meeting of high-level officials from the United States and China to mainly discuss issues of importance, e.g. trade, finance, security, the environment and anything else the Dialogue members deem important between the countries. China was represented by Vice Premier Wang Yang and State Councilor Yang Jiechi who chaired the Dialogue. The US was represented by Secretary of State John Kerry and the Secretary of the Treasury Jacob Lew. This year the Americans co-chaired the talks. Moreover, the talks were basically broken up into two tracks with Wang and Lew heading up the economic track and Yang and Kerry handling the strategic track. That year marked the eighth annual meeting between the world's two largest economies (Hamilton 2016, 1–5).

From an international observation, this year's meeting received extreme criticism from some international observers who underscore China's ongoing militarization of the South China Sea (Bittner 2016, 1–3). On the economic front, US companies voiced disappointment with the talks making the argument that doing business with China is a source of continued frustration. They not only cite a struggling Chinese economy, but they also make the case that China continues to practice protectionist economic policies. In addition, the Chinese officials pushed back when Secretary Lew demanded that Beijing reduce industrial capacity. The underlying theme in this instance centered on the need for US officials to keep pressing the issue of Chinese overcapacity. Lew emphasized the simple fact that China is flooding the global market with steel and aluminum as well as many other manufactured products. A number of China economic watchers claim that China is living in a fantasy that will do interim damage to its own people. China's 2008 government intervention came with a huge price tag; provincial and local government businesses borrowed excessively to invest in unrealistic industrial projects based on a global demand that never materialized.

Estimating global demand is never easy due to global exogenous variables, but in this instance, China had been fooled by its own previous success and now it faces debt problem and overcapacity problems. Unfortunately, these are not easily rectified. At this point in China's economic history, it needs to create a much stronger social safety net to help affected workers with retraining for jobs in its service sector, but this is a very tenuous situation for China. In order for China to transition itself to more of a domestic service economy would involve a steep reduction in its exports which in turn would reduce its foreign exchange reserves resulting in less free cash flow to subsidize its basic industries: mutually conflicting conditions.

The two-day dialogue continued and on day two, Secretary Lew pressured the Chinese to specifically cut back on its glut of steel production. Lew made the argument that China's efforts to glut the steel market have resulted in damaging and serious consequences brought on by below market steel prices for steel producers in the US and the EU. As the time of writing, the US recently hit Chinese steel makers with countervailing subsidies (duties) and anti-dumping duties on Chinese steel.

In response to US pressure, President Xi Jinping agreed to "redouble efforts" to decrease the overcapacity found in China's steel industry, but at the same time, he made no mention of specific measures or details on how China would accomplish this. And virtually no agreements were reached on China's overcapacity in the manufacture of aluminum either. Lou Jiwei, China's finance minister, underscored the role of "market forces" as the catalyst to reduce overproduction and he re-emphasized China's response to global prices (US Department of the Treasury 2016).

However in international finance, a significant development did come out of the 2016 talks. For the first time, China agreed to allow the American banks to clear renminbi-denominated transactions. Under the agreement China's central bank will allow American banks to clear renminbi-denominated trades up to a quota of $52 billion per year. This is included in China's Renminbi Qualified Foreign Institutional Program. According to a release from the US Treasury Department, China and the United States reiterated their position on exchange rates; both agreed to "refrain from competitive devaluation and targeting exchange rates for competitive purposes". As for the international financial system, the US Federal Open Market Committee (FOMC) through Secretary Lew told the Chinese authorities that FOMC policies will be prioritized in such a way that its overall effect will be sensitive to and allow for ramifications to the international financial system.

China simultaneously agreed to continue with its industrial and service sector reform policies by promoting structural adjustments. In that way, the Chinese government can also expand domestic demand for household consumption by increasing structural funds allocated for the domestic economy. China also took it a step further and claimed that going forward all of its investments will be high quality and driven by the private sector.

In May 2016, slowing global demand reduced Chinese exports to 4.1 percent year over year, but according to the Chinese officials its imports had increased substantially, but no data was released and it's too early to retrieve data from China's National Bureau of Statistics. With that said, this may suggest an improvement in China's domestic economy. Overall, China's central bank released its economic growth forecast for 2016 and it came in at 6.8 percent. That number is substantially higher than most of the analysts' forecasts who follow China on a regular basis.

Given the political climate of the 2016 presidential election in the United States, Chinese officials voiced deep concern about the rhetoric of President Donald Trump. China's main concern is the talk of possible protectionist trade policies. On the other hand, the Obama administration hoped that the general election discourse would be the catalyst for more liberal foreign investment policies in China underscored by the Bilateral Investment Treaty (BIT) between the United States and the People's Republic of China. The Bilateral Investment Treaty, according to the US Trade Representative, should have allowed for more liberalized investment policies going back to 2011.

At that time, Obama administration officials complained that China had roughly 100 sectors in the Chinese economy that are closed to US investment. The Obama administration went on to say that number has to come down substantially for the bilateral treaty to function the way it was designed. That was in 2011. Unfortunately, in 2017 and not much has changed. On June 20, 2016

Treasury Secretary Lew claimed that the jury is still out concerning the merits of China's latest negative list. He further stated that Beijing negotiations relative to the bilateral treaty remain one important barometer in terms of a realistic commitment to open its economy to foreign competition.

Following Secretary Lew's press release, the US Trade Representative's office in Washington announced that talks between the United States and China continue to be encouraging after both countries exchanged new ideas on the subject (Lawder 2016, 1). When President Xi visited President Trump in April 2017, the two leaders renamed the annual Strategic and Economic Dialogue. Beginning in 2017, the annual meeting will be called The US–China Comprehensive Economic Dialogue. The 2017 meeting took place in July 2017 and the following joint press release was issued by Secretary Ross and Secretary Mnuchin on July 19, 2017:

> We thank Vice Premier Wang and the Chinese delegation for making the journey to Washington for this first session of the US – China Comprehensive Economic Dialogue.
>
> We also extend our gratitude to Secretary Perdue, Ambassador, Ambassador Branstad, Chair Yellen and Director Cohn for their participation in these meetings.
>
> China acknowledged our shared objective to reduce the trade deficit which both sides will work cooperatively to achieve.
>
> Since the Presidential Summit, the first 100 days made progress on important issues including credit ratings, bond clearings, electronic payments, commercial banking, and liquefied natural gas. Also, this is the first time since 2003 that the Chinese have allowed imports of beef.
>
> The principles of balance, fairness and reciprocity on matters of trade will continue to guide the American position so we can give American workers and businesses an opportunity to compete on a level playing field. We look to achieving the important goals set forth by President Trump this past April in Mar-a-Lago.
>
> (Office of Public Affairs, July 19, 2017)

US businesses complained as far back as 2011 that the Chinese authorities restrict foreign ownership in important economic sectors: financial services, health insurance, audio-visual and so on. As was previously mentioned, the Obama administration claimed that the Chinese government had over 100 sectors of its economy virtually closed to US investment and these were pretty much the same complaints the Obama administration voiced in 2011 some five years earlier.

For the last 25 years, on an annual basis, America has imported hundreds of billions of dollars more in goods from China than the US exports to China. China continues to build its industrial capacity to levels much greater than its domestic demand. Its dramatic overcapacity in sector after sector has had detrimental effects on industrial producers in the West, e.g. steel, aluminum, glass, solar, paper and so on. These Chinese basic industries are subsidized directly by the Chinese government and each industry follows the dictates of the government. In the face of global overcapacity and declining demand, China still keeps producing at overcapacity levels. When US officials question their methods, it's always the same answer: an ongoing pledge to dramatically increase efforts to reduce overcapacity, but with no new initiatives or specific measures. The result of this economic relationship between China and the West has been a decline in profits for Western firms; devastating job losses and a deluge of imports from Chinese companies who are not managed entirely by the profit motive. Trade cases have been filed against China for violating WTO regulations in product after product and each time China loses; it reinvents itself by changing its subsidizing strategy in order to dump other products. The overcapacity issue has been raised numerous times at each Strategic and Economic Dialogue meeting by the United States.

The strategy of overcapacity initiated by the Chinese Communist Party sits with the notion that even a moderate level of domestic growth is better than massive Chinese job losses. The strategy is to keep the Chinese worker working and in turn that will keep China's basic industries working even if that result comes at the expense of subsidized overcapacity.

References

Angang, Hu et al., "China's Economic Growth and Poverty Reduction," Center for China Study, Chinese Academy of Sciences, Tsinghua University, 2005.

Angang, Hu et al., interview with Satarupa Bhattacharjya, "Staying with China's War on Poverty," *China Daily*, April 28, 2017, p. 1.

Bittner, Peter, "US-China Strategic and Economic Dialogue: Key Takeaways," *The Diplomat*, June 10, 2016, Tokyo, Japan, pp. 1–2.

Editorial Board, "China Should Shut Down Zombie Businesses to Help Economy," *New York Times*, June 9, 2016, p. 1.

Hamilton, Gilliam, *NSBO China Policy Research*, Beijing, 2016.

IMF, *Global Stability Report*, April 2018.

Lawder, David, "Corrected: US sees China investment talks 'productive' after new offers: USTR," Reuters News Service, June 17, 2016.

Lipton, David, First Deputy Managing Director, "Rebalancing China: International Lessons in Corporate Debt," IMF, June 11, 2016.

Office of Public Affairs, "Statement from Secretary Ross and Secretary Mnuchin Following the US-China Comprehensive Economic Dialogue," July 19, 2017.

Taplin, Nathaniel, "Shrinking China Bond Issuance Relieves Some Upward Pressure on Yields," Reuters News Service, Beijing, June 17, 2016.

US Department of the Treasury, "US-China Strategic and Economic Dialogue," 2016, available at www.treasury.gov/initiatives/Pages/china.aspx.

World Bank, "Overview-China," Beijing, June 14, 2016.

5 China's currency manipulation

America's two political parties rarely agree on anything, but the one thing that unites them is their anger about China's alleged currency manipulation. Perhaps spurred by the strong dollar and the first sign that it's taking its toll on US net exports, congressional Democrats and Republicans are once again considering legislation to counter what they view as China's unfair currency undervaluation. As for the European Union, the EU authorities repeatedly make the argument that there is a link between the soaring deficit and China's currency undervaluation. Moreover, the EU administration makes the case that China promotes exports and discourages imports by fixing its exchange rate to the US dollar (part of the basket China has been using since 2005) below the renminbi's real value (Lawder 2016, 1).

Recently the Chinese authorities have devalued its currency by approximately 4.4 percent, which underscores China's propensity to manipulate its currency in a concerted effort to make its exports less expensive. This is a pivotal issue between China's trade with the United States and the European Union. Senior officials

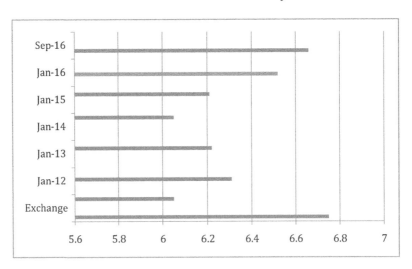

Figure 5.1 US Dollar to Chinese Renminbi (RMB) exchange rate chart
Source: Author with data from the Federal Reserve Bank

in the US and the EU have blatantly confirmed China's currency manipulation. Currency manipulation has been at the very heart of China's trade attacks on manufacturing in the US and the EU.

Figure 5.1 shows that the Chinese renminbi (RMB) against the US dollar had an exchange rate of 6.314 RMB to the US dollar in January 2012 and when the Chinese economy began to slow, the exchange rate increased to 6.52 in January 2016. As the time of writing on November 28, 2017, the exchange is 6.61 RMB to the US dollar. This is an important issue and it's timely indeed especially in the United States given that the new Republican President has used China's currency manipulation as one of his campaign platforms. Currency manipulation is, to sum it up succinctly, the efforts to keep export prices low by government intervention in the foreign exchange market and it is the single most important issue in international economic policy.

Last year, the US Senate rejected an amendment by Senators Rob Portman (R) and Debbie Stabenow (D) that would have put currency manipulators in a very awkward position. The Obama administration has responded to pressures from Congress by making the case that it's better to bring exchange rate provisions into trade negotiations, but ironically, the administration did not want compulsory restrictions relative to currency manipulation included in the proposed Pacific trade agreement, which the Trump Administration has since withdrawn from (Klein 2015, 1).

For the most part, currency manipulation is very difficult to determine and more than likely, most governments don't know currency manipulation even when they see it. The chart on the previous page shows that the solid line represents a strengthening renminbi; in fact, the renminbi has strengthened 35 percent against the dollar over the last ten years which should represent an increase in the price of Chinese exports to the West by more than one-third. On April 29, 2016 the US Treasury Department issued a report to Congress entitled: "Foreign Exchange Policies of Major Trading Partners" (US Department of the Treasury Office of International Affairs 2016). The report targets five countries in particular: China, Japan, South Korea, Taiwan and Germany. Each one of these countries meets at least two of the three factors that verify whether a country has developed Forex policies that give it an unfair competitive advantage over the US.

The report is the result of a bipartisan Act passed by the Congress in 2015 entitled: Trade Facilitation and Trade Enforcement Act of 2015. The US is looking to protect its own interests. No matter what the world economic community may claim, currency devaluation has become a major instrument employed by a number of countries to stimulate exports resulting in greater economic growth. Incorporated in the report is a monitoring list of countries. The list also pinpoints three specific criteria used to determine unfair currency practices: 1) a substantial bilateral trade surplus with the United States, 2) significant account surplus and 3) persistent one-sided intervention in the foreign exchange market. In practical terms, a trade surplus greater than $20 billion or a trade surplus larger than 0.1 percent of US GDP; a trade surplus with the US that's greater than 3 percent of that country's GDP and purchases of foreign currency greater than 2 percent of that country's GDP over a 12 month period.

As the time of writing, no country meets all three of the criteria, but all five meet two of the criteria. According to the Act if any one of the five meets all three criteria the President and the Secretary of the Treasury will immediately inform the responsible officials in that country that in terms of continued trade it has to adopt the policies necessary to reverse its currency undervaluation. Otherwise, the President can impose a number of penalties, which include severing that country's ties to funds from the Overseas Private Investment Corporation. The President can engage the IMF (the organization charged with preventing currency manipulation) to do due process with that country; or the President can reconsider that country's participation in trade agreements with the United States.

In terms of China's currency manipulation, one sticking point stood out in 2016 when China devalued the renminbi. The report underscores the harsh criticism from the US Treasury. Moreover, the report details China's heavy intervention in the Forex markets during the same time frame. The report further emphasizes demand in the emerging market economies. Weak demand in a great many emerging market economies especially in China is center stage in the very difficult transition taking place currently in China as its economy transitions from investment export-led to consumer-led growth. The primary concern for most emerging market economies – growth deceleration – has resulted in massive capital outflows, which puts downward pressure their currencies. Although growth in the West has been far from robust, the relative strength of the dollar and the euro against most emerging market currencies has weakened the emerging market currencies even more over the course of the past 18 months on a trade weighted basis. However, the West is certainly not immune; weakening foreign demand has put a damper on Western economic growth.

During 2017, there has been a significant number of emerging market central banks who purposely intervened in currency markets in an effort to prevent their currencies from further depreciation against the dollar and the euro resulting in a steep reduction in global foreign exchange reserves. Financial markets in general were unusually volatile due to China's change in its exchange rate policy in 2016. Furthermore in China, a combination of falling oil prices and uncertain growth played some part in the aforementioned volatility. Overall, from a global perspective, lower oil prices have impacted the redistribution of current account balances in a great many countries.

Obviously, this has been a benefit to oil-importing countries and in the cases of China, Germany, South Korea and Taiwan, their already large inventories have become even larger. On the other hand, oil-exporting countries have experienced some very serious financial dilemmas.

The report further emphasized that additional support is needed globally to strengthen demand and add stability to global growth expectations. The Obama administration made the argument bilaterally and multilaterally that global economies should utilize each and every policy mechanism at their disposal to help increase global demand. All of our economic ills can be cured if global growth reoccurred, but its being held back by three factors: private sector leverage in some countries is still too high; central banks in some countries are not providing adequate macroeconomic support and in some countries bank lending growth is not anywhere near where it should be to facilitate an increase in growth.

Some economists call for increased investment to stimulate growth, but in most instances, corporations respond to demand. In terms of GDP growth, increased investment will follow demand side economics as opposed to supply side economics (US Department of the Treasury Office of International Affairs 2016, 4). A combination of monetary and fiscal policies is needed to spur demand, but these policies have to be initiated so that each enhances and supports the other. An excellent case in point is the United States. At this time, the US is at near zero interest rates and it has an infrastructure that desperately needs rebuilding. This would have been an excellent time for the US to rebuild its infrastructure with cheap money and spur greater economic growth, which would result in lower unemployment and increase consumer demand. Monetary policy can be forceful (near zero interest rates), but in this case, the US also needs an accommodative fiscal policy.

As was previously mentioned, the US Treasury Department has created a "monitoring list". This includes its trading partners that meet two of the three criteria as specified in the Act that suggest currency manipulation. The monitoring list includes China, Japan, South Korea, Taiwan and Germany. China has by far the largest bilateral trade surplus with the United States at roughly $375 billion and it also has a very substantial current account surplus. According to the report in order to support the renminbi China has recently intervened heavily in the foreign exchange markets. The impetus for this activity was the very strong downward pressure in the renminbi brought on by the unexpected change in 2016 relative to China's foreign exchange policy. Due to the staggering increase in its renminbi depreciation, the negative consequences to its economy were unavoidable and as the third largest economy in the world, this affected global economic growth.

The report further emphasized China's need to have more clarity in terms of exchange rate goals. According to estimates from the US Treasury Department from August 2015 through March 2016 in order for China to support the value of the renminbi, it had to sell more than $480 billion in foreign currency assets. Simultaneously, China had an extremely large trade surplus with the West. All of this leads to the conclusion that an increase in Chinese economic structural reforms is required in order for China to transition itself into a domestic consumption economy. At the same time, it needs to increase its fiscal stimulus to bolster household consumption. Furthermore, the US Treasury Department had also determined that none of the US' major trading partners had manipulated the exchange rate between their currencies and the US dollar to in effect prevent the effective balance of payments adjustments or to obtain an unfair international trade competitive advantage relative to the time frame covered in the report.

The Obama administration was very aggressive in making sure that in terms of international trade there is an even playing field between the United States and its trading partners. Obama made it very clear that no trading partner shall grow its exports based primarily on exchange rates that are constantly undervalued. The US Treasury has made a concerted effort to point out exchange rate issues in a bilateral fashion including the aforementioned annual US–China Strategic and Economic Dialogue and in in-depth discussions at conferences of the G7 and G20 in concert with the International Monetary Fund (IMF).

The US Treasury Department feels that this strategy has produced the right results. In terms of the G20 countries, the United States has technically secured commitments from its members to move expeditiously to more market driven exchange rates. By doing this, each member country will avoid ongoing exchange rate misalignments. Each member agreed to refrain from competitive exchange rate devaluations and they also agreed not to target exchange rates for competitive purposes. As for the G7 countries, which include Japan, the Treasury has been given assurances from all of its members that going forward their monetary and fiscal policies will center on domestic objectives using domestic instruments.

The US Treasury Department has also prodded the IMF for stronger surveillance of its members' exchange rate policies. Consequently, the IMF now publishes an exchange rate assessment for 29 economies and is improving its exchange analysis in its Article IV reports on member countries. And through US leadership, the Trans-Pacific Partnership countries have adopted for the first time trade agreement provisions that address unfair currency practices by explicitly adopting G20 exchange rate commitments and by promoting transparency and accountability. Moreover, the US Treasury Department will constantly monitor the key factors the department uses to determine if an economy has a substantial trade surplus bilaterally with the US; a significant current account surplus and involved in ongoing one-sided intervention in the foreign exchange market. The Treasury will make sure these new reporting and monitoring measures meet the department's objective of creating an indication signal that unfair currency practices may be taking place.

Within the context of both the Omnibus Trade and Competitiveness Act of 1988 and the Trade Facilitation and Trade Enforcement Act of 2015, the Secretary of the Treasury is required to provide reports on the exchange rate policies of the United States' major trading partners to the Congress on a semi-annual basis. These two Acts require the reports to indicate whether any of America's major trading partners have met the three criteria of possible currency manipulation previously mentioned. The reports also have to indicate if any of these trading partners have met any of the three criteria and if they have, the reports are required to identify the criteria.

Fiscal consolidation within the last few years has weighed on the overall economic activity in the United States, but that's been moderated a bit and in the second half of 2016 federal government spending added 0.1 percentage point to US GDP growth. State and local government expenditures added a comparable increase in overall GDP growth in 2016. The 2017 forecast for federal government spending should make a meaningful contribution to overall GDP growth while state and local government spending should result in a small net positive for the year. Inflation in the United States is relatively low for the first half of 2017.

The consumer price index (CPI) increased by 0.9 percent during the year ending March 2017. This is in comparison to a 0.1 percent decline during the year ending March 2016.

In January 2016, China made the decision to set the valuation standard for its renminbi to a five-year low which set off a currency war between China and the European Union. That reinforced the sentiment of the EU financial community: since August 2015, the Chinese authorities believe that in order to bail out its anemic industries, China needs a low-valued currency to drive more of its exports. Coincidentally, in January 2016, market forces drove down the value of the euro not the European Central Bank (ECB) as the Chinese authorities suggest. By the same token, China made the same exact suggestion a year earlier, when market forces drove down the value of the Japanese yen and that depreciation was not the result of a concerted effort by the Bank of Japan. In the depth of the 2008 financial crisis, market forces drove down the currency values of both the United States and the United Kingdom, but obviously no one complained about that depreciation. A lower-value dollar and a lower-value pound didn't result in fewer exports to either the US or the UK.

Countries who peg their currency to another one are attempting to keep their currency's value at the same exchange rate of the currency they're pegging. For example, there are roughly 66 countries that peg their currency to the US dollar or use the dollar as their own legal tender. The US dollar is the world's reserve currency, as established under the 1944 Bretton Woods Agreement. However, the second in line in terms of the world's reserve currencies is the euro with 25 countries who peg their currency to the euro. Some of those countries are in the EU, but not in the Eurozone. For the purpose of explaining a pegging mechanism, the US dollar peg is perfect for explanatory purposes. A dollar peg uses a fixed exchange rate. That is a guarantee from a country's central bank that the bank promises to give you a fixed amount of its currency in return for a US dollar. In order for a country to maintain a dollar peg, that country would have to have a large inventory of US dollars. Normally, countries that peg their currency to the US dollar are usually countries that sell large amounts of exports to the United States.

These are usually goods that are manufactured in their home country and exported to the US. In that light, foreign companies receive payments in US dollars and then those dollars are converted into their domestic currency by a domestic bank in order to pay their workers and domestic suppliers. The bank then sends those dollars to their respective central bank. Central banks usually use these dollars to purchase US Treasury debt instruments, bills, notes or bonds. In that way, the central bank receives interest on its dollar holdings. If for any reason the bank needs to raise cash, it will sell the Treasury debt instruments on the secondary market.

Normally, a country's finance minister will monitor its currency exchange rate in relation to the dollar's value. If for any reason, the home currency falls below the peg, the minister needs to raise its value and lower the dollar's value. This can be facilitated by selling US Treasury debt instruments increasing the Treasury supply on the secondary market. At that point, the minister would use the cash received to purchase domestic currency. This lowers the value of the country's supply of US Treasuries, which in turn lowers the value of the US dollar.

China uses a fixed exchange rate as opposed to an exchange rate system, e.g. Forex or FX. China's wants to keep the renminbi low. In that way, China's exports are more competitive. There isn't anything novel about China's currency maneuver. In fact, most countries try to do the same thing, but at this point, no country has the wherewithal to keep its currency fixed like China. China's currency strength is derived from its exports to the United States and the European Union. China's exports to the West consist mainly of consumer electronics, textiles and machinery. Moreover, there are a number of companies from the West that ship raw materials to Chinese factories for manufacturing that is much less expensive than in their own countries. Most of the finished good are then shipped back to the West.

The result of all this business is that China receives both dollars and euros as payments for manufacturing finished goods. Obviously, these funds are then deposited into Chinese banks and exchanged for the renminbi. The deposit banks then send the dollars and euros to the Chinese central bank where they are stockpiled into China's foreign currency reserves. By doing this, China reduces the supply of dollars and euros available for trade resulting in upward pressure on both currencies. In most instances, China will use these funds to purchase US and EU government securities. China's central bank wants these funds to be invested in safe securities and in both instances; these securities are among the safest in the world. This will also strengthen the dollar and the euro, reducing the value of the renminbi.

In terms of a trade surplus, China had a combined trade surplus with the West of roughly $527 billion in 2016. This is $527 billion of extra free cash flow and of course the Chinese government is free to do whatever it wants with it.

Tables 5.1 and 5.2 point out the enormity involved in the global Forex markets. The yuan plays an essential role in maintaining China's economic competition throughout the world. Historically, the Chinese authorities pegged the yuan to a basket of currencies where the US dollar is the dominant currency which prompted a "reference rate" that kept the yuan's value in a 2 percent trading band

Table 5.1 All data reported in millions of US dollars – average daily volume 2015

Instrument	Amount Reported $USD m	Change Previous Year	Percentage Change
Spot Transactions	374,957	–195,762	–34.3
Forward Transactions	174,675	–45,775	–20.8
Foreign Ex Swaps Transactions	219,677	–19,713	–8.2
Over the Counter Options	39,941	–24,927	–38.4
Grand Total	**809,250**	**–286,177**	**–26.1**

Source: Author with data from the NY Fed

Table 5.2 Total monthly volume September 2015

Instrument	Amount Reported $USD m	Change Previous Year	Percentage Change
Spot Transactions	8,249,064	−4,877,461	−37.2
Forward Transactions	3,842,767	−1,227,611	−24.2
Foreign Ex Swaps Transactions	4,832,963	−672,937	−12.2
Over the Counter Options	878,659	−613,280	−41.1
Grand Total	**17,803,453**	**−7,391,289**	**−29.3**

Source: Author with data from the NY Fed

against the dollar's value, resulting in an exchange rate of 6.25 Chinese yuan to the US dollar.

However, on August 11, 2015, China abruptly changed its policy to allow the yuan greater market volatility. At that point, its so-called "reference rate" would equal the previous day's closing value between the renminbi and the dollar on the Forex markets, but the next day the yuan's value immediately fell 1.9 percent. The following day the yuan fell even further to approximately 6.3845 to the US dollar resulting in China's intervention in a concerted effort to stop the yuan's rapid decline. This put the yuan in a holding pattern at roughly 6.389 to the US dollar and by August 12, 2015 it had weakened to 6.4064 yuan against the USD, but the yuan continued to fall and by January 11, 2016 its value was hovering around 6.58055 to the USD (*The Wall Street Journal* August 25, 2015). This change in monetary policy was prompted by China's big push to have its currency included in the world's official foreign exchange reserve currencies of the IMF, which also includes the US dollar, the euro and the British pound. This took effect on November 30, 2015. Three years ago the central banks of the European Union and People's Republic of China created a bilateral currency swap agreement that included roughly 45 billion euros and 350 billion renminbi (RMB). Both the EU and China had signed numerous currency swap agreements with other nations, but this was the first one between the EU and China.

In terms of the underpinnings of a currency swap agreement, in economics it really is nothing more than a derivative tool. A bilateral currency swap agreement takes place when two nations exchange set amounts of their respective currencies. Any interest earned on the funds is exchanged in a series of payments usually semi-annually based on the initial funds exchanged. This particular currency swap agreement between China and the EU matures in 2016. At the time of maturity, the 45 billion euros and the 350 billion renminbi will be returned to the original central banks that had issued the initial funds along with any unpaid interest.

This was China's third largest currency swap after Hong Kong and South Korea and it followed similar agreements with the United Kingdom, Australia and Brazil. According to a statement issued by the European Central Bank (ECB), the swap arrangement was established to facilitate the rapidly growing bilateral trade and investment between the euro area and China (Noble 2013, 2). The currency swap was originally designed as a financial backstop for two nations that trade on a continuous basis – it's more of an insurance policy and it may not be needed all the time. It's called a bilateral agreement, but in this particular case, this is more of a multilateral agreement between China and the Eurozone countries comprised of 19 nations and over 340 million people. On the one hand, it's a symbolic effort for the countries in the Eurozone that focus on huge exports like Germany and on the other, it's one more step in China's attempt to internationalize the renminbi a fixed rate currency pegged to the US dollar.

At the time, the People's Bank of China (China's central bank) said that this effort will provide the underpinnings for liquidity support needed to facilitate the development of the RMB market in Europe. This was a concerted effort by the Chinese authorities to encourage overseas use of the RMB in trade settlements (Noble 2013, 2). According to HSBC CEO Stuart Gulliver, China expects that approximately 50 percent of its trade will be settled in the renminbi by 2020 (Yip 2015, 1). Moreover, the renminbi is becoming increasingly important for investors as well as trade settlements, but unfortunately, China's current problems extend far beyond China's currency prowess. Since the last half of 2015, China's currency valuation has been steadily falling. At first the devaluation was a welcome effort expecting to increase Chinese exports, but in reality, it is completely insufficient to cope with the challenges facing China's economy, a subject that will be covered extensively later in the book. For the purposes of this chapter, it's important to cover in separate stages the mechanics of China's currency leading up to surprise devaluation in the last half of 2015. First, China's concerted effort to firmly control the value of the renminbi involves setting a daily rate for the renminbi against the US dollar. China's traders have a free hand to make the renminbi stronger or weaker by 2 percent each day, but China's central bank more often than not ignores the market signals when it sets the rate for the following day. Ironically, there are times when the central bank will set the renminbi stronger against the dollar when the market signals a much weaker renminbi. Furthermore, China's central bank claimed that going forward it will put the previous day's trading into its foreign exchange calculations. Moreover, the People's Bank of China makes the argument that this effort will put the RMB more in step with the exchange marketplace (Yip 2015, 1).

However, this whole effort is underscored by China's slowing export sector and overall economic growth looks sluggish and anemic especially by China's historical standards. In fact, the month before China announced its currency devaluation in 2015, Chinese exports dropped 8.3 percent from 2014 according to China custom officials. The maneuver here resulting in a weaker renminbi was to facilitate China exporters in selling their goods overseas, which didn't work. At that point, Beijing sent notice to the rest of the world that the Chinese economy is slowing dramatically. That was a feeble attempt to put the Chinese economy back on track and at the same time it created an unfair disadvantage for the Western corporations. In the West, this will more than likely draw additional criticism that Beijing keeps its currency artificially low to help its own manufacturers; a claim that received added impetus during the US 2016 presidential election (Tejada 2015, 2).

The Chinese currency devaluation in 2015 had a ripple effect on central banks around the globe. It inadvertently added extenuating pressure on them to either lower rates or to keep them artificially low in order to facilitate their export sectors and the initiation of a preventive measure against the destabilization of capital flows. Recently, commodities markets have been rattled by the economic slowdown in China. In addition, the devaluation accelerated capital outflows from China back to the West adding additional strength to an already strong US dollar.

In September 2015, President Xi Jinping visited the United States and President Obama and this move added more stress to an already stressful relationship between the US and China. The following is a synopsis of what transpired in conversations between President Obama and President Xi which were the subject of a joint press release from the White House on September 25, 2015: In terms of the economic relationship between China and the United States, both countries agreed to accelerate their work towards a high-standard Bilateral Investment Treaty (BIT) which would create more of an even playing for American companies operating in China. Moreover, both Presidents Xi and Obama made a commitment to a set of principles for trade in information technologies, which include the protection of innovation and intellectual property. President Xi underscored his commitment to accelerate market reforms that should avoid further devaluation of the RMB. Furthermore, he would like China to play a major role in upholding a rules-based system that underpins the global economy (Office of the Press Secretary, the White House September 25, 2015).

From a long-term perspective, this complicates China's statement to the world economic community that it intends to create a more liberalized economy. Creating a renminbi where its value is determined more by market forces is certainly a good move, but the move is contrary to China's stated long-term goals of looking for more dependable sources of growth. However, on the surface, this maneuver in particular looks like it's designed more to enhance Chinese exports than anything else. This is where the West has a difficult time creating a purposeful dialogue with China. The Chinese authorities' claim their economy is going to transition itself into more of a consumer driven-service sector economy, but at the same time, the Chinese government is trying to conjure up ways to devalue its currency in order to increase exports. This may be their way of experimenting with a socialist market economy, but for the rest of the world that depend on a free market economy this becomes a source of undeniable concern. Currency manipulation is a top issue especially in the United States. President Trump continues to rant on about China's currency manipulation making the argument that it sucks the blood out of the United States (Mozur September 16, 2016). However, in April 2017, President Xi met with President Trump at his private club at Mar-a-Lago. The details of their meeting were vague but we do know that the conversations between the two leaders mainly focused on North Korea.

From 1995 to 2005, the exchange rate for the Chinese renminbi against the US dollar was 8.3 renminbi to one US dollar. At that time, there were some in the academic community that made the argument that this was an artificially depressed value for the renminbi in a concerted effort to purposely make Chinese exports to the United States cheaper and the same held true for the European Union. By comparison, the low Chinese exchange rate made goods and services from the West more expensive, putting the West's manufacturers at a distinct disadvantage. However, this particular exchange rate method was eliminated in 2005 by the Chinese authorities in favor of an exchange rate based upon a basket of currencies, which includes the US dollar and the euro. For a short time during the 2008 crisis, China reinstated the dollar peg and not long after that, the renminbi ties to the dollar loosened even further and its value was determined by market forces involved in the makeup of a basket of currencies.

However, in August of 2015, China devalued the renminbi against the dollar by a staggering 3.5 percent, sending off a splattering of criticism from world economic leaders making the argument that a currency war was going to ensue. The devaluation against the dollar was sparked by a weakening Chinese economy. In 2015, China experienced the lowest economic growth rate in over 25 years. In that year, its growth rate came in at 6.9 percent and there are some in the world academic community that even think that number was inflated. Chinese publicized growth rates have always come under suspicion. So in many instances, economists will use proxies to verify China's publicized growth rates, but that effort can be extremely tenuous at best. Thirty days prior to China's August 2015 devaluation against the dollar, Chinese overall exports declined by roughly 8 percent. The reason is obvious. China's weakening economy has put downward pressure on the renminbi and when you combine that with its decision to measure the renminbi against a larger basket of currencies that in itself devalues the renminbi even further against the US dollar. Within the last few years, there has been nothing less than excessive confusion on Chinese currency evaluation in relation to the ongoing charge of Chinese currency manipulation. For example in May of 2014, the Peterson Institute of International Economics argued that based on China's current account balance and the real effective exchange rate, the renminbi is not undervalued. Fourteen months later, the Chinese authorities devalued the renminbi against the US dollar by 3.5 percent (Miner 2016, 5).

Adding to the confusion of China's currency manipulation, news outlets like the prestigious *Financial Times* of London in January 2016 ran an article on its front page highlighting the concerns over China's economy after the RMB hit a five-year low (Blitz 2016, 1). That's true. In January 2016, the renminbi hadn't been that weak against the US dollar in five years. It had depreciated roughly 7 percent since its strongest point in 2014. However, there are some economists who claim that statement is somewhat misleading. They cite the Nominal Effective Exchange Rate (NEER), which claims that in the last five years the RMB in NEER valuations has actually appreciated approximately 25 percent. If this measure is correct, China's currency is near its strongest level. Their arguments focus on the exchange rate of the RMB against China's major trading partners which they claim is actually of greater importance. In 2016, trade between the United States and China totaled $578. 32 billion and trade between the European Union and China in that same year totaled $558.11 billion. In that year, China had a trade surplus with the United States of roughly $347.18 billion and in that exact same time frame China racked up a trade surplus with the European Union of $180.87 billion which gave China a total trade surplus with the US and the EU of $528.05 billion. Converting the EU euro to the US dollar, the above data was provided by the US Department of Commerce and the Directorate-General for Trade, the European Commission. China's 2016 total GDP was $11.02 trillion. The combined trade between the United States and the European Union with China amounts to $1.36 trillion or roughly 12 percent of China's total 2016 GDP.

References

Blitz, Roger, Jennifer Hughes and Patrick McGee, "Concerns over China's economy after currency nears 5-year low," *Financial Times*, January 7, 2016.

Klein, Michael W., "What you may not know about China and currency manipulation," Brookings Institution, *The Wall Street Journal* Opinion, May 22, 2015.

Lawder, David, "Corrected: US sees China investment talks 'productive' after new offers: USTR," *Reuters News Service*, June 17, 2016.

Miner, Sean, "Renminbi Series Part 1: A Primer on China's Currency," Peterson Institute for International Economics, China Economic Watch, March 16, 2016, p. 5.

Mozur, Paul and Jack Ewing, "Rush of Chinese Investment in Europe's High-Tech Firms Is Raising Eyebrows," *The New York Times*, September 16, 2016.

Noble, John, "European Central Bank and China strike currency swap deal," *Financial Times*, Hong Kong, October 10, 2013.

Office of the Press Secretary, the White House, Joint Press Release President Obama and President Xi, September 25, 2015.

Tejada, Carlos, "5 Things to Know About China's Currency Devaluation," *Wall Street Journal World*, August 10, 2015.

US Department of the Treasury Office of International Affairs, Report to Congress, "Foreign Exchange Policies of Major Trading Partners of the United States," April 29, 2016.

The Wall Street Journal, "China Intervenes to Support Tumbling Yuan," August 25, 2015, p. 18.

Yip, Bobby, *Reuters New Service*, "Half of China's total trade to be settled in yuan by 2020," Hong Kong, March 4, 2015.

Part III
Foreign direct investment

6 US foreign direct investment (FDI)

In terms of a historical perspective, surprisingly there's really not that much US foreign direct investment in China in spite of the fact that these two countries are the largest two economies in the world. In fact, US foreign direct investment in China amounts to only 1 percent of all US foreign direct investment (FDI) abroad. Moreover, in recent years capital flows in the form of US foreign direct investments to China have been hovering around zero. The United States is by far the largest recipient of foreign direct investments and in spite of that fact, Chinese foreign direct investment in the US is much lower than would be expected for the second largest economy in the world. However, in recent years, foreign direct investments from China to the US have increased significantly and if the current pace continues, in a relatively short period of time China will have a larger position of foreign direct investment in the United States than US investment in China (IIF 2017).

It should also be noted that the small amount of US foreign direct investment in China can be attributed to the following: poor protection of property rights and this includes intellectual property rights resulting in limited benefits US firms can receive from their brands and their technologies. There are some sectors within the Chinese economy that would be of significant interest to US firms, but the Chinese authorities impose severe restrictions on investments by foreign corporations. In terms of the G20 countries, China is by far the most restrictive about foreign direct investments in many of its sectors especially in its economic sectors where a great many foreign corporations could very easily excel. When it comes to foreign direct investment in China, it is definitely not an even playing field, but that will be covered in greater detail later in the book. As the time of writing, China and the United States are still in negotiations for a Bilateral Investment Treaty, which if it ever comes to fruition, could substantially increase investment in both countries, however, this treaty has been eight years in the making. In March 2016, former Commerce Minister Chen Deming said in a brief statement that both sides "are almost finished with negotiations over a key investment treaty" (Tiezzi 2016, 1–2). After nine rounds of talks in 2013, both the US and China announced they were ready to engage in "substantive BIT negotiations". And now three years later, they're almost finished. Earlier this year at the Boao Forum for Asia, Chen claimed that both the US and China have resolved the key issues that have dogged negotiations in the past. Both have also agreed that any disputes that arise within the Bilateral Investment Treaty (BIT) will be subject to third-party arbitration at the World Bank.

On August 1, 2016 the US–China Economic and Security Review Commission issued the following report:

> A US-China Bilateral Investment Treaty (BIT) is unique among other existing BITs insofar as it will have to balance the interests of two world powers that are both capital-importing and capital-exporting nations. It will not only determine future investment relations between the world's two biggest economies, but will also set the precedent for US investment relations with other major developing countries. While a US-China BIT could potentially unlock sizable benefits, a number of significant challenges – many of which are unique to China's involvement – complicate the debates around a prospective US-China BIT. This report briefly summarizes each country's history with BITs, identifies potential challenges in moving forward with negotiations, and highlights potential implications of the US-China BIT for the United States. Drawing on the 2012 US Model BIT, the evolution of China's BIT practice, and China's 2012 BIT with Canada, this report concludes by a number of questions US policymakers should consider.

According to the US-China Business Council, US foreign direct investments in China have remained relatively stable. The Council claims that since 2008, FDI in China coming from the United States ranged between $2.7 billion and $4.1 billion annually. With that said, Chinese foreign direct investments in the United States have soared in that exact same time frame. In 2008, China's FDI in the US was less than $1 billion, but in 2014, that number had skyrocketed to $11.9 billion and that was actually a decline from the 2013 number which was $14 billion (Tiezzi 2016, 1–3).

Both countries obviously have different objectives. According to the Institute for International Finance, American business feels constrained in China due to China's devastating restrictions on foreign corporations in China. US corporations hope that the proposed BIT will relax some of these restrictions in an effort by the Chinese government to open more of its economic sectors to foreign corporations. On the other hand, Chinese companies would like to see an investment process underscored by the elimination of bias and excess oversight from the Committee on Foreign Investment in the United States (CFIUS). At this point, foreign firms cannot invest in a whole host of industries in China. The list includes, but is not limited to genetically modified agricultural products (GMOs), domestic partial delivery services, publishing houses, news outlets and television stations. Some sectors are restricted, but joint ventures may be allowed with a Chinese partner who has majority ownership. A few years ago, the Chinese government established the Shanghai Free Trade Zone which was intended to be an experimental zone with much less restrictions than the rest of China, but even that experiment came with a lengthy negative list of restricted industries which include telecommunications, automobile manufacturing and banks.

The consensus among many business executives is that China lately has been becoming less receptive to foreign direct investments, e.g. the latest rule prohibits any firm with foreign direct investment from publishing content online. According to the US-China Business Council's 2015 China Business Environment Survey, China has repeatedly made commitments to open its markets, but in reality, very little progress on that issue has been made. Ironically, in sectors where foreign investment is allowed, the Council claimed that more than 80 percent of US companies make the case that their Chinese competitors are given preferential treatment. That sentiment is for Chinese competitors who are private enterprises. In terms of state-owned enterprises, 97 percent of the survey respondents claim that their SOE competitors receive a blatant competitive boost from the Chinese government.

The US-China Business Council has always been an outspoken proponent for the conclusion of the BIT. However, the Council wants a treaty with clear stipulations that provide equal treatment of each country's investors and a very short list of exceptions. Moreover, the Council makes the case that these are key items that could make an immediate and tangible impact for both economies. Historically, China has also had an economic history of highlighting its domestic firms as "international superstars" which involves promoting them and protecting them from foreign domestic competition. According to China's Commerce Minister, Gao Hucheng who recently stated that the United States and China have basically agreed to the text of the BIT, but he said the same thing in March 2016. This is the typical cat and mouse government deliberations; the leaders of both countries toast each other in a photo op and together they make all of these very positive statements, but afterward in a separate setting each starts to back-pedal. In March of 2015, Gao made it a point to say that the actual negative lists – the economic sectors that will be off limits to foreign investment – would be a challenge. On the surface, it doesn't appear that China and the United States are any closer to the finalization of a Bilateral Investment Treaty than they were in 2013 and now with the election of President Trump, the viability of a US-China BIT is anyone's guess. China is a socialist market economy. It's a mixed economic system that attempts to highlight the typical features of both open market and planned economies. The term socialist market economy was used for the first time in 1992 during the XIV Congress of the Chinese Communist Party to outline the new goals in relation to ongoing economic reforms, but by its very nature a socialist market economy evokes several factors of instability. For instance, it has created a convoluted system in which private and state-owned companies compete in a marketplace underscored by open-market prices and planned-economy prices where protection of property rights is usurped by communist ideology and state intervention comes at the expense of competition. Foreign direct investment in Chinese non-financial sectors increased 3.8 percent year-on-year to CNY343.55 hundred million in the first five months of 2016. From January to May, investment in the services sector was up 7.0 percent to CNY241.8 hundred million, representing 70.4 percent of total FDI. In contrast, foreign investment in the manufacturing sector fell 3.2 percent to CNY98.8

hundred million accounting for 28.8 percent share. In the Ministry of Commerce of the People's Republic of China's latest FDI report it showed China with a total of $122.3 billion in FDI as of November 10, 2015 (MOFCOM 2016). In 2014, China received capital inflows totaling $119.6 billion. This was an increase from 2013 of 1.7 percent. One interesting fact considering the stability of FDI levels since 2010, China overall is still an attractive destination for foreign capital flows. According to KPMG (2015, 24–40), the Report makes the case that although the Chinese economy is in a downtrend, in absolute terms, China is still a very significant market for FDI. New opportunities are steadily arising from increased development, industrial restructuring and augmented consumer consumption. Apparently, the most significant development in terms of FDI capital inflows is the growth in FDI in China's service sector. Included in the 2014 FDI tally was $66.2 billion for China's service sector an increase of 7.8 percent year-on-year. At this point, China's service sector in terms of FDI is greater than its manufacturing sector. The recent growth of the service sector underscores China's transition away from an export led manufacturing economy to more of a domestic consumption economy. China's manufacturing sector is always going to play a major role in China's economy and China will never function primarily as a service economy. For one thing, its population is too large, but if China can succeed in its domestic consumption effort that in itself will artificially increase the standard of living for a large part of the Chinese populace. In many developed countries the service sector accounts for well over 60 percent of GDP, but in China that number is less than 50 percent.

The recent development of China's service sector can best be attributed to China's emerging sizable middle class. Over the last 20 years, China's domestic consumption has changed dramatically for the better. From health care, to education to financial services, China's citizens have much more disposable income than they have ever had and that leads to demand for high quality services. Simultaneously, the Chinese government has been actively encouraging a shift in its overall economy from savings to an increase in domestic consumption. On the other hand, in 2014, China's manufacturing sector began to show a weakened trend. For example, in 2010, FDI directed toward China's manufacturing increased by roughly 6 percent, but in 2014 the FDI directed toward manufacturing in China declined by 12.3 percent.

At this point, overcapacity is the primary concern of the manufacturing sector in China, which as previously mentioned is the direct result of a planned economy with little or no consideration for global demand. Other important concerns about China's manufacturing sector include: environmental protection standards, increasing costs and a tighter labor market. Moreover in 2014, Central China experienced an increase in FDI growth of roughly 7.5 percent and at the same time, Eastern and Western China registered increases of 1.1 percent and 1.6 percent respectively. The year 2014 marked the third year in a row where Central China's manufacturing based experienced larger increases in FDI growth over Eastern and Western China. While the eastern provinces still receive a much larger share of FDI, Central China has clearly become a very popular investment destination.

Figure 6.1 Provinces and municipalities of China
Source: D-maps

There is an ongoing stream of companies relocating or expanding operations in Central China the result of comparatively lower labor and land costs underscored by a much-improved infrastructure.

According to China's National Bureau of Statistics in terms of regional definitions, Eastern China consists of the municipalities of Beijing, Tianjin and Shanghai. Also included are the provinces of Liaoning, Hebei, Shandong, Jiangsu, Zhejiang, Fujian, Guangdong and Hainan. Central China comprises the provinces of Heilongjiang, Jilin, Shanxi, Anhui, Jiangxi, Henan, Hubei and Hunan. The autonomous regions and provinces of Western China include: Inner Mongolia, Guangxi, Tibet, Ningxia, Xinjiang and Uyghur. China's statistics bureau further claimed that the provinces of Western China include: Sichuan, Guizhou, Yunnan, Shaanxi, Gansu and Qinghai. Western China has only one municipality: Chongqing Municipality.

A brief look at Figure 6.1 will clearly show that Western China is a much larger landmass than Central China and Eastern China, but without a doubt, Eastern China is the most populous and Central China is now the destination of choice for the largest increase in foreign direct investment. Another telltale sign of FDI includes mergers and acquisitions (M&A). China inbound M&A in 2014 reveals a downward trend since 2009, but 2010 marks the largest M&A activity in China with the completion of 908 deals with a dollar value of $57.8 billion.

In 2009, China put together 801 deals representing a value of $38.8 billion. M&A activity in 2011 experienced a decline in the amount of deals from 908 in 2010 to 810 in 2011, but the value per deal was much larger so the total value amounted to $56.5 billion in 2011 down slightly from the 2010 total value of $57.8 billion.

The year 2012 experienced a steep decline in M&A amounting to 564 deals representing a total value of $35.1 billion down sharply from 2011 where China put together 810 deals with a total value of $56.5 billion. In 2013, the downward trend flattens out a bit to 586 deals totaling $37.6 billion not really that much different from 2012, but 2014 faced yet another a sharp decline representing only 447 deals with a total value of $26.7 billion. All total in the four-year period beginning in 2010, China's M&A went from 908 deals representing a value of $57.8 billion in 2010 to 447 deals with a value of $26.7 billion in 2014 a decline of over 50 percent in both categories.

A closer look at the data shows that the "single most important contributor to the decline in the overall inbound M&A" was the real estate sector, which declined from $8.36 billion in 2013 to $4.31 billion in 2014.

This squares with the anemic property market in China in that same time frame. The finance sector experienced a significant drop in FDI from 2013 to 2014. In 2013, there were three M&A bank deals each with a total value in excess of $1 billion and in 2014 there were no M&A deals even close to that size in the finance sector. Also in 2014, there was a steep decline in inbound M&A for the consumer goods sector from $2.53 billion in 2013 to $450 million in 2014.

It was also noted that there was a sharp decline in large-scale inbound M&A transactions in 2014. The top ten inbound M&A transactions averaged around $890 million each representing a drop of roughly 24.3 percent from the 2013 levels. In fact, there were only two M&A deals in 2014 valued in excess of $1 billion on the top ten list. That number was somewhat disturbing; in 2003 that number was remotely close, but that was a time in China when the SARS (severe acute respiratory syndrome) outbreak negatively impacted foreign investment activities substantially.

Going forward FDI growth is expected to advance in the service sector beyond 2014. This will help facilitate China's effort to rebalance its economy away from manufactured exports to more of a domestic economy and investment-led growth. In this effort, China claims that it will open its service sector to foreign investment. In this way, China hopes to establish a multiplier effect in concert with its own ongoing expansion investments. Along these lines in 2014, the Chinese authorities initiated a whole host of new policies relative to its anticipated increase in FDI for its service industries. To that end, China's central government created new policy guidelines, which allow foreign investors better access to the Chinese market for financial services. This is supposed to facilitate foreign banks and other financial institutions more of an even playing field in terms of competition with their Chinese counterparts. China's efforts to remove such barriers began in 2012. Moreover, in 2014, the Chinese government set up a pilot program that allowed full foreign ownership of private hospitals in seven major cities and provinces. The aforementioned reform measures combined with the large aging population in China should attract a significant number of foreign investors into China's health care market, which has a $1 trillion estimate by 2020. Attracting foreign investment for Chinese health care will not be an easy endeavor. Most health care systems in the advanced economies are very expensive with the United States at the top of the list. Health care in the West requires a significant investment in very sophisticated, specialized hospital equipment and it also requires access to very expensive pharmaceutical products. Cost will be at the heart of China's reformed health care system. How will the Chinese authorities fund a health care system for its people in both the urban and rural areas who have never had access to even the most basic health care? When it comes to an increase in access to health care, there is always a correlation between the actual access and funding the access. An increase in access results in an increase in cost (Burns 2013, 2).

China's overall rising labor and resource costs have deterred a number of foreign investors from allocating additional FDI to China in general. In fact, some foreign investors have taken it a step further and relocated their production of low value-added products to other low-cost nations. However, the high-tech sector has proven more resilient. China's chip industry is a good case in point. China is one of the world's leading manufacturers for cellphones and other handheld devices. In that light, the Chinese market for these devices is among the largest in the world. To that end, Silicon Valley's Intel Corporation in September 2014 paid up to $1.5 billion for a 20 percent interest in two of China's largest mobile chip manufacturers. All of this underscores the Chinese government's commitment to transition itself from low value-added products to high value-added products. The Chinese authorities are encouraging foreign investment by welcoming foreign participation in this important transition. In order to emphasize this commitment to its high-tech sector in 2014, the Chinese government initiated a number of new policy guidelines in its effort to increase FDI to its high-tech sector. The previously mentioned new policies for this sector include: Opinions on accelerating the transformational and innovative development of state-level economic and technological development zones. Opinions on accelerating the development of science and technology service, which should boost more FDI in high-tech services and advanced manufacturing in high-tech products.

In order to facilitate the aforementioned new policies, the Chinese central government has instructed local governments to also update their existing industrial policies. A very good case in point is the government of the Hunan province. In 2014, the government of the Hunan province issued a new industrial policy that foreign companies will receive favorable treatment if foreign companies invest in the construction of high-tech industrial parks or if a foreign corporation establishes research and development (R&D) centers in Hunan Province. This new policy is spelled out in explicit detail in its 2015 Opinions on accelerating the development of industrial zones of high and new technologies.

In order to support these new initiatives, on January 19, 2015, China's Ministry of Commerce released the Draft Foreign Investment Law. This new law replaced three existing laws related to foreign investment – the Law of the

People's Republic of China (PRC) on Foreign-capital Enterprises, the Law of the PRC on Chinese-foreign Contractual Joint Ventures and the Law of the PRC on Chinese-foreign Equity Joint Ventures. The new law is supposed to be designed so that it gives foreign investors easier access to Chinese markets, but in all fairness, it really gives foreign investors access to "specific" Chinese markets. For the most part, the new law will allow foreign investment into economic sectors where the Chinese do not have the technological wherewithal to create certain kinds of research centers or it does not have the production expertise to produce certain (mainly high-tech) products.

In support of the above statement the so-called new Draft Law will still be subject to the management method negative list, meaning that the foreign investor must adhere to the traditional approval procedures while the projects not listed on the negative list, the foreign investor only needs to file regular documentation with the Chinese authorities in charge of foreign investments. Moreover, the new Draft Law is supposed to contain provisions that create more of an even playing field for foreign investors. A closer look at the new Draft Law shows that the status of foreign investment companies will not be based on the percentage of ownership, but on the controlling party.

Foreign companies operating in mainland China which are owned by foreign investors shall be considered foreign enterprises. On the other hand, Chinese companies owned and controlled by Chinese investors shall have the status of a domestic company. This kind of rhetoric makes it clear that it will be much more difficult for a foreign investor to use a Chinese enterprise as a shield to operate in China and gain benefits if they own a minority stake but exercise *de facto* real control. There are some provisions inside the new "Draft Law" that overlap with certain provisions found in China's Bilateral Investment Treaties (BITs) which China is currently in prolonged negotiations with a number of countries including the United States and the European Union and there are certain provisions inside the new Draft Law that contradict certain provisions within the proposed BITs with the US and the EU. These issues will be up in the air until the actual specifics are precisely detailed in the respective Bilateral Investment Treaties. China is currently asking for input on the details of its proposed new investment law. The end result will likely impact a number of foreign investors currently operating in China and abroad. On the surface it appears that China is poised to open its investment environment considering its new reform initiatives plus its proposed investment treaties or its suggested free trade agreements especially with the West. Most of the so-called pundits make the case that China's investment environment will improve significantly in the short term. They further claim that the Chinese authorities have initiated any number of initiatives to create a more conducive environment for foreign investment in the coming years.

In terms of foreign investment initiatives, in the 2013 and 2014 Plenum meetings (which are also called the Third and Fourth Plenum meetings respectively), the Third Plenum meeting stated that the 'market' should play a much bigger role in the Chinese economy. With that said, the meeting's participants indicated that there should be less government intervention which will lead to a marketplace based on fair competition in the future. Moreover, the Fourth Plenum embraced the rule of law principles in order to facilitate an improved regulatory environment for corporations operating in China.

Additionally, the Chinese Government's Central Economic Work Conference that took place in December 2014 publicly announced that China will give foreign companies broader market access to specific service and manufacturing sectors. This is a concerted effort on the part of the Chinese government to stabilize inbound investment and improve investment quality. Moreover, investments worth less than $300 million in a joint venture controlled by Chinese investors no longer require approval from the National Development and Reform Commission (NDRC).

Two to three years later and nothing has changed. The same complaints from foreign companies operating in China keep coming to the surface. The complaints are the same that we discussed earlier. China has done nothing to create a more even playing field for foreign investors. In the case of the NDRC, though approval is no longer required for a joint venture, the Chinese company involved in the joint venture must still be a majority shareholder and the company still is required to register with the NDRC.

And if the Chinese company involved in the joint venture is subsidized by either the Chinese government or a local government, which there is a high probability that it is, then every detail about the joint venture must have government approval. With that said, a $300 million inbound investment in a joint

Table 6.1 China's outbound and inbound FDI 2010–2015

$US Billions						
140						
						131 In
120				122 In	123 In	124 Out
	101 In	118 In	115 In	117 Out	119 Out	
100						
			84 Out			
80						
	72 Out	77 Out				
60						
40						
20						
0						
	2010	2011	2012	2013	2014	2015

Legend
Out = Outbound FDI
In = Inbound FDI

Source: Author with data from the National Bureau of Statistics

venture isn't really large enough to attract the big foreign players and it's far too big for the smaller-sized foreign companies.

Table 6.1 provides a much clearer picture of what's taking place inside the Chinese economy. The gold dust years were obviously from the early 2000s to 2011. In 2012, China's economy started a downward trend. Inbound and outbound FDI provide a much better picture of China's economy than the actual GDP growth numbers published by China's Ministry of Commerce. In July 2016, China once again changed its GDP calculation for the second time in less than a year, resulting in and adding credence to foreign investors' doubts about China's data accuracy.

In June 2016, the China International Capital Corporation (CICC) one of China's leading investment banking firms once again lowered its GDP 2016 forecast for China from 6.9 percent to 6.7 percent and its 2017 GDP growth forecast has also been reduced from 6.8 percent to 6.7 percent. According to CICC, the expected monthly GDP growth in the second half of 2016 will be flat in line with no more interest rate cuts from the People's Bank of China (China's central bank). The CICC has an interesting history. It is very well connected indeed. It was incorporated in China in 1995 as a joint venture between the China Construction Bank, Morgan Stanley in New York, China National Investment and Guaranty Co Ltd, GIC in Singapore and the Mingly Corporation in Russia. It was the first Sino-foreign joint venture investment bank in China. This was a joint venture between three state-owned companies and two private companies: Morgan Stanley and the Mingly Corporation. Over the years with the exception of GIC in Singapore, the original joint venture partners sold their interest in the firm. In 2015, CICC was converted into a joint stock company with limited liability and its top three shareholders were Huijin, GIC and TPG. In November 2015, CICC completed its own IPO on the Hong Kong Exchange.

As mentioned earlier in this chapter, US FDI in China is relatively modest, which confuses many of the world's financial analysts considering the size of China's economy relative to the rest of the world. However, an analysis of American FDI criteria shows firsthand that China in many respects does not meet the minimum requirements for most US corporations in relation to outbound FDI. In many instances, China does not meet the necessary investment criteria that US companies require in order to establish outbound FDI. First, US outward investments are very sensitive to property rights and the rule of law and this includes intellectual property rights. More often than not, US corporations are for the most part technology leaders which results in the very important protection of trademarks and patents. Historically, and according to the World Governance Indicators, China has repeatedly demonstrated a poor record on property rights and the rule of law and over time – the situation has only gotten worse. And while China encourages inbound FDI for manufacturing, it prohibits foreign investment in financial services, mining, telecom and media just to name just a few sectors. According to the Organisation for Economic Cooperation and Development (OECD), China is much more closed to FDI than any of its emerging market counterparts, e.g. Brazil, India, and South Africa and China is definitely much more closed than either the United States or the European Union. Ironically, the Chinese sectors that were previously mentioned that would be of particular interest to the West are for the most part closed to Western FDI.

At this point, there are some multinational corporations from the United States who are very big players in China, but a close look at their investment outcomes underscores the obstacles involved in foreign direct investment in China for US corporations. First is the Caterpillar Corporation. In 2012, Caterpillar announced its $677 million purchase of ERA Mining Machinery Ltd. Its investment bankers billed this purchase as a coup for Caterpillar and it soon became the cross-border deal of the year. Caterpillar is the largest maker of tractors and excavators in the world. ERA was the holding company for Zhengzhou Siwei Mechanical & Electric Equipment Manufacturing Co Ltd. Zhengzhou is one of China's major manufacturers of hydraulic equipment for coal mines and Siwei was Caterpillar's entrée into China's huge coal industry. In January 2013, Caterpillar's lawyers uncovered major accounting problems at the headquarters of Siwei. After a very lengthy audit, Caterpillar said it had discovered "deliberate, multi-year, coordinated accounting misconduct" (Baldwin and Ruwitch 2014, 1). Consequently, Caterpillar fired Siwei's chairman, Wang Fu, and the company took a non-cash goodwill impairment charge of $580 million or roughly 86 percent of the purchase price. Later additional audits by Reuters and interviews with former employees, board members, bankers and advisers, showed that accounting problems were widespread and rampant at that company prior to the purchase by Caterpillar, but Caterpillar chose to look the other way and move expeditiously to close the deal. Eighteen months after Caterpillar's board approved the deal it had become a case study in how a foreign company with decades of experience in China can still struggle in that market. The case study also highlighted the fact that multinational corporations are willing to accept risks they may otherwise avoid just to get a foothold in China (Baldwin and Ruwitch 2014, 2). Needless to say, the Siwei purchase triggered a number of shareholder lawsuits against Caterpillar and they're still ongoing. In the meantime, Siwei has been on an ongoing downward trend since the purchase and it had received no new orders in 2015. The company also announced that it had furloughed 50 percent of its workforce. This is out and out fraud, but when there's a very tepid rule of law, things like this take place. To add additional insult to Caterpillar's ineptitude, the fired former CEO of Siwei said that indeed his books were a mess, but he committed to no wrongdoing. In fact, he is now pursuing the creation of a similar company with an identical name in the same business. As of this writing, he is yet to build a factory, but he claims that when he does, he'll be able to take most of Siwei's old customers with him (Baldwin and Ruwitch 2014, 2). The agonizing part of this particular story is that the Caterpillar Corporation is not new to the Chinese business landscape. In fact, it employs over 20,000 Chinese employees in a number of manufacturing facilities, R&D centers, and parts centers in order to facilitate a viable dealer network.

The following are the chain of events leading up to the Siwei acquisition. In 2011, Caterpillar purchased Bucyrus International for $8.8 billion, an Ohio mining and earth-moving company with substantial Chinese operations. In this case, the deal clincher here was Bucyrus' significant Chinese operations, but following the acquisition, the company was slow in the design and manufacture of new specialized equipment for the Chinese mining market. Consequently, Caterpillar's Bucyrus operation in China lost market share. Research shows that the Bucyrus acquisition was the precursor for the Siwei debacle (Baldwin and Ruwitch 2014, 2). Caterpillar did not want to make the same mistake in China's coal mining industry especially since China has the largest coal mining operations in the world. A former Caterpillar executive, Anthony Farmer explains unequivocally that in China local companies particularly state-owned companies prefer locally made products (Baldwin and Ruwitch 2014, 2). Within that context, Caterpillar thought Siwei looked attractive. Originally, it was a state-owned company, but at that point, it had become a public company listed on the Hong Kong Exchange under the ERA name, which made it much easier for a foreign company like Caterpillar to purchase.

Siwei was an expert in the manufacture of hydraulic arms that keep underground mines from collapsing. Consequently, Caterpillar viewed the purchase of Siwei as a very lucrative proposal considering that 80 percent of China's coal mines are underground plus Siwei had a very good relationship with the Chinese government. In fact, the Siwei manufacturing facility was visited twice in 2012 by the leader of the Chinese Communist Party in Zhengzhou. On the surface, it appeared that the idea had been fully examined by two of Caterpillar's executives, Steve Wunning the president of Caterpillar's mining division in Peoria and Ed Rapp, Caterpillar's Chief Financial Officer. Both men made a positive presentation to the company's board in October 2011 and the Caterpillar board expressed support for the proposal and in November 2011, the Caterpillar board of directors approved the acquisition for up to $964 million (Baldwin and Ruwitch 2014, 3).

Ultimately, this particular Chinese venture cost Caterpillar shareholders hundreds of millions of dollars; the result of significant accounting mismanagement, incomplete product and manufacturing capabilities, dereliction of duties by Siwei's executive management, and obviously Caterpillar's inability to really comprehend China's overall business practices with respect to that country's grasp of the rule of law in spite of the fact that Caterpillar had done business in China for over two decades. A few years ago General Electric (GE) created a joint venture with state-owned Aviation Industry Corporation of China (AVIC). The primary product in this deal was GE's flight simulator which was considered the best in the aviation industry: a next generation technology, though GE's executives are well aware that access to the world's second largest economy often comes at a very high cost. The cost includes, but is not limited to the transfer of the very technologies that the United States cite as essential to their future economic viability. GE is no different than the other American multinational corporations who must decide which technologies should be included in the one-sided joint ventures with Chinese state-owned corporations. These corporations have to determine how to protect their technologies from being stolen or misused by their Chinese partner who has majority control of the joint venture.

The decision makers have to worry continuously about software piracy. This conclusion is substantiated by the earlier industrial manufacturers who saw replicas of their product group in the marketplace shortly after entering into partnerships with their Chinese counterparts.

This particular joint venture is more of a double-edge sword. In the joint venture agreement with AVIC, the avionics created by GE technologies will be an essential part of the new Chinese commercial airliner and it will no doubt be in competition with Boeing in the United States and Airbus in the European Union. This has created a groundswell of stern criticism from the industrial manufacturing sectors in the West considering that both are struggling to maintain a manufacturing base. Yet the General Electric executives who made the decisions to go ahead with the joint venture claim they have no second thoughts. They argue that the Chinese aircraft market is booming and the deal was too good to pass on even if it means that GE will have to share an avionics technology that should be considered an indispensable part of US national security. This was your typical shortsighted management decision on the part of a few key executives of a multinational corporation to boost short-term profits. "We are all in and we don't want it back," said Lorraine Bolsinger, then chief executive of GE Aviation Systems. The chief executive claimed that the chance to be part of developing a major new aircraft is not to be missed, even if all the jobs will be in Shanghai or elsewhere in China (Schneider 2015, 1). Time and again, American business leaders have questioned GE's logic in risking the long-term strategic advantages of a technology transfer deal for a short-term gains, GE's management publicly argues that this is not the case. They claim they negotiated rigid protections in their contract with AVIC. Furthermore, GE management argues that their joint venture with AVIC has very strict limitations about employing Chinese nationals who have a military or intelligence background. This kind of nonsense is more wishful thinking than anything else. They do a technology-transfer deal with a state-owned enterprise in a country that virtually has no rule of law and the GE management team in charge makes the case that the aforementioned joint venture has very strict limitations about employing specific Chinese nationals in their manufacturing facilities in China (Schneider 2015, 2).

Many studies by the United States Chamber of Commerce have deeply criticized China's state policies of transferring technology from abroad in order to advance technological and manufacturing capabilities with a de-emphasis on cheap labor. The Chamber further points out that China is at a crossroad; its demographics are making it imperative for the Chinese authorities to acquire and develop technologies to produce higher valued products and services. In that light, China's wage scale is rising and its population has leveled out plus the younger people in its workforce are in decline (US Chamber of Commerce 2016, 7–8).

The multinational corporations like General Electric make the claim that the so-called "colonial" model of manufacturing products in the advanced economies and selling them to the developing markets is an outdated method of global economics. According to information from the US Commerce Department exports to China in 2015 supported over 500,000 US jobs, but that number was minuscule compared to the imports from China to the United States that resulted in a $350 billion trade deficit for 2015 (McGregor 2016, 15–16).

In terms of a colonial model of manufacturing products in the advanced economies, Germany's trade balance with the United States is second only to China which is truly amazing considering that Germany's population is much smaller than China's 1.3 billion. Germany has created a manufacturing economy that emphasizes the integration of capital and knowledge where the end result is both maximum production accompanied by maximum efficiency. Further research on this subject shows that the German manufacturing sector enhances its efficiency with the use of small family owned and mid-sized manufacturing firms with no more than 500 employees. These firms are known as the "German Mittelstand". Many of these successful companies are characterized by independence and/or family ownership. This is in accordance with Germany's Federal Ministry of Economics and Technology.

Thanks to Germany's very successful vocational trade school system, the Mittelstands employ highly skilled workers that tend to stay with the same company for decades and they are encouraged and buffeted by a banking system that is mandated to fund local businesses as opposed to risky investment maneuvers. The German Mittelstand contributes nearly 52 percent of total German output. Furthermore, these firms account for around 37 percent of the overall German GDP, which in 2015 was approximately $3.85 trillion. The training provided by the German Mittelstand makes a significant contribution towards the comparatively low level of youth unemployment in Germany, which is 7.20 percent as of June 1, 2016. The idea behind the German Mittelstand is stakeholder capitalism as opposed to shareholder capitalism (FMET 2016, 1). The German Mittelstand does not have to be concerned with shareholders so consequently they're able to focus on long-term growth and development, but even Germany's large public corporations, e.g. BMW, continue to invest heavily in Germany as insurance for future profits.

Since the Chinese economic reforms in the 1990s, some of America's largest public companies have invested confidently in China only to limp away a few years later in a daze about what they had experienced. These failures had nothing to do with incompetence. In fact, most were Fortune 500 companies with very successful track records, e.g. Home Depot, eBay, Google, Mattel, and so on. None of these firms are new to international investments and they've all succeeded in their other global investments, but not in China.

Some of these companies failed because they didn't understand the domestic customer environment or they were unable to compete with the local competition. Each industry is different so it's virtually impossible to generalize, but with each failure surfaced a uniform pattern: the inability of each firm to fully comprehend just how different and cut-throat the Chinese markets really are. Most foreign operation failures in China are the direct result of not understanding China's very complex legal system (Hermann 2016, 2). On the surface, Home Depot thought China would be the ideal place for do-it-yourself (DIY) stores.

All of the prerequisites were in place: millions of new homeowners, a growing middle class, and the Chinese culture of parsimony and independence. In 2006, Home Depot acquired a Chinese firm with 12 stores. Home Depot set about stocking these stores with tools and DIY materials, but that business model never got off the ground in China. Consequently, after six years of hemorrhaging money Home Depot China shut its doors for good and in the process, it terminated 850 Chinese employees. In retrospect, Home Depot's failure in China resulted from several factors. First, the company's timing was wrong; by the time the company set up shop in China, its competitors had a very significant advantage and the Chinese economy was in a downward trend. Second, the Chinese housing market is as much investment speculation as it is a Chinese domicile. That's the nature of the Chinese housing market. A large percentage of Chinese homebuyers are property speculators who hope the home price inflates; they're not in the business of home improvement (*China Daily Mail* 2015, 2).

Third, and this is what Home Depot should have learned from Best Buy; the Chinese customer doesn't like big boxy warehouses away from the city's main shopping center. Finally, and this proved to be the firm's main fatality; Home Depot tried to Americanize the Chinese DIY customer, forgetting that labor is so cheap that most homeowners just hire a handyman.

In the case of Mattel, this was solidly a planning failure. Their store in Shanghai was too big, too expensive and too confusing for the typical Chinese shopper. For whatever reason, Mattel tried to mix adult trinkets with children's dolls and toys. The Mattel store opened in 2009 with an investment of over $30 million and after a very brief period of losing huge sums of money, it closed its doors to the House of Barbie in 2011. In 2004, eBay bought a Chinese company, EachNet and immediately switched its platform to an eBay platform. Its main competition was Taobao and that company allowed its buyers and sellers to talk to one another prior to the sale, but eBay did not have a mechanism in place to facilitate conversations between buyers and sellers which turned out to be its fatal flaw. This is Chinese culture; the Chinese customer wants to talk to the owner prior to the secondhand sale. Two years and millions of dollars later, eBay closed its China operation leaving Taobao with a 95 percent market share. Finally, Google's entrée into the Chinese marketplace, this is, by far, the most studied and complicated failure of any American company in China. In 2009, Google in China announced that the company's Chinese servers had been hacked. At that point, the company moved its servers to Hong Kong which resulted in a steep decline in Google's market share in China: from a 30 percent share all the way down to a paltry 3 percent. At the very heart of this huge mistake was politics. This debacle goes all the way back to 2006 when Google launched a search engine in China with no blog, no Gmail, no software and no YouTube.

From the beginning, the Chinese government told Google that it had to censor certain internet content. The Chinese government requires all official Internet Service Providers (ISPs) to self-censor in order to remove illegal content from search results. After the company moved its servers to Hong Kong, Google publicly disclosed that it would no longer censor on behalf of the Chinese government. In 2008, the Chinese authorities outright demanded that Google increase its censorship of its autofill search suggestions. In 2009, Google discovered a breach of its servers which was traced back to the Chinese government. The hackers not only stole sensitive corporate information, but they also went through all of the accounts of suspected activists and dissidents in both China and Tibet and immediately afterward, Google moved its search engine servers to Hong Kong.

In this case, the lessons for Google were very difficult to comprehend, but nonetheless, they were extremely significant. At the end of the day, the message here is very loud and very clear. Foreign companies who want to do business in China will either have to rigidly follow the dictates of the Chinese government and engage in some distasteful, unsavory business practices or as in the case of Google, exit the country.

References

Baldwin, Clare and John Ruwitch, "Special Report: How Caterpillar got bulldozed in China," *Reuters News Service*, January 23, 2014.

Burns, Lawton R., "Ticking Time Bomb: China's Healthcare System Faces Issues of Access, Quality and Cost," *Knowledge @ Wharton*, June 26, 2013.

China Daily Mail, "Why big American businesses fail in China," June 3, 2015, p. 14.

Federal Ministry of Economics and Technology (FMET), "Germany is Europe's economic driving force," Federal Ministry of Economic and Technology website, July 11, 2016, available at www.bmwi.de.

Hermann, Steffen, "Stakeholder Management-Long term business success through sustainable stakeholder relationships," TNS Infratest, Germany website, July 11, 2016, available at www.tns-infratest.com/.

Institute of International Finance (IIF) website, Washington, DC January 25, 2017, available at www.iif.com/.

KPMG China, "China Outlook 2015," January 2015, Shanghai, China.

KPMG China, "China Outlook 2015," January 2015, Shanghai, China.

McGregor, James, "China's Drive for 'Indigenous Innovation' A Web Of Industrial Policies," Global Regulatory Project, Publications and Reports, US Chamber of Commerce Website, July 11, 2016, pp. 15–16, available at www.uschamber.com/sites/default/files/legacy/reports/100728_chinareport.pdf.

Ministry of Commerce, the People's Republic of China, (MOFCOM) press release, July 24, 2016.

Schneider, Howard, "GE 'all in' on aviation deal with China," *The Washington Post*, August 22, 2015.

Tiezzi, Shannon, "Are China and the US Close to Sealing an Investment Treaty?" *The Diplomat*, March 24, 2016.

US Chamber of Commerce, "Competing Interests in China's Competition Law Enforcement," Publications and Reports, US Chamber of Commerce Website, July 11, 2016, pp. 7–8.

US–China Economic and Security Review Commission (CESRC), "Policy Considerations for Negotiating a US-China Bilateral Investment Treaty," August 1, 2016.

7 European foreign direct investment

The following is an overview of the European Union-China relations from 1975 onwards. From this overview, the reader will have a clear view of the economic and political relationship between the EU and China. The following analysis will focus on the outbound FDI to China from the EU's three largest economies: Germany, the United Kingdom and France. As mentioned earlier, the United Kingdom just passed a voter referendum to leave the European Union: Brexit. However, historically as the second largest economy in the EU, the UK has played an important part in the economic and political success of the Union.

The EU and China represent two of the three largest economies in the world. Consequently, both have a serious interest in creating an equally comprehensive economic partnership where both the EU and China benefit. In 1975, formal diplomatic ties between the EU and China were officially established resulting in the creation of a 40-year broad-based framework of bilateral relations. To this end in 1998, the EU and China established their annual EU-China Summit which today accounts for over 60 substantive and sectoral dialogues. In 2013, the EU-China 2020 Agenda for Cooperation was adopted, focusing on the topics of development, sustainable development, peace and human interactions.

Over the years, both the EU and China have changed substantially. China's unparalleled economic growth over the last 25 years has catapulted that country into both a domestic and international phenomenon giving China more weight on international issues. According to the European Commission, this should underscore the major opportunities present in EU-China cooperation, specifically creating EU jobs and economic growth and providing China with the means to support and enhance its economic reform program. Accordingly, the High Representative and the European Commission issued a joint communication on the elements for a new EU strategy on China on June 22, 2016.[1] The communication points out the long-term benefits for both EU and Chinese citizens. China and Europe traded with one another 20 years ago, but they would not have been considered large trading partners. However, today the EU is China's largest trading partner and after the United States, China is the EU's second largest. The trade between the EU and China amounts to well over 1.5 billion euros per day. In 2016, EU exports to China totaled 170 billion euros and Chinese imports to the EU amounted to over 350 billion euros resulting in a Chinese trade surplus with the EU of over 180 billion euros. That amounts to 180 billion euros of free cash flow for China in 2016. Within the boundaries of the EU-China High-Level Economic and Trade Dialogue, the EU and China analyze important key issues involved with trade, e.g. investments, services, procurement and intellectual property rights, reciprocity, and the ongoing progress in China's announced so-called economic reform program. The EU is extremely interested in Chinese reforms that give the market more of a decisive role in the leveling of an even playing field.

In 2016, the EU's foreign direct investment into China amounted to roughly 16 percent of the total FDI inflows. However, if an even playing field were to ever occur in China, this number could be increased dramatically. The EU capital outflows into China amounted to only 4.5 percent of the total EU capital outflows. Both sides are in the midst of negotiating the Comprehensive Agreement on Investment (CAI). The CAI's mandate is to improve the protection of investments, market access and the investment climate for EU investors in China and for Chinese investors in the EU. At the most recent EU-China Summit, both sides confirmed their serious interest in each other's important investment initiatives: the Investment Plan for Europe and the One Belt, One Road Initiative. In 2015–2016, the EU and China established the EU-China Connectivity Program. This particular program facilitates and promotes cooperation in infrastructure which involves financing, interoperability, logistics and maritime and rail links throughout the Eurasian continent. Moreover, increased cooperation for research and innovation plays a very big role in the EU-China relationship. Reciprocity is key. Reciprocal access to the research and innovation of both sides is essential to ensure the appropriate funding programs. All of this is part of the EU's Horizon 2020 program, which promotes long-term joint research and innovation partnerships in very strategic areas of common interests.

Horizon 2020 is the largest EU Research and Innovation program ever with nearly $100 million of funding available over a seven-year period (2014–2020). This is in addition to the private funding this endeavor will attract. The goal of Horizon 2020 is to create breakthroughs, discoveries and world-firsts by taking great ideas from the laboratory to the marketplace. Its threefold emphasis is excellent science, industrial leadership and solving societal changes underscored by the intended development of the European Research Area. Two areas of deep concern for the EU are China's positions on the rule of law and human rights. The European Union has a firm commitment around the world for the promotion of human rights. Time and again, the EU has expressed profound concerns over human rights issues in China.

The EU and all of its member nations will continue to prod the Chinese authorities to promote human rights among its citizens in conjunction with the creation of an environment where the rule of law is at the heart of a civilized society. An EU-China Human Rights Dialogue takes place every year. The EU Special Representative for Human Rights Stavros Lambrinidis visited China twice in 2016 for specific human rights violations. In defense of the EU, at the most recent EU-China Summit, both sides expressed a common interest to better understand the other's legal systems. The 17th EU-China Summit agreed to set up an EU-China Legal Affairs Dialogue with a view to further enhance EU-China cooperation on a broad range of issues using mutual learning and exchanges of best practices on the rule of law. The first dialogue was held in Beijing on June 20–21, 2016.

In terms of global governance, the EU would like China to support global standards and institutions and at the same time, promote effective multilateralism among the global economies. At the core of this proposition obviously are the G20 countries and the World Trade Organization (WTO). The EU and China play very important roles in both of these organizations. The G20 and the WTO are the catalysts in finding solutions to global challenges within the global economy. The EU would like China to become more involved with the WTO policies on multilateral initiatives relative to an open trading system.

On July 13, 2016 and later in June 2017, Jean-Claude Juncker, President of the European Commission, warned China in no uncertain terms that it must cut steel production. If not, China will be frozen out of the World Trade Organization (WTO). China has received word that it has to cut back its steel production overcapacity – which results in the dumping of excess production into the EU – or lose its membership in the WTO. Jean-Claude Juncker and Donald Tusk, President of the European Council, delivered this stern message at a joint press conference in Beijing.

Juncker further stated that he very deliberately explained in precise detail to his Chinese colleagues that China's overcapacity in steel production presents extremely serious and detrimental problems for the EU and for Europeans in general. In a further elaboration, Juncker argued that China's overcapacity steel production is more than double the steel production of the entire EU and that in itself should amplify the challenges faced by the EU steel manufacturers and the thousands of steelworkers employed by the EU steel industry. Earlier, China applied for Market Economy Status (MES) in the EU through the WTO, but as of this writing the European Commission's decision on China's market economy status has not been made. Juncker made it perfectly clear that the EU will hold firm on its international obligations, but the continuation of China's steel dumping into the EU will not be tolerated.

Juncker further stated that on July 20, 2016 the Commission would initiate an orientation debate on the impact assessment of Article 15 of the WTO accession agreement with China relative to MES in the EU. According to the by-laws of the WTO, if China were granted MES in the EU that would make it much more difficult for the EU to bring anti-dumping cases against Beijing so if the EU were to agree to give China MES that could be detrimental.

Under Section 15 of the Chinese WTO Accession Protocol, China is treated as a Non-Market Economy (NME) in anti-dumping proceedings. This takes place if Chinese firms cannot prove they operate under market economy conditions and for the most part, they cannot. NME status in anti-dumping proceedings is the possibility to use other methodologies to determine normal value of the good, instead of using domestic prices to compute the dumping margin.

This enhances the proceeding by adding additional leverage. Generally, NME methodologies are used in the determination of normal value result in much higher anti-dumping duties (Middleton 2016, 1).

Since 2003, in light of the aforementioned much higher duties combined with the indisputable fact that China is subject to more anti-dumping investigations than any other WTO member, the mission of the Chinese authorities is to obtain MES, making this one of the country's major foreign policy objectives. China is attempting to make the argument that under the Section 15(d) of the WTO Accession Protocol, the provision mandates the expiration of its NME methodology after December 11, 2016 and according to China's interpretation of the WTO by-laws, the EU is legally obligated to grant MES to China after that date. There's nothing even remotely close to this interpretation within the WTO by-laws. With that said, China's understanding of Section 15(d) may not hold (Puccio 2015, 1).

As China increases its efforts to obtain MES, international criticism is making the case that China is either unable or unwilling to make difficult economic reforms. When China devalued the renminbi and bailed out its stock market, this sent a signal to the global economic community that China may be in the process of reversing its earlier public statements about allowing market forces to have a free hand. China is still under the impression that the MES should be automatic; yet in spite of its claim, there are a number of EU trade experts who make the case that China cannot achieve MES until their trading partners are convinced that the Chinese exporters are not benefiting from government subsidies. According to the Washington-based Economic Policy Institute (EPI), Chinese Market Economy Status would generate an even larger surge in Chinese exports to the EU eliminating a minimum of 1.6 million to 3.5 million manufacturing jobs within the European Union.

The following is a more detailed explanation of the EPI's findings. It's estimated that any decision by the EU to grant China MES would increase manufactured imports from China to the EU by between 25 percent and 50 percent from their 2011 base level in the first three to five years following Chinese MES designation. First, China MES would increase Chinese commodity exports to the EU by between 71.3 billion euros and 142.5 billion euros or even more resulting in an increase in EU trade deficits which reduces EU GDP by between 114.1 billion euros and 228 billion euros (1 percent to 2 percent of GDP) in the first three to five years eliminating 1,745,400 to 3,490,900 EU jobs (Scott and Jiang 2015, 1–15).

The Paper further shows that the biggest job losses would take place in the four largest EU economies, Germany (319,700 to 639,200 jobs lost); Italy (208,100 to 416,000 jobs lost); the United Kingdom (193,400 to 386,800 jobs lost) and France (183,300 to 366,800 jobs lost). These four countries would also be the hardest hit when measured by jobs at risk as a share of total employment though the rankings shift slightly with Italy at the top (jobs at risk constituting 0.9 percent to 1.9 percent of total employment followed by Germany (0.8 percent to 1.7 percent of total employment), France (0.7 percent to 1.5 percent of total employment) and the United Kingdom (0.7 percent to 1.4 percent of total employment). The next four countries, in terms of total jobs at risk are Poland (145,100 to 290,100 jobs), Spain (136,600 to 273,300 jobs), Romania (100, 100 to 200,100 jobs) and the Netherlands (52,000 to 104,000 jobs).

The question about granting China Market Economy Status is currently under consideration by the European Union and other members of the WTO including the United States. In the case of China, this is a very precarious undertaking on the part of the EU and other WTO members. First, in a China with a MES "designation" under an anti-dumping investigation, investigators would be required to begin with the tenuous presumption that the prices and costs in China are effectively market driven which would result in much lower or even zero duties in anti-dumping cases.

Moreover, should the EU grant MES to China, the EU would in essence eliminate its forthcoming duties on tens of thousands of Chinese manufactured products that are government subsidized either directly or indirectly in terms of the actual depressed costs. At that point, Chinese exporters could lower prices substantially without fear of engendering anti-dumping complaints.

Furthermore, there is a consensus building among a great many EU economists that should the EU grant market economy status to China, the result would be an even bigger flood of Chinese exports to the EU, but by far the most important prediction is that the EU would have few defensive economic tools in place to defend itself against Chinese product dumping. A decision to grant MES to China would expose producers in the European Union, the United States, and other countries to a flood of cheap products from China. Granting China market economy treatment would leave European manufacturers with few tools to protect themselves.

As the time of writing, China has massive amounts of overcapacity in a wide range of industries. This is the direct result of enormous amounts of government subsidies, a concerted effort by the Chinese national, provincial and local governments designed to support a dynamic Chinese export growth strategy. Consequently, China is massively overproducing: steel, plate glass, chemicals, solar panels and a number of other industrial products. However, the most damaging effects of this particular strategy to its trading partners is China's excess export production, normally priced at below market prices, resulting in an unfair competitive advantage to the importing countries.

For example, China's steel production glut is negatively affecting the profitability of the global steel industry. The reader should keep in mind that this is not a one-off issue; this is what takes place in all of China's basic industries. With that said, China's current non-market economy status evokes rules where the cost and pricing of China's exports are evaluated closer to the Chinese exporters real costs and pricings which is technically the last line of defense for China's trading partners in terms of anti-dumping laws. Going back to China's initial entrée into the WTO, Chinese exports to the EU had an average annual increase of roughly 11 percent per year and this is in spite of the EU's ongoing treatment of China as a non-market economy. If the EU granted China MES, reputable sources estimate an additional increase in addition to the one mentioned above of another 5 to 10 percent in Chinese exports to the EU within the first three to five years (Dalton 2015). The incremental increase in Chinese exports to the EU would be the result of both an increase in exports to the EU that are currently subject to anti-dumping regulations; (lower duties equal lower prices) and an increase in Chinese exports to the EU of other products in the same sectors along with other vital sectors in line with China's five-year plans. The hypothetical grant of MES to China by the EU would underscore the lack of any EU defense against "dumping" resulting in no disincentives for not dumping on China's part.

The overwhelming negative on the question of whether to grant China MES sits with the potential EU jobs that will be put at risk. According to the most recent estimates by the Economic Policy Institute, the jobs that will be eliminated in the EU by granting China MES which result in increased exports from China include 478,600 to 957,300 direct jobs in the EU competing industries. In terms of indirect jobs at risk and mainly in the EU supplier industries, e.g. manufacturing, commodity and service industries are currently estimated to be between 537,100 to 1,074,100 indirect jobs (EC 2013).

The particular macroeconomic model used by the Economic Policy Institute in this analysis measures the historical relationships between output and employment enhanced by the increase in manufactured exports from China to the EU if China is granted MES. In this instance if the EU grants China MES, the model estimates that EU jobs at risk will amount to between 0.9 percent and 1.8 percent of the total EU workforce or between 1.7 million and 3.5 million EU jobs assuming Chinese exports to the EU increase by 25 percent to 50 percent, not a very encouraging prospect.

The model further analyzes the EU jobs at risk by industry. Obviously, the sectors with the biggest amount of job loss exposure would fall into manufacturing. Within the manufacturing sector, the largest losses would occur in textiles and apparel which have a job loss risk estimate of 7.8 percent to 15.5 percent of total industry employment or 187,000 to 374,000 EU textiles and apparel jobs at risk. The other manufacturing sectors with large numbers of jobs at risk are computer, electronic and optical products 9.2 percent to 18.3 percent of total industry employment or somewhere between 143,900 to 287,000 EU jobs at risk.

Furthermore, the model used in this scenario also shows that the reductions in trade balance have a multiplier estimate on GDP of 1.6 with each euro reduction in the EU balance of trade dropping GDP by 1.6 euros, which is the equivalent of the US infrastructure spending multiplier. This is a conservative estimate for the EU, which normally has multipliers applicable for government spending in 2.0 range. Given the 1.6 euros criteria a 100 billion euros increase in the trade deficit results in a GDP reduction of roughly 160 billion euros within the three to five year origination period following the initial EU MES grant to China in 2016 or later. The model also underscores the assumption that each percentage-point decline in GDP results in a reduction of total employment by 0.9 percent. In essence, the macroeconomic model used in these analyses establishes the total effects of trade modification relative to output and employment. According to the EU-China FDI Monitor data, there was a substantial slowdown of European FDI into China in 2016. Technically, the Monitor records FDI investing of European companies into China. The transactional value of the 2016 EU FDI went from nearly $4 billion in Q1 to $2 billion in Q3 and Q4 representing a 50 percent reduction in EU FDI into China. Moreover, the annual value of EU FDI transactions in China declined from about $13 billion in 2014 to $10 billion in 2016, a drop of 23 percent. However, these figures are partially distorted by USD/EUR exchange rate movements and the decline in EUR terms was less pronounced (from EUR 9.9 billion to 9.3 billion, about 9 percent).

With that said, the investments in multi-year green field projects remained flat, but stable and this includes a Lego plant worth roughly $471 million in Jiaxing. Lego's first production began in Q4 of 2014. Total spending on China's green field projects by the EU amounted to approximately $640 million. This number is somewhat higher than that amount in Q3, but still on the lower end of quarterly averages in recent years. At the risk of being redundant, a green field investment is a form of foreign direct investment where a parent company builds its operations in a foreign country from the ground up. In addition to the construction of new production facilities, these projects can also include the building of new distribution hubs, offices and living quarters. As opposed to a brown field investment where leasing existing facilities and land results in relatively lower expenses, green field investment forwarded by multinational corporations entail higher risks and higher costs associated with building new factories or manufacturing plants (RHG 2016, 3–4).

Developing countries tend to attract prospective companies with offers of tax breaks, subsidies and other incentives to set up green field investments. While these concessions may result in lower corporate tax revenues in the short term, the economic benefits and the enhancement of local human capital can deliver positive returns over the long term. "Green field investment" refers to a project where a company builds the entirety of its operations in a foreign market from scratch, or a so-called green field (Investopedia NY n.d.).

These projects are foreign direct investments that provide the highest degree of control for the sponsoring company. In these projects, the company's plant construction is done to its own specifications, employees are trained to company standards and fabrication processes can be tightly controlled. This type of involvement is completely different than indirect investments where companies may have little or no control in operations, quality control, sales and training.

In terms of the major risks involved with green field investment, the company's relationship with the host country would be at the forefront. As a long-term investment, any situation or domestic events that would result in the corporate investor having to exit the host country prior to the completion of the green field project could be financially devastating. Other risks include: construction overruns, building-permit problems and human resource problems where the assessment of resources and local labor is difficult to comprehend. Though these are smaller risks, they can still be very expensive to the firm's bottom line. Most corporations contemplating a green field investment will hire the services of a domestic consultant to assess and research feasibility and cost-effectiveness prior to initiating an investment. Otherwise, the entire investment may end up being a very costly experience.

Other major new EU projects in China include: the expansion of Shell's JV with CNOOC in Guangdong, a Blüthner piano plant, AstraZeneca R&D facilities and a very large investment by a major German chemical company BASF in a catalyst plant along with an elaborate expansion of its BASF's current R&D center. The data shows that the biggest reason for the decline in EU investment into China in Q4, 2015 is the record low number of acquisitions. Unfortunately, there were only two deals with a total of $22 million and included in that amount is a $20 million leasing company acquisition by BMW in Germany.

On the surface, it appears that autos and chemicals are the dominating force behind EU investment in China, but for the most part, this is a long-term, multi-year investment strategy, e.g. Volkswagen's plants in Tianjin and Foshan both of them have a completion date of 2018. In terms of the EU ranking of investment countries and this is the same as the previous four quarters, Germany and France lead the way followed closely by the United Kingdom and the Netherlands. Going forward, there are only a few M&A transactions pending, e.g. Rexel's acquisition of an automation systems company, Maxqueen in Shanghai. However, the largest green field project pending is the second expansion of Lego's plant in Jiaxing, which will increase its employees from 600 to well over 2,000 by 2017.

Table 7.1 is the result of the EU-China FDI Monitor. This is a monitor that keeps track of and notes in real time all of the transactions taking place pursuant

Table 7.1 EU FDI transactions in China by industry, Q3 2014–Q1 2016

Quarterly Investment Values in USD million							
4,000							
3,500	$3.7B BS						
3,000							
2,500							
2,000			$2.2B A		$2.3B BS		$2.1B BS
1,500	$1.5B A	$1.6B A		$1.6B A	$1.3B A	$1.6B A	$1.5B A
1,000	$1.1B CH	$1.2B CH					
500			$501M CH	$502M CH	$720M CH	$801M CH	$790M CH
0		$0 BS	$0 BS	$0 BS		$0 BS	
	Q3 2014	Q4 2014	Q1 2015	Q2 2015	Q3 2015	Q4 2015	Q1 2016

Industry Legend
Autos-A
Business Services-BS
Chemicals-CH

Source: Author with data from the Rhodium Group 2016

to EU FDI earmarked for China. The Monitor was developed by the Rhodium Group in New York in conjunction with the "China Economic Observatory" Project for the Director-General Trade, European Commission (DG Trade). The China Observatory FDI Monitor describes in explicit detail the EU FDI capital outflows into China transaction by transaction in real time.

Transactional data is broken down by the aggregation of relevant and/or similar transactions under a specific group heading. The dataset covers acquisitions and green field investments in two directions: by Chinese investors in the EU-28 and the EU-28 investors in China. The data are updated on a quarterly basis with detailed commentary on recent patterns and specific transactions. On 18 October 2013, the Council on Trade of the European Commission authorized the Commission to initiate a very comprehensive trade agreement, which the genesis of this goes back to December 2005. At that time, the Council authorized the initial negotiations. Consequently, the negotiations of a proposed EU-China investment agreement were formally launched at the EU-China Summit on November 21, 2013 in Beijing.

Removing market access barriers and investment, investor protections are the basic tenants of this agreement in both the EU and the Chinese markets. In a concerted effort to create a single comprehensive investment treaty between the EU and China, this agreement will replace the previous bilateral investment treaties with each of the 28 EU individual member states and China. At this point, ten rounds of negotiations have been held. Negotiations between the EU and China for an upgraded version of the 1985 Trade and Economic Cooperation Agreement began in 2007, but they have been in limbo since 2011. This is clearly the result of a mile-wide divergence between the Agreement's so-called mandates relative to the overwhelming expectations of the participants on both sides. By now, the reader should have a clear understanding about the difficulties of economic and investment treaty negotiations between sovereign nations. The efforts contained in these negotiations become an extremely cumbersome, complex, time-consuming endeavor, which may or may not ever come to fruition.

As mentioned in the opening of this chapter, a detailed analysis of the capital outflows of the three largest EU economies: Germany, the United Kingdom and France will commence. Over the past 20 years, German investment in China underscores the importance of China's economy relative to Germany's largest corporations. Consequently, German investment in China has grown steadily each year. In fact by 2014, the German capital stock position in China had grown to a total amount of over 48 billion euros. Germany is one of China's top ten foreign investors nearly doubling its foreign direct investment and it has focused heavily on its very capital intense automotive industry. German FDI to China has outgrown total FDI to China by an average of 20.5 percent annually and that number is over three times greater than the average FDI growth to China of roughly 6.1 percent between 2010 and 2016. All of this data confirms that China overall is an important destination for German capital outflows. Most German investments are concentrated in three main economic centers: Shanghai, Beijing and Guangzhou/Shenzhen. It's in these three economic centers where 90 percent of German FDI is invested. The remaining 10 percent is scattered throughout the northeastern provinces of Liaoning and Jilin around the cities of Shenyang and Changchun. Moreover, there are some small clusters of German manufacturing in the western provinces of Sichuan and Chongqing. The key industries for the German companies with operations in China include: automotive, machinery, services, chemical, electronics and plastics/metal. The previous key industries were arranged according to their size or percentage of German FDI. As previously mentioned, there are a total of 5,200 German companies operating in China with 51.7 percent of those companies operating in the Yangtze River Delta Cluster comprised of four main cities: Shanghai, Suzhou, Taicang and Kunshan. Its key industries include according to size are: (1) automotive, (2) machinery and (3) chemicals. The second largest region German manufacturing region in China is the Bohai Economic Rim Cluster which represents 18.3 percent of German operating companies located in the cities of Beijing, Tianjin, Dalian and Qingdao and its key industries according to size are: (1) machinery, (2) automotive and (3) services. The third largest cluster for German manufacturing in China is the Pearl River Delta Cluster representing 12.9 percent of German companies operating in China with manufacturing operations in four main cities: Guangzhou, Shenzhen, Zuhai and Dongguan and its key industries according to size include: (1) electronics, (2) plastics/metals and (3) machinery.

The fourth largest cluster of German companies operating in China is the Northeastern Emerging Cluster representing 3.7 percent of the German companies operating in China and its key industries according to size are: (1) automotive and (2) machinery with manufacturing plants in the cities of Shenyang and Changchun. Germany's final manufacturing cluster in China is the Western Emerging Cluster which accounts for 1.8 percent of the German companies operating in China in the cities of Chengdu and Chongqing and its key industries according to size are: (1) automotive and (2) machinery. The services sector in Germany's Bohai Economic Rim Cluster is the third largest in terms of key industry size of the German companies operating in China, but for whatever reason it's only represented in the Bohai Cluster. In summary, the 5,200 German corporations currently operating in China represent a total investment of 48 billion euros. These German corporations operating in China employ 1.1 million workers (mainly Chinese) who work in the following key industries according to size: (1) machinery, (2) automotive, (3) services, (4) chemical (5) electronics and (6) plastics/metal. In terms of FDI from the United Kingdom to China, the UK is expected to quadruple its current investments in China by 2020. According to King & Wood Mallesons, the global law firm in London, foreign direct investment from the UK to China totaled almost 6.7 billion pounds in asset stocks in 2016 and the firm expects that to increase to 26 billion pounds by 2020. In 2016, the UK contributed roughly 1 percent of China's total foreign direct investment.

According to the firm's estimates, that amount will increase to 2 percent by 2020 only with a much larger total.

Although UK investment into China is expected to increase quickly, it will still be dwarfed by capital outflows into China from Hong Kong, Singapore, Japan, Taiwan, South Korea and Germany. Moreover, UK FDI to China will take place mainly in the financial services sector in the form of asset stocks (equities) as opposed to investments by other EU members in China's industrial manufacturing sector.

There are two reasons that facilitate UK investment into this specific Chinese sector: removal of Chinese restrictions on trading the renminbi and China's very public commitment to reform its financial markets. The reader should also keep in mind that the London financial center is one of the leading financial hubs in the world and foreign direct investment in asset stocks is completely different from FDI directed towards the construction of a manufacturing facility that will employ thousands of domestic workers. In its attempt to change investor perceptions, the Chinese government has made reforms that should make investment in China much easier. The Chinese authorities have identified a variety of areas that need foreign investment. In this way China can meet domestic demand and successfully rebalance its economy towards quality growth. (Burn-Callandar 2016, 1) This is a very important subject that helps facilitate the book's main thesis and it will be discussed in very explicit detail in the Conclusion. In terms of France in China, French investment in China goes back well over 30 years; the overall stock assets of France in China is currently running around 17 billion euros. This involves more than 1,200 French companies operating in China and these companies employ approximately 500,000 workers. However, since the 2008 financial crisis, French outbound FDI to China has declined dramatically. For example, outbound French FDI to China in 2008 was a negative $125 million; in 2009 that number rallied back to $100 million; in 2010 French FDI to China dropped back down to $24 million; in 2011 French FDI to China amounted to $92 million and in 2012 according to the United Nations Conference on Trade and Development total French FDI to China amounted to $13 million and this is in spite of a very user-friendly strategy in place on the part of the Paris financial center (Burn-Callandar 2016, 1).

In 2015, the Paris financial consortium intensely increased its effort to establish a formal trading platform to facilitate the Chinese renminbi in trade and financial transactions. However, according to the World Investment Report from the UNCTAD, French outbound FDI in 2015 was roughly $25 billion and in 2016 that number was $43 billion, but in both years French outbound FDI went to only developed economies. Coincidentally, more than 40 percent of all payment between France and China are denominated in the renminbi. China is France's second largest supplier of goods and services and China is the number three destination for French exports outside of the EU (Burn-Callandar 2016, 1). The following is a list of the top ten French multinational companies currently operating in China: Total, AXA, BNP Paribas, GDF Suez, Carrefour, Crédit Agricole, Société Générale, Électricité de France, Peugeot and Groupe BPCE.

Note

1 European Commission (EC), in the first year, this would represent an increase in imports from China of approximately 7.5–15 billion euros. In this regard, note the EU imports of solar modules and cells from China alone increased by more than 7 billion euros in 2011 (more than 7 percent of all EU imports from China in that year), an increase of about 50 percent from imports in 2010. See Commission Regulation (EU) No 513/2013 of June 4, 2013, OJ 2013 L 152/5, recitals 110 and 113.

References

Burn-Callandar, Rebecca, "UK to quadruple investment in China within five years," British Chamber of Commerce in China, China-Britain Business Council, King & Wood Mallesons, London, 2016.

Dalton, Matthew, "EU Lawyers Favor Market-Economy Status for China Next Year: Designation Would Lead to Lower Tariffs on 'Dumped' Chinese Exports," *The Wall Street Journal*, June 9, 2015.

European Commission (EC), Commission Regulation (EU) No 513/2013, June 4, 2013, OJ 2013 L 152/5, recitals 110 and 113.

European Commission (EC), "EU-China Relations," Brussels, 22 June 2016.

Investopedia, reference New York, NY, n.d., available at www.investopedia.com.

Middleton, Rachel, "Jean-Claude warns China it must cut steel production or be frozen out of the WTO," *The Guardian*, London, July 13, 2016.

Puccio, Laura, "Granting Market Economy Status to China," European Parliamentary Research Service, Brussels, November 2015.

Rhodium Group, "EU-China FDI Monitor: 4 Q 2015 Update, Public Version," January, 2016.

Rhodium Group (RHG) for Director-General Trade, European Commission, "China Observatory EU-China FDI Monitor," March, 2016.

Scott, Robert E. and Xiao Jiang, "Unilateral Grant of Market Economy Status to China Would Put Millions of Jobs at Risk," Economic Policy Institute, EPI Briefing Paper #407, Washington, DC, September 18, 2015.

8 China foreign direct investment in the United States

China's capital outflows literally soared for the first half of 2016 and the United States is one of China's top destinations for its foreign direct investment. Within the first six months of 2016, Chinese FDI to the US amounted to well over $18 billion. This was a threefold increase compared with the same time frame in 2015. The bulk of this FDI was invested in private sector acquisitions in technology, consumer-oriented assets as well as services. China's 2016 FDI also included capital-intensive green field projects in manufacturing and free-standing real estate.

From a quarterly perspective, Chinese FDI to the United States amounted to $8.3 billion in the Q1 2016 and $10.1 billion in Q2 2016. This brings the total Chinese FDI to the US in the first two quarters of 2016 to $18.4 billion compared to Chinese FDI to the US of $6.4 billion in the first half of 2015, but here's the real narrative: the total Chinese FDI to the United States for 2015 was $15.3 billion. At the time of writing, for 2016, China is on track to increase its FDI to the US by well over 100 percent (Hanemann and Gao 2016).

The majority of the incoming capital from China to the United States in 2016 went into either mergers and/or acquisitions (M&A). All total so far for 2016, there were 55 completed acquisitions with a dollar value in excess of $17 billion. In terms of green field projects, China's investment efforts in very capital-intensive projects in manufacturing and real estate have increased dramatically compared to previous years. There are some in the global financial community who are making the case that the precipitous increase in capital outflows from China into the West are more the result of a capital flight into safe havens. These experts further claim that these capital flights are the direct result of the increasing uncertainty about global currency exchange rates combined with the immediate economic and political outlook in China.

From an investor's perspective, China has had a spectacular economic run for many years and as its domestic economy improves, domestic costs keep increasing resulting in smaller margins for domestic investments making foreign investments more attractive. While the aforementioned negative factors are certainly important, it's equally important to remember that China's recent capital outflows to the West are categorized as strategic investments. More than 80 percent of all Chinese FDI transactions in the US in the first half of 2016 can be characterized as strategic investments. The sectors attracting the largest strategic investments were consumer goods: (Haier's acquisition of GE's appliance unit for $5.6 billion), entertainment (Wanda's purchase of Legendary Entertainment for $3.5 billion), ICT (acquisition of Omnivision Technologies by a Chinese consortium for $1.9 billion) and automotive (Ningbo Joyson's acquisition of Key Safety Systems for $920 million).

In July 2016, Chinese financial investments in the United States amounted to $3.5 billion. The Chinese categorizes these investments as investments "primarily for financial returns" in the first half of 2016 and most of these are large real estate assets in coastal cities in the US, e.g. 1285 Avenue of the Americas, New York, NY; 61 Broadway, New York, NY; Park Lane Hotel, New York, NY and 755 Sansome Street, San Francisco, CA. Moreover, the lion's share of these investors is private. In fact, private Chinese investors accounted for more than 72 percent of total FDI investment in the US in the first half of 2016.

It should also be noted that the dramatic increase in Chinese outbound FDI for 2016 has set off political reactions by the Chinese authorities as well as the host economies. Due to the continued decrease in China's Balance of Payments brought on by the sudden huge increase in Chinese outbound FDI, the Chinese regulators have increased their scrutiny significantly. On the one hand, the Chinese authorities continue to support "external liberalization", but on the other, their concerns about capital outflows have clearly increased. In fact, China's State Administration of Foreign Exchange (SAFE) as well as other monetary regulators has taken direct measures to so-call "manage" foreign exchange outflows.

Table 8.1 Chinese FDI transactions in the United States by industry

$USD millions

	Q4 2014	Q1 2015	Q2 2015	Q3 2015	Q4 2015	Q1 2016	Q2 2016
10,000							
9,000							CPS
8,000							
7,000	HB					ICT	
6,000					CPS		
5,000		FS ICT				REH	
4,000		REH				E	HB ICT
3,000				HB CPS			REH FS
2,000	REH		HB FS	E FS	FS E REH		
1,000	A CPS E	A FS E	A ICT E	A FS REH	ICT HB		A

Industry Legend

A	Autos	HB	Health and Biotech
CPS	Consumer Products and Services	ICT	Info & Communication Tech
E	Entertainment	REH	Real Estate & Hospitality
FS	Financial Services		

Source: Author with data from the Rhodium Group 2016

Clearly, those measures have sidetracked or even terminated a number of in-process transactions, but equally important they have also increased the anxiety level on behalf of Chinese businesses who question their ability to close deals. That kind of a business environment drives up risk premiums and reverse break fees for Chinese buyers. In the United States, a huge uptick in Chinese deals combined with the past presidential election has generated various and assorted responses from US lawmakers about specific individual transactions taking place within their representative states.

However in the presidential election, both Clinton and Trump were not restrained in terms of taking a tough stance on US-China trade relations, but with that said, neither candidate mentioned the huge spike in Chinese FDI entering the United States. On the other hand, US regulators have slowed a number of transactions in compliance with regulations from the Committee on Foreign Investment in the United States (CFIUS) and other regulatory agencies, e.g. Fidelity & Guaranty Life, Ironshore and Syngenta. In spite of cancelations of some high profile proposed transactions, e.g. joint venture to develop high speed rail service between Los Angeles and Las Vegas and Zoomlion's bid for Terex, the value of announced, but not yet completed Chinese investments in the US was still close to an all-time high of $33 billion at the end of June 2016. On the surface, it appears that unless the US takes action to limit the flow of Chinese capital into the US, China's annual investment of $25 billion will become the norm beginning in 2017. Pending M&A transactions add up to more than $23 billion including HNA Group's $6 billion bid for technology distributor Ingram Micro; Anbang's $6.5 billion acquisition of Strategic Hotels; Apex Technology's acquisition of Lexmark for $3.6 billion; and HNA's bid for Carlson Hotel for an estimated $2 billion. Currently, pending investments in green field projects add up to $9.5 billion, mostly driven by real estate developments in New York and California, but also projects in automotive (such as Yenfeng's plants in Tennessee and South Carolina or Faraday Future's expansions in California and Nevada) and materials (Jushi's glass plant in South Carolina and Sun Paper's paper mill in Arkansas).

On the surface, it appears that interest in increased FDI from China into the United States remains strong, but it should also be said that future outbound Chinese FDI into the US will be subject to Chinese regulations and other external factors, e.g. Brexit, related US dollar strength, and any other geopolitical shocks. Any of these factors will exacerbate Chinese outbound capital flows in the short term. However, the biggest drawback to increased outbound capital flows from China in the near future will be increased Chinese regulatory scrutiny particularly in transactions that involve large amounts of foreign exchange as well as transactions that involve financial activities.

Future FDI from China to the West will also be in accordance with the slow pace of China's economic reforms and the shallow progress of China's reluctance to further open its economy to foreign investment. Undoubtedly, these will set off negative reactions from the host economies that will more than likely strengthen their own regulations relative to inbound capital flows from China. The recent increase in Chinese acquisitions in the West has already provoked a number of countries to express a deep concern about the inequalities found in China's marketplace compared to the openness of the Western markets.

Chinese outbound capital flows to the US have been regularly taking place over the past three decades. This is the perfect segue for a brief background and an overview of Chinese investment in the United States. The China-US economic relationship is without a doubt the most significant economic relationship of the 21st century. For years, China had been a top recipient of foreign direct investment from the advanced economies. However in the past decade, China has aggressively accelerated its FDI into the developed countries due primarily to China's development of its domestic economy. In terms of Chinese FDI to the United States, China has experienced a wave of difficulties based primarily on national competitiveness, security concerns and lack of transparency. On the surface, security concerns and lack of transparency on China's part have resulted in a "trust" problem for the United States.

According to Brookings Senior Fellows Ken Lieberthal and Jonathan Pollack in their "Campaign 2012" paper advising the president, they indicated that the Sino-American relationship had fallen "well short of expectations" since President Obama's November 2009 visit to Beijing. Given the trust deficit and continued concerns about unfair practices between the two countries, many of the long-term economic and trade policy objectives have not yet been addressed or resolved. Most of the US concerns stem from China's reluctance to allow the renminbi to free-float and appreciate against the US dollar, government subsidies, funding for government-controlled firms and US companies' inability to gain full access to China's domestic markets (Aoki et al. 2014). Going back to the period 2001–2007, Chinese FDI into the US averaged roughly $500 million per year with the exception of the acquisition of IBM's PC business in 2005 for $1.75 billion, which was later renamed Lenovo. After 2007, the trend in Chinese FDI destined for the US tilted upward in terms of deals and dollar size. Much of this can be accounted for and incentivized by the huge trade surplus China runs with the United States over the years. The Chinese trade surplus became the catalyst for China's proactive approach for investment opportunities in the United States.

Moreover, from 2007 onward the Chinese government encouraged its public and private corporations to "go global" for diversity purposes to expand technology, resources, brands and management skills. The huge sums of outbound Chinese FDI to the United States provoke a wide range of implications for the overall American economy which includes politics and national security. Donald Trump, the newly elected US president, has made US-China trade and China's mergers and acquisitions of US based corporations the centerpiece of his administration.

Trump applied the fear factor claiming that US-China trade is basically a one-sided effort where China has the advantage with a huge trade surplus with the US that gives the Chinese treasury free cash flow in US dollars and at the same time the US-China trade imbalance has cost America millions of well-paid manufacturing jobs. Trump further claims that American manufacturing cor-porations cannot compete in price with government subsidized corporations in China who are manufacturing product in that country and selling it in the United States.

From an academic perspective, foreign direct investment should be beneficial for both the home country as well as the host country. It affords firms the oppor-tunity to explore new markets and it provides a different business acumen from the home country which usually results in increased efficiency through econo-mies of scale and adaptation leading to specialization. When selling into a foreign market, it's also imperative to have a domestic presence. On the one hand, FDI is supposed to generate more competitive prices and more choices for consum-ers. Moreover, foreign investment usually increases the local employment base and local tax revenues, but this applies more to green field projects. If it's an acquisition with no expansion, it's merely a zero-sum game. FDI should enhance knowledge through employee training in conjunction with technology transfer and research and development activities.

On the other hand, according to Sophie Meunier at the Woodrow Wilson School, Princeton University, Chinese outbound FDI to the US creates unprece-dented challenges to the US government. Historically, foreign direct investment normally flowed from an advanced economy to an emerging market economy, but with China reversing that trend and emerging as a global player in terms of outbound FDI, this reversal of fortune has created a great deal of uncertainty. Moreover, from a political perspective, Chinese corporations operate under an authoritarian political regime and this in itself is particularly disturbing to the US authorities (Meunier 2012).

More to the point, Chinese corporations even when they claim they're private are, for the most part, not very transparent. According to estimates by the US government, nearly two-thirds of Chinese FDI originates from state-owned enterprises or state-controlled corporations. This reinforces the US government's suspicion that these enterprises are less concerned with commercial goals and more interested in completing a political strategy. Consequently, there is a great deal of anxiety on the part of US authorities that Chinese investment in the United States is a serious risk that could enable state and/or corporate espionage.

In terms of entry, most Chinese FDI destined for the United States takes the form of a proposed green field project; for the most part, these funds are usually used to establish sales offices or the creation of more efficient distribution chan-nels in order to facilitate Chinese trade with the United States. In fact before 2009, Chinese green field projects were more the norm rather than the excep-tion, but now mergers and acquisitions have a much larger total deal value. There are more green field deals, but the total deal value is much smaller.

According to the Rhodium Group, between 2000 and Q2 2017 Chinese out-bound FDI to the United States amounted to $80.9 billion with a total 1,270 deals. Of these deals, 755 were green field deals with a total value of $7.2 billion and 515 acquisitions with a total value of over $73 billion. In that same period of time, Chinese outbound FDI to the United States invested in 15 industrial sectors: Agriculture & Food 21 deals, total value $7.4 Billion; Automotive 127 deals, total value $4 billion; Aviation 16 deals, total value $736 million; Basic Materials 46 deals, total value $709 million; Consumer Products & Services 108 deals, total value $6.58 billion; Electronics 62 deals, total value $753 million; Energy 109 deals, total value $10.5 billion; Entertainment 43 deals, total value $$7.7 billion; Finance & Bus. Services 74 deals, total value $$4.2 billion; Health & Biotech 105 deals, total value $3.6 billion; ICT 199 deals, total value $13.5 billion; Ind. Machinery & Equip. 84 deals, total value $919 million; Metals & Minerals 33 deals, total value $1.4 billion; Real Estate & Hospitality 146 deals, $15.5 billion, and Transport & Infrastructure 97 deals, total value $3.5 billion (RHG 2017, 1).

Geographically, outbound China FDI to the United States between 2000 to Q2 2017 was invested in most all of the states with California, Texas and New York receiving the largest amounts of Chinese FDI. Research shows that access to natural resources was always a pivotal reason to attract Chinese outbound FDI since the early 2000s. However, in 2005 the tide changed for Chinese outbound FDI to the West (advanced economies); at that point, more and more Chinese firms became interested in acquiring foreign technologies and managerial skills.

A 2005 survey by China's National Bureau of Statistics showed there were basically three motivations that attracted Chinese FDI: increase market share (56 percent); technology and brands (16 percent) and resources (20 percent). This explains the transition for Chinese FDI to the United States from the green field projects of the early 2000s to acquisitions beginning in 2005 (National Bureau of Statistics 2005). Clarification is needed about China's state-owned enterprises or state-owned and state-holding enterprises. According to the National Bureau of Statistics, the term state-owned enterprise is an enterprise owned by either the central government or a local government of China, which includes wholly owned state-funded firms. This definition is used basically for balance sheet information, e.g. asset statistics presented by the Chinese Ministry of Finance in relation to local and central state-owned enterprises and this is precisely where Chinese transparency becomes a problem. This definition does not include other enterprise ownership forms such as shareholding cooperative enterprises, limited liability corporations, joint operation enterprises or shareholding corporations whose majority shareholders are either the Chinese government (local and/or central) or public organizations.

Surprisingly, research also shows that the World Trade Organization (WTO) has no specific rules or regulations concerning the different classifications of enterprises. For whatever reason, the WTO is more concerned with the rights and obligations of its member nations than ownership of various and assorted enterprises. Unfortunately, this is a short-sighted position which would be perfectly fine if each FDI enterprise were privately or publicly held with no government ownership. However, in the case of China where enterprise ownership can be a convoluted mixture of any combination of local or national governments and a private corporation, this is unsettling and creates consternation and concern on the part of the host countries relative to those countries' national security.

In its "Report of the Working Party on the Accession of China", in reference to state-owned and state-invested enterprises, Section 6 Article 43, the WTO made the following case: The Chinese representative to the WTO argued that state-owned enterprises operate in accordance with rules of a market economy. Essentially the Chinese government would not dictate and administer the human, finance and material resources in conjunction with operational activities, e.g. production, supply and marketing. The prices of the commodities produced were decided by the marketplace. Furthermore, the representative argued the state-owned banks had been commercialized and lending to state-owned enterprises took place under market conditions. He further claimed that China increasing its ongoing reform of state-owned enterprises in an effort to establish a modern enterprise system (WTO 2001, 8–9). The WTO Working Party Report is basically a draft written with information provided by the nation-state applicant prior to that country's accession into the World Trade Organization. In essence it's a commitment made by the nation-state applicant to the members of the WTO that will take place immediately upon membership acceptance into the WTO. More importantly according to China's entrée Working Party Report, China's commitment to its fellow nation-state members has not exactly been fulfilled. Thus, the reluctance on the part of the United States, the European Union and other countries to grant China Market Economy Status (MES) in December of 2016 as discussed earlier in Chapter 7.

The turning point in US-China bilateral investment occurred between 2011 and 2013. It was in that time frame that China's investments in mergers and acquisitions (M&A) in the United States exceeded the value of US investment in China. China's corporations are set to increase their investments in the US evidenced by the tripling of China FDI to the US in the first half of 2016. In spite of China's recent economic slowdown, China is still a dominant exporter of manufactured goods and its GDP growth is growing at a faster rate than most other nations.

At the time of writing, China's central bank holds roughly $3.21 trillion in foreign exchange reserves. (USCESRC 2015, 4) Chinese foreign exchange reserves came in at $3.2 trillion in June of 2017 slightly up from $3.19 trillion in May and above market expectations of $3.17 trillion. Yet, a year earlier, reserves were higher at $3.69 trillion. Foreign exchange reserves in China averaged $860 billion from 1980 until 2016 reaching an all-time high of $3.99 trillion in June 2014 and a record low of $226 billion in December 1980. Foreign exchange reserves in China are reported by the People's Bank of China. Between August 2014 and February 2015, the US-China Economic and Security Review Commission conducted a series of telephone and email interviews with over a dozen US state officials in an effort to determine China's US investment strategies relative to the US' 50 states. The aforementioned interviews were supplemented by an analysis of media and industry reports, quantitative data on trade and investment flows and state government economic websites. The Commission's principal conclusions are as follows: each state's investment promotions vary dramatically and there are roughly 25 states with investment offices in China.

On the surface, it is strikingly apparent that in the Southern US Georgia and the Carolinas are extremely active in terms of investment outreach to China. In the US Southwest, energy commercial activity takes place in a big way and receives a great deal of Chinese investment, but on the whole does very little to lure Chinese investment. Moreover, the Commission also found that the Chinese authorities have reduced restrictions on outbound FDI to the US. This was based primarily on the steady economic growth in the United States since the 2008 financial crisis and it also reinforces the notion that China's central bank would like to diversify its very large foreign exchange reserves. The Commission later uncovered another related concern: China's extensive use of the US's EB-5 visa program. This program in particular allows foreign nationals as well as their family members to receive conditional green cards in exchange for investments in the United States of $1 million or more. The EB-5 visa program has generated a huge number of Chinese applicants to the extent that the applicant vacancies were actually filled prematurely in 2014 and 2015, but that was only part of the problem. The Commission also found a number of instances where fraud on behalf of the Chinese applicants was involved, casting doubt on the ability of the US authorities to properly screen Chinese EB-5 investors.

China's business investment in the United States takes on a broad spectrum of commercial entities ranging from light manufacturing operations that take advantage of cheap US energy prices as well as farm goods to corporate acquisitions in the automotive sector and research and development (R&D) projects in the health care and pharmaceuticals sectors. Because Chinese investments involve any combination of private and state-owned companies, its direct effects on job creation can be conflicting depending on the issuance of EB-5 visas. It should also be noted that for the most part Chinese investors are less experienced than other international investors and they tend to seek the advice of state officials rather than private consultants on legal matters concerning local and national laws on employment, employee benefits, building infrastructure, and so on.

The Commission further decided that Chinese investment in the United States needed closer consideration by the US authorities. These considerations include: improved regulation of the EB-5 visa program, federal programs are in a better position to assist local governments in the identification of Chinese investment opportunities and risk assessment relative to infrastructure and technologies; an appropriate regulatory framework in concert with local research can make a contribution to US-China R&D cooperation which can result in a mutually beneficial relationship; adherence to US labor and environmental laws and in terms of bilateral market access, trade, and the overall balance of payments. Chinese investment in the United States is not sufficient to rebalance the bilateral economic relationship.

The Commission's last consideration is by far the most important. Bilateral market access by US corporations in China is highly restrictive and the overall Chinese regulatory environment tends to favor Chinese corporations as opposed to the open-door policy for Chinese corporations operating in the United States.

US trade to China is subject to the same one-sided restrictions. With the exception of specific commodities, e.g. agricultural, minerals, energy and so on, US manufactured goods are subject to the same protective measures in US-China trade. In terms of balance of payments, the US trade deficit with China is currently running approximately $350 billion per year. This provides the Chinese government with $350 billion per year in free cash flow and for the US-China Economic and Security Review Commission to argue that Chinese investment in the United States is not sufficient to rebalance the bilateral economic relationship is certainly an understatement.

In 2015, China shook up the global economic markets when large amounts of money started to flow out of its country. The amount was estimated at close to $1 trillion; this evoked growing skepticism that China had deep-seated monetary problems and its reputation as a driver of global economic growth became questionable. Global doubts lingered around the world about Beijing's capability of turning around its slowing economy and repair its unraveled financial system, but new data shows that in the interim China has been able to slow the vast sums of money leaving the country.

In March 2016, China's hoard of foreign exchange reserves actually grew for the first time in five months. China's foreign exchange reserves topped $3.21 trillion made up of US dollars, euros, pounds and other foreign currencies. These accumulated reserves are the direct result of China's ability to manage the value of its currency over the years. China watchers use the value of China's foreign exchange reserves as a proxy for money moving in and out of the country (Bradsher 2016, 1).

At this point, it's not clear if China again will start to send vast sums of money around the globe in the form of FDI. As for the United States, Chinese investment so far in 2016 has tripled from 2015. However, there are those who argue that Chinese FDI to the US is driven partially by fear about a downtrend in the Chinese economy. At the point of being redundant, it's more about diversification away from the Chinese markets than anything else. Most of these firms have saturated the Chinese market. So when any of them experience a market downturn, they're constantly reminded that what they need is more diversification or new markets. In April 2016, the People's Bank of China stated that its foreign exchange reserves increased by $10.3 billion in March. Earlier in the year, China's foreign exchange reserves declined by $28.6 billion in February and the bank also experienced a decline in foreign exchange reserves in January of $99.5 billion and this was on the heels of an even larger decline of foreign exchange reserves in December of $107.9 billion. Simultaneously, a gradual decline in the renminbi was taking place from mid-December through January 2016. On the same note in March 2016, the Federal Reserve Bank sent a signal to the global economy that the chances of an interest rate increase for the balance of 2016 were not very good, resulting in a weaker dollar. This should have never happened.

In China, Zhou Xiaochuan, the governor of China's central bank made a number of public statements in late February that the bank saw no need for a further decline of the renminbi against the dollar. According to the People's Bank of China that helped stabilize China's foreign exchange reserves in March which in turn led to the previously mentioned increase in reserves in March. Also in March, the total value of the foreign exchange reserves in US dollars increased to $3.21 trillion. Part of the China's foreign exchange reserves are denominated in euros and an almost equal amount are denominated in yen and it was in that same exact month that the euro and the yen strengthened against the US dollar. If not for the US dollar valuation effect, China's foreign exchange reserves would have declined between $20 billion and $30 billion in March 2016.

A lot of economists in the US claimed that China will try to prevent any big declines in the renminbi until after the US presidential election in November 2016. They believed this because they're sure China didn't want a weakened renminbi to become a US presidential election issue especially on the part of the Trump Republicans. Moreover, the renminbi was slated to join the International Monetary Fund's (IMF) basket of currencies on October 1, 2016 making it very clear that China will do whatever it can do to support its currency in the interim.

Moreover, President Obama attended 2016's G20 meeting in Hangzhou, China on September 4–5. Most of Wall Street thought that a possible renminbi devaluation before the upcoming G20 meeting was highly unlikely and it turned out that they were right. China has emphasized and re-emphasized the prestige associated with hosting the G20 and it's doubtful the Chinese authorities would want to turn the meeting into an argument over its currency.

In recent months, the Chinese government has placed large bets in the Forex markets that the renminbi will stay very close to its current exchange rate in the immediate future. This was done primarily to offset large hedge fund bets on the other side who were taking the position that China will allow the renminbi to devaluate further. Along the same lines, the IMF has been applying pressure on China's central bank for several months to disclose the traded value of the contracts China owns which bets on the continued strength of the renminbi. Finally, China's central bank acquiesced and disclosed the traded value, which came in at $28.9 billion as opposed to the total hedge fund bets on the other side of $2.44 billion a factor of almost 12 adding increased speculation about currency manipulation.

In 2017, a report written by the National Committee on US-China Relations and the Rhodium Group unveiled a detailed tally of the operations of Chinese affiliated companies operating in the United States. The report underscored the impacts of these Chinese investments in each region, state and congressional district. With over $30 billion in pending deals thus far, 2017 should be another record for Chinese foreign direct investment (FDI) into the United States. The report further stressed the increased scrutiny by US regulators and members of Congress (Rosen and Hanemann 2017, 1–3).

The appropriate regulators and the various committees in the Congress have a responsibility to the American people that the legitimate concerns about Chinese FDI are addressed and discussed in explicit detail. And this effort needs to be accomplished without the influence of political rhetoric from the candidates in an election year. The US has to be very careful not to create needless impediments in terms of job creation relative to investment inflows from China. At the same time, it needs to fully understand the ramifications of China's investment methodology to determine if this methodology is used for commercial purposes or does it increase China's national strategic interest. The 2015 patterns affected the ranking of cumulative Chinese FDI by Congressional district. New York District 12, California District 12 and New York District 10 were already in the top 15 in the previous year and moved further up. Texas District 19 was another big recipient of Chinese FDI in 2015 moving that district into the top 15 ranking. However, Texas District 27 mainly in Corpus Christi, Texas and Iowa District 4 in Northwest Iowa dropped out of the top 15 Congressional districts for 2015 Chinese foreign direct investment.

Moreover between 2000 and 2015, the top 15 Congressional districts that received cumulative Chinese were: New York District 12, New York City, $5.21 billion; North Carolina District 04, Raleigh-Durham Triangle, $3.36 billion; Illinois District 7, Chicago, $3.35 billion; Virginia District 4, Eastern Virginia, $1.98 billion; New York District 10, New York City, $1.93 billion; Texas District 7, Houston, $1.87 billion; California-District 12, San Francisco, $1.72 billion; Texas District 23, Southwest Texas, $1.64 billion; Oklahoma District 3, Northwest Oklahoma, $1.59 billion; Kansas District 03, Kansas City, $1.53 billion; Texas District 19, North Texas, $1.37 billion, Massachusetts District 6, Northeast Massachusetts, $1.35 billion; California-District 17, San Jose, $1.26 billion; North Carolina District 7, Southern North Carolina, $1.25 billion; Texas District 9, Houston, $1.09 billion.

In total, Chinese companies employ well over 90,000 American workers. In 2015 alone, Chinese companies operating in the United States added over 13,000 new employees to their US payrolls. This was an increase in excess of 14 percent over 2014. With a 2016 total of over 90,000 American employees working for Chinese companies operating in the US, that number represents a threefold increase in just three years. Chinese US acquisitions in 2015 made up the majority of the added jobs in that year. In 2015, Chinese acquisitions included a number of purchases of medium sized US companies mainly in labor-intense industries, e.g. automotive parts manufacturing and financial services. Contrary to popular belief, employment patterns in 2016 tend to support an earlier finding by the Committee that new Chinese business acquirers have a tendency to increase their local labor force after the initial acquisition. This is in direct opposition to those who claim that Chinese investors acquire US companies and then relocate the acquired assets to China.

The following examples will shed more light on the aforementioned employment patterns uncovered by the National Committee on US-China Relations: Smithfield Foods added 1,500 additional employees after its 2013 acquisition by Shuanghui. Nexteer went from 6,000 employees to over 10,000 employees within two to three years after it was acquired by Aviation Industry Corporation of China (AVIC) in 2010. In terms of China's green field projects in the United States relative to US employment, there is no comparison with

Chinese acquisitions. The creation of new American jobs from China's green field projects in the US remains very small in comparison. Green field projects in the US are basically start-ups by foreign corporations engaged in the same business only in their home countries, but they really can't be compared to mergers and acquisitions (M&A). US acquisitions by a foreign corporation involve the buying and selling of a "going business" and the chances of failure are remote, but green field projects may or may not reach fruition.

The following is a list of the top 15 Congressional districts in terms of total jobs provided by Chinese companies in the United States, 2015: North Carolina District 7, Southern North Carolina, 7,640 jobs; Michigan District 5, Central Michigan, 5,330 jobs; North Carolina District 4, Raleigh-Durham Triangle, 3,890 jobs; Virginia District 4, Eastern Virginia, 3,800 jobs; South Dakota District 1, South Dakota at large, 3,400 jobs; Iowa District 4, Northwest Iowa, 3,320 jobs; Missouri District 6, Northern Missouri, 3,190 jobs; Nebraska District 3, Western and Central Nebraska, 2,280 jobs; Illinois District 7, Chicago, 1,960 jobs; Illinois District 17, Northwest Illinois, 1,710 jobs; California District 17, San Jose, 1,600 jobs; California District 12, San Francisco, 1,360 jobs; New York District 12, New York City, 1,230 jobs; Kentucky District 5, Eastern Kentucky, 1,220 jobs and California District 33, Los Angeles, 1,120 jobs. Technology and talent are the two most important factors driving Chinese acquisitions of US firms. This is readily apparent by the growing number of transactions in information and communication technology, e.g. Integrated Silicon Solutions; automotive, e.g. Henniges Automotive, Burke Porter Machinery and Stern Rubber; aviation, e.g. Align Aerospace and United Turbine Corporation; and health and biotech, e.g. Cytovance Biologics and NextCODE Health.

Most Chinese acquisitions that involve information and communication technology, automotive, aviation and health and biotech are small to middle-sized companies and that's a very good strategy on the part of the United States considering that there are any number of industrial sectors in China that are totally off limits to American corporations.

References

Aoki, Yohsuke, Dong Liu, Shaoyu Sun, Tian Wang, Xi Wang and Annie Yang Zhou, "Chinese Foreign Direct Investment in the United States," Columbia University School of International and Public Affairs, Capstone Project for Joshua Meltzer, The Brookings Institution, New York and Washington DC, January, 2014.

Bradsher, Keith, "China Stanches Flow of Money Out of the Country, Data Suggests," *The New York Times*, April 7, 2016.

Hanemann, Thilo and Cassie Gao, "Chinese FDI in the US: Tripling Down on America," *Rhodium Group*, New York, 2016.

Meunier, Sophie, "Political Impact of Chinese Foreign Direct Investment in the European Union on Transatlantic Relations," Princeton University, May 2012.

National Bureau of Statistics, "Investment Climate Management," Beijing, January 2005.

Rhodium Group (RHG) for Director-General Trade, European Commission, "China Observatory EU-China FDI Monitor," 2017.

Rosen, Daniel H. and Thilo Hanemann, National Committee (NC) 2017 on US-China Relations and the Rhodium Group, "New Neighbors 2017 Update: Chinese FDI in the United States by Congressional District," April 24, 2017.

US-China Economic and Security Review Commission, (USCESRC) "2015 Annual Report," Washington DC, December 2015.

World Trade Organization (WTO), "Report of the Working Party on the Accession of China," October 1, 2001.

9 China foreign direct investment in Europe

In 2017, a combination of Chinese state-owned and private corporations' FDI to Europe totaled over $23 billion and that included Switzerland and Norway as well as the European Union. That number was $8 billion more than Chinese FDI to the United States. However, in the latest report authored by Baker McKenzie data suggests that Chinese FDI to the West may be slowing. With that said, new Chinese investment increased by 28 percent in 2015 based upon the $18 billion in Chinese FDI to Europe in 2014. Though the 28 percent increase in Chinese FDI to Europe in 2015 was impressive, the 2014 Chinese FDI to Europe represented a 100 percent increase over 2013 (Jones 2016).

Most of the world's central banks including the European Central Bank (ECB) have expressed concerns about China's current economic conditions, which have been a drag on global financial markets. This is probably the biggest reason why the ECB is expected to announce a new round of economic stimulus into the Eurozone imminently. Recently, there have been a number of criticisms voiced by some of China's wealthiest businessmen about China's state-owned enterprises. One Chinese businessman in particular, Wang Jianlin, supposedly China's richest man, makes the case that state-owned enterprises lack international management standards. Moreover according to Michael DeFranco, Chair of Baker McKenzie's M&A practice, "These are turbulent times and yet we see Chinese companies acting with confidence and continuing to make major moves in Europe and North America" (Jones 2016).

However, it should also be noted that Chinese FDI in the Eurozone only was up 37 percent in 2015 representing an increase of over $4 billion to $17.1 billion compared to $12.5 billion in 2014. Interesting enough, Italy who doesn't exactly have a star-studded stellar economy received the most FDI from China in 2015: $7.9 billion. That number, for the most part, amounted to one acquisition by ChemChina for Pirelli, the fifth largest tire company in the world. Moreover, France received the second largest amount of Chinese FDI in 2016 totaling over $3.6 billion, which involved a number of large acquisitions in the tourism and infrastructure sectors. Currently, Chinese investment to the West is in line to surpass its 2015 number. During the first six weeks of 2017, Chinese corporations announced a potential $70 billion in acquisitions in the West.

In total, Europe appears to be a pivotal destination for Chinese outbound foreign direct investment (OFDI). This reinforces the obvious shift in Chinese OFDI away from emerging market economies to the advanced economies. China's aggressive efforts for increased investment in the EU is a stark contrast with the stagnant or even diminishing EU investment in China by European Companies, thus the surface intent of the EU-China Bilateral Investment Agreement (BIA) (Hanemann 2016).

As mentioned earlier, diversification is the driving force for the surge in OFDI to Europe, which is in direct response to the changing economic realities in China. The early stage of structural adjustment combined with the growing domestic volatility has increased the pressure on Chinese corporations to diversify and prepare for greater competition on the home front resulting in an increased eagerness for risk taking through international expansion. Moreover, 2016 marked an obvious shift in Chinese OFDI to Europe towards a more diverse mix of industrial sectors, e.g. advanced services, brands, consumer products and high technology.

At this juncture, a discussion outlining the reasons why Europe has become more attractive to Chinese investors is in order. The 2008 financial crisis marked a critical moment for the Chinese government. It was at that time when the Chinese government started aggressively buying Eurobonds and simultaneously, it started making sizable investments in infrastructure companies at very competitive valuations. A good case in point is Greece's Port of Piraeus. After the Chinese government acquired a 67 percent interest from the Greek Port Authority, the port and its operation were taken over by China's Cosco Holding Company.

EU economies like Germany, France, Italy and the United Kingdom have a number of small to medium-sized companies who are niche players in their respective fields backed up by some of the best technologies in the world. Consequently, these companies set the stage for China to enhance its home companies through acquisitions in the above four countries in the automobile industry, food, transport, energy, luxury brands, travel and entertainment resulting in the transfer of know-how to their home country with the intention of creating world-class enterprises.

In 2016, relations between the EU and China were much less competitive and confrontational than the US-China relationship. Unlike the United States where the Committee on Foreign Investments evaluates each foreign transaction in terms of national security, the EU didn't have anything in place to perform a similar task, but recently the European Commission has stepped up its analytical apparatus in terms of Chinese OFDI to the EU relative to EU national security.

In the late 1990s, Beijing made a political decision to deploy capital flows away from China. It was exactly that political decision made by the Chinese government that served as a catalyst for individual business decisions to employ outbound FDI especially in its state-owned enterprises in order to transfer know-how and technology to its respective home companies in China. In terms of Africa and Asia, China's investments center around natural resources, but in the case of the EU, China's foreign investments focus on acquisitions that include brands, knowledge and technologies which will facilitate China's footprint in that region, enhanced by massive financial assistance from state-run banks and sovereign wealth funds.

The increase in Chinese transactions has also increased bilateral relations between China and individual EU nations. Interesting enough, there are 16 EU countries that meet with China annually to discuss future investment – this is called the "16+1". There's no question; China is very clever at pitting one country against another using its outbound foreign direct investments as an instrument of debate. Historically, European companies would fight one another for a larger market share of the Chinese consumer market, but now they seem to compete with one another for a larger share of Chinese capital through OFDI to their respective country.

Obviously, nothing moving on the global stage does so without challenges and that holds true for China's investments in Europe. Research shows that human resources in Europe have historically presented a complex issue for Chinese investors. The Chinese investor often finds it very difficult to relinquish power to European managers. In those particular situations, the challenge becomes even more complex for everyone when the European employees become more like window dressing. There have been other instances where the Chinese tend to manage their European operations carelessly while the headquarters in Beijing analyzes the synergies or lack thereof.

Job creation tends to be another unknown. It's very difficult to estimate how many Europeans work for Chinese companies due to a lack of transparency on the part of Chinese companies in general, especially state-owned enterprises. Estimates range anywhere from 40,000 to 70,000 employees. Another issue that has surfaced in terms of Chinese OFDI to the European Union is that Chinese state-owned enterprises have access to cheap credit. Moreover, they view their investments in Europe as a way to diversify away from their home operations or to move capital out of China. Consequently, the Chinese investor tends to invest liberally, but not efficiently, e.g. most wineries in France and Italy were purchased by the Chinese at extravagant valuations.

In Europe as well as in the United States, debate has begun to reach a high pitch among many of the EU's policymakers and European society in general about the long-term benefits of Chinese investment. All of this was brought on by the uneven playing field with respect to the Chinese markets for EU corporations. For whatever reason, China's public relations along with its general communications effort is not always good and when that happens, it's not very well received, e.g. many people in Germany and Italy have a negative view of China and Chinese investments in the EU. With that said, there are those in the EU corporate community who would like to think that if the proposed bilateral investment treaty is signed either this year or next, that this will improve the one-sided trading relationship between the EU and China (Le Corre and Sepulchre 2016).

The European automotive industry ended up being the top destination for Chinese OFDI in 2015 thanks to the Pirelli acquisition followed by commercial and industrial real estate and the hospitality sector: Louvre Hotels and Club Med; smaller cutting-edge information and telecommunication technology companies: NXP Semiconductors and RF Business, and financial services: SNS Reaal's insurance unit and Banco Espirito Santo's investment banking unit. Coincidentally, in terms of an aggressive interest, Chinese corporations have really picked up the pace in sectors that are still off-limits to foreign investors in China underscoring the political environment of unequal market access. An area where the West has amplified serious concerns for at least three decades and in reality, we're really no further along on that subject than in 2001 when China was allowed entrée into the World Trade Organization (WTO).

An excellent case in point is China's financial services sector. Corporations from the EU have been extremely frustrated with their inability to do business in China's financial services sector on an even playing field with the local competition. Given China's recent growth in OFDI to the EU for acquisitions in this sector, this should give the EU a leg up in terms of demanding fair competition in the Chinese market within the context of bilateral negotiations.

Another area that crossed the political divide is China's services industry in Europe. Recently, Chinese companies operating in Europe have been successful at selling service contracts that couple with infrastructure investments. Some examples of these transactions include: the Hinkley Point nuclear power plant and the Swansea Bay tidal lagoon in the United Kingdom, railway construction in Hungary and power plants in Romania. Obviously, transnational security concerns are at the forefront of potential political problems on the part of the EU, but with that said, this should also provide the EU with an opportunity to integrate China into relevant international agreements, e.g. OECD rules on export financing and the Government Procurement Agreement under the World Trade Organization (WTO).

The bulk of Chinese OFDI to the EU comes from state-owned companies and this seems to be the norm rather than the exception as new foreign financial opportunities increase, the role of Chinese state capital relative to OFDI to Europe increases. On the whole, private Chinese firms have also increased their OFDI to the EU. In 2016, OFDI to Europe from private Chinese companies amounted to $7.2 billion. Even though that's a record high, it's still a far cry from the $23 billion total Chinese OFDI to Europe for 2016. The European Union will probably struggle with the idea that Chinese state capital is funding the bulk of Chinese OFDI to Europe. On the one hand, it provides ample opportunity for Europe to advance new and much-needed projects especially in infrastructure development in Eastern Europe, but on the other hand, China's aggressive push to fund OFDI to Europe has the potential to undermine Europe's integrity and interfere with EU sovereignty. Moreover, this kind of an arrangement also stands in the way of the EU's firm commitment to discipline Chinese government subsidies.

Furthermore, state-owned capital has the potential to crowd out private capital and it could eliminate private investors who operate under market principles. In April 2016, a landmark decision from the European Commission paved the way for much greater regulatory scrutiny in terms of Chinese state-owned companies attempting to make acquisitions of European assets. After the Commission's review of a proposed joint venture between EDF in France and China's state-owned General Nuclear Power (CGN), the Commission ruled that CGN was not at all independent from China's central administrator for state-owned enterprises: the State-owned Assets Supervision and Administration Commission (SASAC). At that point, the European Commission decided that it did have the authority to make a decision if the joint venture should be approved or not.

For the Commission to reach a decision, it had to take into consideration not only CGN's revenue, but also the combined revenue of all the Chinese state-owned energy enterprises in order for the proposed joint venture to come under its jurisdiction. The reader should also note that the European Commission has exclusive authority over antitrust issues in the EU. Though the ruling received little notice by the general public when it was released in April 2016, the law firms advising Chinese companies issued a series of warnings to their clients. From a legal perspective, their lawyers advised them that the decision could mandate Chinese SOEs to file for European Union merger clearance regardless of their size in Europe. This alone creates an additional barrier which at the very least will delay proposed mergers and acquisition by Chinese state-owned companies.

From a political perspective, this new development comes on the heels of a total spending spree by Chinese companies of over $200 billion in mergers and acquisitions during the past 18 months across the world. Most of these companies are Chinese state-owned enterprises which generate enormous consternation and concerns by government officials in the EU as well as the United States. The very rapid advance of Chinese companies in Europe has triggered deep concerns on the part of high-level government officials in France and Germany. President François Hollande has stated publicly that he is completely against the prospect of Shanghai-controlled Jin Jiang buying controlling interest of Accor, the French hotel group.

The previously mentioned CGN-EDF acquisition was approved by the European Commission in March 2016, but it was the full analysis presented by the Commission showing why it reviewed the transaction that drew all of the attention. The unprecedented CGN transaction is the first time the Commission has said publicly that with respect to Chinese state-owned enterprises the Chinese government is so pervasive that it has become imperative that all SOEs in a given sector should be treated as a single entity. Shortly after the CGN-EDF deal was concluded the European Commission issued a brief statement on the matter that basically claimed that the Commission evaluates a state-owned enterprise on the basis of independence regardless of its national origin. The Commission further stated that it does not dictate rules in its cases, but its job is to make findings based on facts uncovered over a specific period of time. Moreover, there are some European and US policy officials who have raised concerns that China's FDI push presents national security risks. Thus the creation of the Committee on Foreign Investment in the United States (CFIUS). This committee in particular scrutinizes each and every foreign investment in the US and there have been times in the last two decades when the Committee has blocked the transaction entirely. Given the fact that roughly 70 percent of all Chinese FDI involves a state-owned enterprise, global law firms are advising their Chinese state-owned clients to consult with the European Commission first before proceeding with a merger or an acquisition in Europe even if the company believes that the proposed transaction does not meet EU M&A thresholds. This advice makes special reference to any transaction that involves China's energy sector.

It should also be noted that failure to file for approval from the European Commission will result in inordinate penalties, e.g. the European Commission fined Marine Harvest, a Norwegian salmon processor, 20 million euros for merging with a competitor without prior approval from the European Commission or any lower regulatory body. According to Nicholas French, co-head of China antitrust practice at the law firm Freshfields Bruckhaus Deringer in London, "This certainly sets down a marker for future cases. If the SOE is in the energy sector, they would have to show some concrete evidence to rebut the Commission's analysis" (Reuters 2016).

Companies who do file for an M&A review by the Commission will probably be subject to longer than normal delays in the pending transaction as the Brussels Commission analyzes and determines the control structure of the Chinese SOE. Given China's very strict state secrecy laws, this may be a difficult proposition. Historically, Chinese investors have invested heavily in the EU's big three economies: Germany, the United Kingdom and France which combined have received an average of $5 billion to $10 billion of Chinese OFDI per year. These three continued to be a major destination for Chinese OFDI to the EU in 2015. Interestingly, the big story starting in 2015 was the amount of Chinese OFDI headed towards other parts of Europe. In 2015 for the very first time, Southern European economies accounted for almost half of all the Chinese OFDI to the EU. Chinese OFDI to Belgium, the Netherlands and Luxembourg (the Benelux countries) also increased substantially over the past two years. Moreover, there are pending infrastructure projects in Eastern Europe that could give Chinese OFDI to that part of Europe a dramatic increase if they come to fruition.

Competition for Chinese OFDI among the countries in the European Union has intensified. Virtually every member-state within the EU has had high-level discussions with Chinese investors in an attempt to create more bilateral investment. China is more than happy to use its state-owned enterprises' OFDI as an incentive to accomplish its foreign policy initiatives and goals with member-states within the EU. The following list will include all 28 nations-states that comprise the entire European Union. Each country will be identified followed by Chinese outbound FDI into that country between 2000 and 2015 in euros: United Kingdom, EUR 15.2 billion; Italy, EUR 11.2 billion; France, EUR 9.5 billion; Germany, EUR 7.9 billion; Portugal, EUR 5.5 billion; Netherlands, EUR 5.3 billion; Belgium, EUR 1.7 billion; Spain, EUR 1.5 billion; Hungary, EUR 1.9 billion; Sweden, EUR 1.6 billion; Romania, EUR 741 million; Austria, EUR 506 million; Luxembourg, EUR 495 million; Poland, EUR 462 million; Greece, EUR 405 million; Bulgaria, EUR 222 million; Czech Republic, EUR

207 million; Denmark, EUR 134 million; Ireland, EUR 108 million; Finland, EUR 103 million; Malta, EUR 69 million; Slovakia, EUR 40 million; Lithuania, EUR 32 million; Cyprus, EUR 31 million; Estonia, EUR 23 million; Slovenia, EUR 8 million; Croatia, EUR 4 million; and Latvia, EUR 3 million (IIF 2017, website). Though Germany was not the largest recipient of Chinese OFDI, research shows that it experienced the most constant inflows of Chinese OFDI in the past five years. In 2015, Chinese OFDI to Germany dropped a bit, but it was not a significant amount: EUR 1.2 billion compared with 2014 at EUR 1.4 billion. However, as of February 2016, Germany has a backlog of pending transactions with Chinese investors amounting to EUR 2.5 billion, which tells the rest of the global economy that Germany has sustained appeal to Chinese investors.

In 2015, the automotive and machinery sectors continued to drive Chinese OFDI in Germany accounting for more than EUR 400 million, e.g. acquisitions of WEGU Holding and Quin, an increased stake in KION by Weichai. KION is a manufacturer of forklifts and warehouse technology. Research and development continued to play a big role in Chinese investment to Germany in 2015 which included new facilities in advanced component materials for Kangde Xin and R&D contracts in biotechnology with KTB Tumorforschungs, a free-standing research institute in Germany. In 2015, Chinese OFDI also went into R&D for rail technology, mobile device innovation and electric vehicles with an assorted group of German research institutes.

Surprisingly, Germany has also become increasingly attractive to Chinese financial investors who are looking for stable long-term returns. Returns in the upper end emerging market economies would be much greater as opposed to the near zero or negative returns in either the EU or the US. With that said, safety may account for a large part of the Chinese investors' decision. Moreover in 2015, China's sovereign wealth fund took a position in Germany's largest operator of gas and service stations (Tank & Rast), but the exact details of this investment are unavailable as of writing.[1] Another interesting observation took place when the Chinese conglomerate made a significant investment (non-FDI) in KTG Agrar. This is a very large agricultural company with vast farming interests in Eastern Germany and Eastern Europe and the investment details are also unavailable.

KTG Agrar is a publicly traded company on the Frankfurt Exchange. For whatever reason, it's always a very interesting transaction when one government invests in another country's natural resources. KTG Agrar has been in the farming business for over 20 years and has over 46,000 hectares under cultivation, but what really caught my attention was its stock price. On August 5, 2015, the KTG Agrar SE share price closed at EUR 16. On August 5, 2016 the KTG Agrar share price closed at EUR 0.59 – a fraction of the EUR 16.0 representing an unbelievable decline over a 12-month period. The pending investments in Germany by the Chinese investment community in 2016 point to a substantially growing interest in Germany's machinery, environmental technologies and financial services sectors. Given the current state of Chinese government encouragement along with the creation of financing vehicles such as the new "industry 4.0" fund, these positive investment factors should further increase Chinese invest-ments in German R&D and advanced manufacturing assets in the foreseeable future. However, there are some sticking points in terms of Chinese OFDI for 2016, which includes China's ongoing conflict with capital flight in tandem with China's overall bad debt position that could present short-term risks for 2016. China's pending transactions in early 2016 in Europe are certainly a positive sign for the continuation of Chinese investment in Europe in 2017.

The current volatility of China's markets is worrisome and when that nega-tive factor is combined with the downward pressure of the USD/CNY exchange rate, the outlook for a continued boom in Chinese OFDI to the West could be at risk for the balance of 2016, but that's doubtful due to the large amount of pending transactions in the pipeline in Europe. No chapter on this subject would be complete without a solid discussion on China's largest acquisition ever. In an effort to improve China's domestic food production, state-owned ChemChina agreed to a $43 billion bid for the world-class seeds and pesticide group Syngenta in Basel, Switzerland. The deal was consummated and announced by both com-panies on February 4, 2016. This particular acquisition will accelerate a shake-up in global agrochemicals and marks a definite setback for the American chemical giant Monsanto who tried, but was unable to put an acquisition together for Syngenta in 2015.

With a population in excess of 1.3 billion people, China is by far the world's largest agricultural market and given that scenario, the Chinese government wants to secure a solid food supply for its people. Syngenta's product line of top-tier agricultural chemicals and patent-protected seeds will give Chinese agriculture a substantial increase in its basic food production. According to researchers at Kyushu University, due to pollution and poor agricultural practices in the past, only 10 percent of China's available farm ground is fertile. This is the direct result of years of very intensive farming combined with an overuse of agricultural chemicals. Unfortunately, this kind of farming practice has degraded the soil and poisoned the water supplies, which leave China very vulnerable to various crop shortages (Chen 2015, 1–8). Consequently, this is much more than a Chinese acquisition in the European Union; it's the Chinese government attempting to address a major problem in that country: a problem that could result in human disaster. With a slowing Chinese economy, Chinese companies are constantly looking overseas for acquisitions that will add diversification to their product mix and help them increase sales. If completed, the Syngenta acquisition would be twice the CNOOC purchase of $17.7 billion of Canadian energy company Nexan in 2012. Last year, as mentioned earlier, ChemChina acquired Pirelli in Italy for over $7 billion and earlier this year it also announced a bid for Germany's industrial machinery maker KraussMaffei Group for roughly $1 billion.

Interestingly, Syngenta shares are currently trading at around 412 Swiss francs well below ChemChina's bid price of 480 Swiss francs, which is an indication that investors feel there is a possibility the deal will fall through. The Swiss regulators have given a preliminary indication that they were okay with the acquisition, but they did indicate that they want the Swiss retail investors to receive the

ChemChina offer in Swiss francs, which was also underscored with warnings given on foreign exchange risks. In an August 2016 press release, Syngenta's chairman did say that ChemChina will be in the market for more acquisitions in line with China's efforts to bolster its food production. It should also be noted that Syngenta is currently China's largest supplier of crop chemicals with a 6 percent share of a very fragmented market. The main focus of the Chinese authorities at this time is to cut its reliance on food imports while increasing the fertility of its farmland (Syngenta 2016).

In terms of meat consumption, China's combined consumption of poultry, beef and pork has increased by an average of 1.7 million tons per year for the last ten years, which results in further stress on feed grain supplies. Moreover, for the past three years, there has been an oversupply of corn and soybean commodities which has resulted in depressed grain prices resulting in a reduction in purchases on everything from equipment, seeds and pesticides by the farming community in the United States, a major supplier of agricultural products to the world.

A combination of cutbacks and pressure from investors to increase profits has resulted in an ongoing effort by the world's largest agricultural companies to create mergers and acquisitions. Along those lines, DuPont and Dow Chemical announced in December 2015 an all-stock merger with a street value of $130 billion in a first step to consolidate into three separate businesses a move that will set the stage for further consolidation. The downside in this pending acquisition is the United States. Considering 25 percent of Syngenta's sales takes place in North America, this transaction has to be approved by the Committee on Foreign Investment in the United States (CFIUS). There are persistent concerns in the financial markets that they may not approved this deal. However, in a press release of July 22, 2016 via Reuters Syngenta claimed the deal would be done this year (Burger 2016).

At present, some analysts in Europe feel the deal will be completed and they have a "buy" rating on Syngenta justified by the current discounted share price against the offer price resulting in a 20 percent gain to the shareholder if the transaction is completed. Surprisingly according to the prospectus, funding for this acquisition is coming from a range of Chinese investors as well as HSBC and China CITIC International. If approved, this will be China's largest acquisition by the Chinese government.

In 2012, when the EU-China Bilateral Investment Agreement negotiations began both sides wanted to fully understand its potential synergies. This part of the chapter will provide an overview of the current negotiation strategy. From a political and economic perspective, the vigorous expectations within the agreement must be offset by the many challenges and obstacles currently found in EU-China relations in global trade and investments within the context of EU's capabilities.

If properly negotiated, this could be very important for the EU; it offers the potential for the EU to enlarge its global economic footprint, but if it's poorly negotiated, the result will be the usual lopsided EU-China trade and investment regime. In January 2016, representatives of the European Commission and the Chinese Ministry of Commerce met in Beijing for the ninth round of negotiations for the proposed EU-China Bilateral Investment Agreement (BIA). The EU-China BIA negotiations history goes back to the 2008 financial crisis in the Eurozone.

From a historical perspective, EU-China economic relations have centered on trade in goods and services. On the surface, the whole notion of EU-China reciprocal investments evokes a source of vast, untapped potential for both the EU and Chinese economies. There's no question. China is the EU's second largest trading partner, but investments from the EU into China amount to a modest 5 percent of all European investments overseas and only a small part of the total trade volume. On the other hand, Chinese investment into the EU amounts to less than 3 percent of the total FDI flow into the European Union (EC 2015).

The current BIA negotiations are focused on providing market access for EU companies operating in China while felicitating Chinese investment into the 28 EU countries. The intent is an increase in the total outbound foreign direct investments between the European Union and China. EU officials along with the EU business community claim they have good expectations that the EU-China BIA will come to fruition. However, recently the EU-China relationship has not been as robust as it once was.

The proposed EU-China BIA is seen by many as the catalyst in an effort to rekindle a better EU-China relationship. The EU-China relationship began to sour in 2011 when a number of high-level EU officials began to doubt the significance within the wording of the 2003 Comprehensive Strategic Partnership between the EU and China. On a similar note, the multiple dialogues between the EU and China do enhance exchange at various levels of government, but lately the dialogues have come under extreme criticism due to a lack of visible output. If the proposed EU-China BIA is approved, it would represent the first major agreement between the EU and China since 2003.

In spite of the multiple so-called Chinese reform initiatives, there are many in the EU who are skeptical that things will change soon if ever. A good example is the experimental Shanghai Free Trade Zone (SFTZ). This is supposed to include Chinese reform initiatives for free trade, currency liberalization and market determined interest rates, but the reforms have been extremely slow in coming to the surface and the list of sectors which is restricted or off limits to foreign investors is still extremely substantial resulting in diminished expectations for real reform relative to the SFTZ.

In terms of the BIA, the EU wants the agreement to include legal certainty and legal rights with respect to EU corporations operating in China, which includes the protection of EU investments, a reduction of EU investment barriers and an increase in bilateral investment flows. Chinese market access for EU investors still remains the most important consideration for the EU within the context of the EU-China BIA. With that said, a conclusive EU-China BIA depends entirely on the inclusion of significant market access for EU investors in China's marketplace.

Currently, the existing restrictions for EU investors operating in China include very limiting market barriers and unfair competition from the state-owned enterprises sanctioned by the Chinese authorities. None of these issues are a problem for the Chinese companies operating in the EU. The European markets are already open to Chinese corporations or for that matter any foreign investor and EU state-owned enterprises for the most part are non-existent with the exception of a few state-owned enterprises in Eastern Europe. Overall, China's specific objectives within the context of the EU-China BIA include: EU extensive unchanging fortification for Chinese companies, an escalation of EU legal jurisdiction for Chinese investors operating in the EU, assurances by EU authorities that the markets will remain open to Chinese outbound FDI and an increase in the total investment flows between the EU and China. From an economics perspective, it's abundantly clear that the EU has to have increased market access for EU investors operating in China in order for the EU-China BIA to ever take place, but unfair competition on the part of Chinese corporation is equally important. In the unlikely event that the Chinese government will ever really open its markets to foreign investors, unfair government subsidized competition from Chinese corporations will still put the EU investor operating in China at a distinct disadvantage. As for the Chinese investors operating in the EU, China wants to be assured that nothing will change.

Note

1 While we certainly don't know the details of the sovereign wealth fund's (CSWF) investments other than it took place in 2015, but it would be safe to assume that the Chinese government bought in at the high end of the share price range.

References

Burger, Ludwig, "Syngenta sees ChemChina deal done this year, first-half profit disappoints," *Reuters New Service*, July 22, 2016.

Chen, Tinggui, "Equity, Efficiency and Farmland System in China," Department of Agricultural and Resource Economics, Faculty of Agriculture, Kyushu University, May 9, 2015.

European Commission (EC), "Trade Policy – Countries and Regions-China," Brussels, 2015.

Hanemann, Thilo and Mikko Huotari, "A New Record for Chinese Outbound Investment in Europe," Mercator Institute for China Studies & Rhodium Group, Berlin & New York, February, 2016.

Institute of International Finance (IIF) website, Washington, DC, 2017, available at www.iif.com.

Jones, Claire, "Chinese investment in Europe hits $2–3 billion record," *Financial Times*, March 9, 2016.

Le Corre, Philippe and Alain Sepulchre, *China's Offensive in Europe*, Washington, DC: Brookings Institution Press, 2016.

Reuters, "RPT-Chinese state-owned companies face greater scrutiny of EU deals after ruling," June 13, 2016, available at www.reuters.com/article/china-eu-ma-idUSL1N 195008.

Syngenta, "ChemChina and Syngenta receive clearance from the Committee on Foreign Investment in the United States (CFIUS)," press release, August 2016, available at www.syngenta.com/media/media-releases/yr-2016/22-08-2016.

Part IV

Trade balances

10 US trade policies and trade balances with China in the 1990s

Since the 1990s consumer goods prices in the United States have remained relatively stable. Of course, the prices of consumer goods have increased since the 1990s, but the US hasn't experienced any real significant spike in the prices of consumer goods. It's been more of a gradual increase. Other than a sound monetary policy conducted by the Fed the most important reason for this is US international trade with developing countries, mainly China. For every dollar Americans spend on products made in China, the Chinese spend less than 30 cents on American made products resulting in an ongoing US annual trade deficit with China. Currently, China holds roughly $3.2 trillion in foreign reserves mainly in US dollars or US government bonds. Foreign reserves equal excess cash flow.

Ironically in the 1950s and 1960s, the United States was the world's leading export economy. Of course, the Marshall Plan helped provide the needed capital to rebuild Europe and Japan and at the same time, it created a tremendous demand for US manufactured goods and services. During this time frame the US ran a very substantial trade surplus with its trading partners which equaled approximately 1 percent of US Gross Domestic Product (GDP). Moreover in that time period, US strong export demand was drawn from a vast array of industries from low-tech textiles and apparel to sophisticated aircraft and machine tools.

Since the 1970s, the US has transitioned from running a trade surplus with its trading partners to a trade deficit. The reader should keep in mind that this was also a time when Europe and Japan began competing effectively with the US in a variety of industries. Unfortunately, there are a number of ways a trade deficit affects US workers. First, a deepening trade deficit reduces domestic employment. Trade exports create jobs and trade imports eliminate jobs if the imports are in US competing industries especially in manufacturing and other industries producing traded goods.

In 1998, the trade surplus of the 1960s, which amounted to 1 percent of GDP became a trade deficit that surged to 2.9 percent of GDP. Sadly, the continued growth in the trade deficit for the last three decades has destroyed millions of good paying, high skilled manufacturing jobs in the United States which forced workers into lower paying jobs in other sectors, e.g. fast food outlets, restaurants, health service industries and retail stores. In 1998, the United States lost 500,000 jobs in manufacturing alone due to the impact from an increasing trade deficit with China (BLS). According to the Economic Policy Institute, between 1979 and 1994 the rising trade deficit eliminated 2.4 million jobs in the United States. Since then many more jobs have been lost due to trade deficits from NAFTA and China (Scott et al. 1997). Moreover, more than 75 percent of the sum total US trade deficits are essentially derived from China and Japan.

In some ways, China's trade policies mirror Japan's: Chinese government ownership and control of the bulk of its economic resources. China's very extensive network of government controls over economic activity, banking, and trade and foreign exchange flows, all of this combined has created the United States' imbalanced, one-sided bilateral trading relationship.

Figure 10.1 shows that the US trade deficit with China has an upward bias reaching almost 25 percent of the total US deficit in the 1990s. In 1990, the US trade deficit with China was $10.43 billion; in 1991 that number increased roughly 18 percent to $12.69 billion; in 1992 the US trade deficit with China increased to a whopping $18.31 billion representing a 31 percent increase; in 1993 that number came in at $22.78 billion, an increase over 1992 by roughly 20 percent; in 1994 the US trade deficit with China rose to $29.51 billion, roughly a 23 percent increase; in 1995 that number came in at $33.80 billion representing a 13 percent increase over the previous year. In 1996, the US trade deficit with China increased $39.52 billion, an increase of roughly a 15 percent increase over 1995; in 1997 that number came in at $49.69 billion representing a 21 percent increase over 1996; in 1998, the US trade deficit with China was $59.93 billion, an increase of roughly 17 percent over the previous year; in 1999 that number registered $68.67 billion representing an increase of roughly

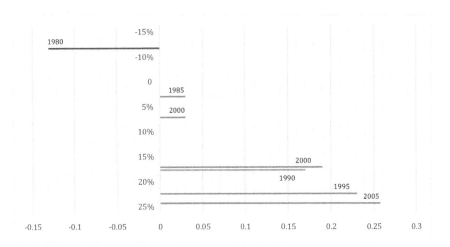

Figure 10.1 China's portion of the total US trade deficit 1980–2005

Source: Author with data from US Department of Commerce

13 percent over 1998; in 2000 the US trade deficit with China jumped to $83.83 billion representing approximately a 19 percent increase over 1999 and an increase by a factor of 8 or 800 percent over 1990 in ten years! I'll cover this in Chapter 12, but in 2015, the trade deficit with China came in at over $367 billion which represented roughly 74 percent of the total US trade deficit.

The only other trading partner with a rapidly expanding trade deficit with the United States is Germany with a trade deficit growth rate of 25 percent per year in the 1990s. The German trade deficit in the 1990s was centered on a combination of macroeconomic, industrial and agricultural trade policies on the part of the US. There were some economists in the 1990s who made the case that even if the United States has large trade deficits with China these simply reflect macroeconomic problems in the US – an indication that the US had a shortage of domestic savings in relation to investments. Moreover, there were some economists who claimed that the US benefits from exporting high-value added goods such as aircraft and computers while importing low-tech goods such as apparel, footwear and toys.

In the 1990s, the truth about trade patterns was much more complicated than today. At that time, the industry that created the largest trade deficits in the United States was crude oil and natural gas which was certainly not a surprise considering that in the 1990s the US imported approximately 50 percent of its petroleum products. However, automobiles and auto parts imports created the second largest trade deficits in the 1990s and the most interesting thing was that these were certainly not low-technology industries by most standards. Other high-technology and/or high-wage industries that also created massive trade deficits in the 1990s included computers, office machines, steel and other blast furnace products, television sets, radios and other electronic equipment. Interestingly, of the top eight trade deficit sectors only three were considered low-technology products by economists in the 1990s: apparel, leather products and toys.

The top eight trade deficit industries in 1997 produced trade deficits of $230 billion, of which China accounted for $49.69 billion or roughly 21 percent. The total $230 billion in trade deficits for those top eight industries in 1997 exceeded the total US deficits in manufactured goods in that year by significant amount. If there were a way to eliminate the trade deficits found in those top eight industries, the result would have been an overall trade surplus for 1997. Between 1991 and 1997, the top eight trade surplus industries were: cigarettes, meat and meat packing products, engines turbines and parts, scientific instruments, photo and optical goods, construction and mining machinery, cash grains and other crops, chemicals and allied products and aircraft and parts. The total trade surplus for the top eight sectors in 1997 was $101 billion.

A closer look at Tables 10.1 and 10.2 shows the trade deficit and trade surplus in 1997. The total trade surplus of the top seven surplus industries was $109.2 billion less than half of the trade deficit of the top seven deficit industries in 1997 of $221.1 billion. It also shows that in 1997 five of the top seven trade surplus industries do involve high-technology and high-wage industries: aircraft, chemicals,

Table 10.1 Top seven US trade deficit industries, 1991–1997

Total deficit of top seven in 1997: $221.1 billion

$US billions					
0					$10.8 B
-10				$20.4 B	
-20					
-30			$40.3 B		
-40					
-50					
-60	$65.2 B	$65.4 B			
-70					
	Crude Pet Nat Gas	Autos & Parts	Apparel	Computer Off M Part	Leather & Leather Pr.

Source: Author with data from the US Department of Commerce

Table 10.2 Top seven US trade surplus industries, 1991–1997

Total surplus of top seven in 1997: $109.2 billion

$USD Billions						
40						
30	$32.5 B					
20		$20.2 B				
			$18.3 B			
10				$10.4 B		
					$9.8 B	$9.7 B	$8.3 B
0	Aircraft & Parts	Chemicals Allied	Grains & Crops	Constr. & Mining M	Scientific Instruments	Engines & Turbines	Meat & Packing

Source: Author with data from the US Department of Commerce

construction machinery, scientific instruments and engines and turbines. The United States was a net exporter of three major commodity products in 1997: cash grains, meat packing products and cigarettes. Unfortunately, commodity markets do not necessarily generate high-wage jobs due to price competition.

Furthermore, the US trade surplus industries between 1991 and 1997 do not reveal any kind of a pattern in terms of sustained growth. Within the US trade surplus industries from 1991 to 1997, only three of the top eight trade surplus industries showed signs of steady growth: meat and meat packing products, engines, turbines and parts, and cash grains and other crops. However, each of the top eight deficit industries from 1991 to 1997 grew steadily in that time frame. That's definitely a pattern in terms of sustained growth, but it's the wrong pattern.

The steady erosion of output and employment in high-wage, high-technologies industries combined with the US' dependence on commodity exports point directly to the failure of the trade and industrial policies to nurture and enhance US international competitiveness in the 1990s. At that time, other countries prospered, but no country more so than China at the direct expense of the United States and the United States' workers. The US government trade policy was the stimulus for corporate outsourcing especially in the 1990s. The Uruguay Round which created the World Trade Organization (WTO) and the North American Free Trade Agreement (NAFTA) soon became a Trojan horse for the interests of multinational corporations. These two agreements set the stage for investor protection through limits on trade-related investment measures, intellectual property rights enforcement and by bringing services trade into the WTO.

The Uruguay Round had many more global ramifications than NAFTA, especially for the United States, Europe and China. It took seven and a half years to complete. By the end, 123 countries were taking part in the agreement, which created the WTO. The agreement covered almost every product from toothbrushes to pleasure boats, from banking to telecommunications, from the genes of wild rice to AIDS treatments. It was quite simply the largest trade negotiation ever and most probably the largest negotiation of any kind in history (WTO 1986–1994).

From a historical perspective, the idea for the Uruguay Round was first discussed at a ministerial meeting of the members of the General Agreement on Tariffs and Trade (GATT) in Geneva in November 1982. That particular meeting fell short of expectations. The conference could not agree on agricultural products and it was thought to be a failure, but in fact, the members agreed to a work program that later formed the basis for the Uruguay Round negotiating agenda. It still took four more years for the members to agree to launch a new round and that finally took place in September 1986 in Punta del Este, Uruguay. The conference accepted a negotiating agenda that included virtually every outstanding trade policy. The meeting extended the trade issues into other new areas, notably trade in services and intellectual property, and the members also wanted to reform trade in the sensitive areas of agriculture and textiles. With all the articles incorporated in GATT up for review, that meeting became the biggest mandate on trade ever agreed and the members gave themselves four years for completion. In December 1988, the members met again in Montreal, Canada for what was supposed to be an assessment of the progress completed at the halfway mark, but the meeting ended in deadlock until the officials met quietly in Geneva in April 1989. Despite the problems in Montreal, the members did agree on a package of early results. In spite of politics as usual, a considerable amount of technical work continued which led to the first draft of a final legal agreement. This draft in particular was compiled by the then director-general of

GATT and it was presented to the members in final form in Geneva in December 1991, but the draft did not contain one exception; it lacked commitments for cutting import duties and opening their service markets. The draft became the basis for the final agreement. Over the next few years, negotiations among the members gyrated between imminent failures to predictions of imminent success. The arguing points were always the same: agriculture, services, market access, anti-dumping rules and the proposed creation of a new institution, which was the genesis for the World Trade Organization (WTO). At that point, the hold-up was between the United States and the European Union.

In November 1992, the US and the EU came to terms on their differences on agriculture. Their agreement became known as the "Blair House Accord". At the end of July 1993, the "Quad" (US, EU, Japan and Canada) reached an agreement on tariffs and market access for goods and services. Finally on April 15, 1994, the Uruguay Round agreement was signed by representatives of 123 governments in Marrakesh, Morocco setting the stage for the creation of the World Trade Organization (WTO). On January 1, 1995, the WTO was established in Geneva, Switzerland. The WTO is the only global international organization dealing with the rules of trade between nations. At its heart are the WTO agreements negotiated and signed by the bulk of the world's trading nations and ratified by their respective legislatures. The goal of the organization is to help producers of goods and services, exporters and importers conduct their business. Today, the WTO's membership totals 164 countries with a budget in excess of 200 million Swiss francs and a staff of 640 employees. Its functions include: the administration of WTO agreements, providing a forum for trade negotiations, settling trade disputes, monitoring national and international trade policies, providing technical assistance and training for developing countries and cooperating with other international organizations. There's no doubt that US trade with China has hurt a great many US workers, but it's been a windfall for US multinational corporations. As of this writing, the Dow Jones Industrial Index and the S&P 500 Index are at record highs, reinforcing the monetary benefits enjoyed by America's largest corporations. The development of new methods to the US-China trade problems must be based on a complete analysis of the US-China failed trade policy currently in place. A thorough analysis on how and why the current trade policy failed is definitely in order. This analysis should begin with a very close perusal of the US corporate influence involved in the US-China trade policymaking process. Twenty years ago on Wall Street, the buzz among the investment banks was the declining influence of US major corporations, but today that sentiment has utterly disappeared.

The obvious competition between the US multinational corporations and the US workers is reflected in the US trade statistics. In 1970, the US produced almost 20 percent of all world exports, but by 1998 that number plummeted to 12 percent and unfortunately today, the US world export percentage is even worse. This is a subject that will be covered extensively in Chapter 12 when the book examines US-China trade relations from 2000 forward. In 1995 after the creation of the WTO, the US multinational corporations played a dominant role in world production by aggressively investing in and building manufacturing facilities overseas. This was facilitated by closing manufacturing plants in the United States and moving production abroad mainly to China. Historically, US multinationals would use their manufacturing facilities in China to serve foreign markets, but after 1995 and the creation of the WTO, they used their manufacturing facilities abroad to serve the United States as well. This was a win-win deal for them. Most of their manufacturing facilities in China were established as joint ventures with Chinese companies. The joint venture manufactured the product under the US company's brand. So, not only did they reduce their labor costs dramatically, they also reduced their overhead by at least 50 percent. The shifting role of East Asia within the context of the global economy is another major factor that impacts US trade deficits. In spite of China's dramatic increase in US trade in the decade 1996–2006, China's share of US global trade deficits has remained basically unchanged in the range of 27 percent to 28 percent. However during the same time period, the share of US global trade deficits of all East Asian countries dropped from 70 percent to 45 percent, but the US trade deficits with the rest of the global economies grew from 30 percent to 55 percent (US Census Bureau 2013). The above paragraph points to that period in US corporate history when outsourcing became the norm rather than the exception and unfortunately it hasn't slowed today. Since the 1990s, US trade policy has been successful in giving the US multinationals the green light for corporate outsourcing. In 1995, the Uruguay Round, which created the WTO and the creation of NAFTA in 1994 significantly enhanced the commercial interests of US multinational corporations. Both agreements guarded foreign investors by limiting trade-related investment standards, providing intellectual property rights enforcement and the initiation of services trade into the WTO by-laws. Simultaneously, new binding dispute settlement mechanisms were enacted relative to the enforcement of international property rights.

These new standards set the stage for an avalanche of US foreign investment especially in China, which needless to say had a devastating effect on US workers mainly in the manufacturing space. Foreign investor rights were given the highest priority in the bilateral and multilateral trade negotiations that followed. The reader should also be aware that as previously mentioned China did not become a member of the WTO until 2001, but it was a nation member of the General Agreement on Tariffs and Trade (GATT) which it joined in 1971 shortly after resumption of diplomatic relations with the United States. Between 1995 and China's entrée into the WTO in 2001, China and the United States were operating under an informal bilateral trade agreement established under the Clinton Administration.

In terms of bilateral and multilateral trade agreements in the 1990s, investor rights were given the highest priority, but input from workers, consumers and environmental groups were largely ignored. Consequently, the 1990s saw these groups form regional coalitions in many regions in the United States that in fact blocked several fast track trade initiatives in those days. Moreover, the financial crises in the early 1990s and then again in the late 1990s served as a constant reminder that globalization had allowed the US corporate community to escape the limits of regulatory statues. These statutes were created after 1930 and brought stability, economic growth and prosperity to a large part of the world for decades, but in the 1990s, the global trading system became unstable by the creation of favoritism towards investor rights while ignoring worker rights, human rights and the environment.

In 1998, some members of Congress agreed the answer to achieve President Clinton's goals was to create a new coalition in support of global integration. This group in particular was established in the Republican Party, but included in the group were a large number of House Democrats. Unfortunately in 1999, the coalition began to unravel when a large number within the coalition deserted the group entirely. In that year, 71 Republicans and 151 Democrats opposed legislation to extend the President's fast track negotiating authority, but President Clinton's 1998 address to the Council on Foreign Relations reflected a new political reality.

From an economic history perspective, right or wrong trade became an obsession for the Clinton Administration and it played an important role in the US economic history of the 1990s. There's widespread disagreement about the assertion made by some policy officials at that time that somehow trade was part of the national consciousness and US trade policies were a big part of US domestic politics and diplomatic relations. In the 1990s, the Clinton Administration took on a very aggressive role in finalizing the Uruguay Round, NAFTA, and the creation of global trade agreements in financial services, telecommunications and information technology. The Clinton Administration launched the Free Trade Area of the Americas (FTAA) and at the same time the Administration elevated the Asia-Pacific Economic Cooperation forum to a greater position of power. The Clinton government was also the driving force in the international financial rescue of Mexico and at a future point in time, East Asia. The Clinton Administration negotiated the US-Jordon Free Trade Agreement and the US-Vietnam Bilateral Trade Agreement.

And it was the Clinton Administration that became the power broker and chief spokesman for China's entrée into the World Trade Organization (WTO). However, by the mid to late 1990s domestic polarization led to a paralysis overseas most notably the collapse of WTO negotiations in Seattle in 1999 where 50,000 raging protestors took to the streets fervently against China's admission into the WTO. When domestic politics got in the Clinton Administration's way, the European Union took on the temporary task of dealing with the WTO on China's behalf.

In the 1900s, trade policy in the United States was integrated into the overall general economy, but when the Clinton Administration took office in 1993, the overriding narrative was "it's the economy, stupid." Prior to the arrival of the Clinton Administration, the 1980s ushered in a harsh macroeconomic imbalance of the free-wheeling fiscal policies of Presidents Reagan and George H.W. Bush combined with the tight monetary policy of Alan Greenspan and a severe erosion of international market share which questioned the competitiveness of the United States in key industrial sectors. Economically, Japan was coming on very strong and the US manufacturers took the position that Japan had to be challenged or copied whenever possible.

Not unlike in the 1980s, in the 1990s America's deficits and a strong dollar reduced US competitiveness vis-à-vis Asian competitors. Also in the 1990s, global trade developments were enhanced by the Clinton Administration's unwavering commitment to fiscal discipline. Simultaneously, the US information technology sector exploded creating a stunning market share performance, which generated an economic windfall in the United States. By the mid-1990s, Japan's economy had deteriorated into a deep economic slump as opposed to the US economy, which was growing at a robust pace enhanced significantly by global trade. In terms of sectoral economic performance, it had become abundantly clear that the US industries that held a cutting edge advantage dominated peer competition all over the world. The 1990s and the Clinton Administration marked a distinct turning point in United States economic history.

On the surface, there are some economists who claim that the Clinton Administration in the 1990s was very strong on trade and there are those who make the argument that its idea of trade was not free trade; early on in the process, the Administration's rhetoric sounded more like results-oriented managed trade. The fact is that the Clinton Administration was strongest on building market opening trade agreements; thus, President Clinton's aggressive push for China's entrée into the WTO. In terms of market opening trade agreements, the 1990s provided the United States with a number of achievements. First, The Reagan Administration initiated the Uruguay Round and it negotiated the US-Canada Free Trade Agreement (FTA) and the US-Israel FTA followed by the Bush Administration that did the initial negotiations for NAFTA. The Clinton Administration succeeded the Bush Administration. Moreover, the Clinton Administration completed negotiations and achieved legislative approval for both NAFTA and the Uruguay Round. And the Clinton Administration completed WTO agreements on telecommunications, information technology and financial services.

There are many in the economics profession who like to make the case that any implementations of trade solutions is basically protectionist and against free trade and then there are those in the same profession who make better distinctions. First, there is a very big difference between initiating protectionist standards on an ad hoc basis and implementing solutions according to US trade laws and WTO rules. Second, the US populace in general tends to think of US trade laws as more of a domestic regulator, which assists in supporting free trade as fair trade. To the average American manufacturing worker, free trade with China has nothing to with fair trade. Those same workers question the so-called regulatory bodies associated with each one of the trade agreements created in the 1990s including the WTO.

When the Clinton Administration took office in 1993, it made a public disclosure about taking an aggressive stance on trade barriers imposed by America's trading partners. And indeed, 1993 to 1995 saw several high profile trade agreements come to fruition. First in terms of US-Japan trade, the development of the US-Japan Framework was followed by an informal trade agreement with China that was supposed to mirror the original framework of the GATT, but with the piecemeal passage of the Uruguay Round legislation in 1994 combined with the proposed WTO dispute settlement system, the United States embarked on a different approach in terms of trade rules enforcement.

After several years of questionable relations in terms of security and trade issues, the Clinton Administration also asserted that it had made moderate inroads in the US-China relationship through a much better trade policy in 1994. The previous years witnessed a series of high profile trade disputes between China and the United States which culminated in a so-called landmark intellectual property agreement agreed to under the threat of sanctions. After Premier Zhu Rongji agreed to China's membership in the WTO, the Clinton Administration used WTO accession as leverage available to the United States against China in an effort to influence China's development and advancing the rule of law in that country. In brief, WTO accession takes place when a country becomes a member of the WTO. The naive intent here on the part of the Clinton Administration was for the US to play a key role in China's domestic reform agenda and advancing its rule of law.

China's entrée into the WTO was supposed to have a profound impact on US-China relations in terms of China's integration into the global economy and into the WTO itself. Along those lines, several interactions transpired relative to trade and foreign policy. For openers, President Clinton and the Republican Congressional leadership actively sought Congressional approval to grant China Permanent Normal Trade Relations (PNTR). This was before China's accession into the WTO was completed, during the President's final year in office in spite of the outward objections from a number of academics who at the time claimed that granting China PNTR and WTO accession would result in economic and political costs that greatly outweighed its benefits.

Moreover, the intricacies involved in the US-Chinese trade negotiations against the backdrop of domestic politics in both countries definitely created a very strained US-China relationship right from the very beginning. Clinton's aggressive push for China's entrée into the WTO combined with the Administrations' concerted effort to obtain Congressional approval to grant China PNTR resulted in a heavy political cost and it displaced other important trade legislation priorities such as debate on the Fast Track Authority.

Furthermore, many see the Clinton Administration and the 1990s as a watershed in the politics of trade, but in order for that observation to have credence a distinction should be drawn between the politics involved in public debate on trade agreements and the trade balance between two countries in terms of a historical perspective. In the case of China as previously mentioned, the United States had run an annual trade deficit with China going back to 1985 some 16 years before China's entrée into the WTO in 2001. Where this mutually beneficial US-China trade relationship went off track is difficult to determine, but ten years later, according to Robert Lighthizer, the former US trade representative in the Reagan Administration, the US trade deficit with China surged 173 percent to $227 billion in 2009 up from $83 billion in 2000. In that same time period the United States lost more than one-third of all its manufacturing jobs: 5.6 million jobs. US wages have declined and the country suffered a financial meltdown. In spite of the US spending trillions of dollars on an economic stimulus program, the country experienced the highest unemployment rate in generations and in 2010, Lighthizer further claimed that these trends are not likely to end (Lighthizer 2010).

On April 8, 1999 speaking to a conference of the US Institute of Peace, President Bill Clinton said in so many words that the United States has an interest in integrating China into global economy and the World Trade Organization. Accordingly, he further claimed that Chinese membership in the WTO will give the United States better access to China's markets and it will enhance China's economic reforms. He went on to assert that China will be forced to lower tariffs which will enable the US to sell American-made cars in China through US dealerships without any technology infringements (Knowlton 1999).

Unfortunately, none of President Clinton's promises have ever materialized. The United States does not have an even playing field in China and China's trading history with the US tells us that it is not willing to abide by the global rules of trade. There are no lower tariffs for manufactured goods from the US and China does not allow automobiles made in America to be sold in China. Anything manufactured or distributed in China by a US corporation is done on a joint venture basis with a Chinese company and under Chinese law the Chinese company must own at least 51 percent of the joint venture. There are multiple sectors that are basically off-limits to US corporations even in a joint venture proposal.

Critics of the Clinton Administration claim the United States made the mistake of treating China as if it were another democracy. In support of their argument they further claim that the General Agreement on Tariffs and Trade (GATT, WTO predecessor) was created in 1947 and it soon evolved into the world trading system. At that time China was excluded from GATT. Though it was never formally put into the GATT by-laws, the founding 23 members of GATT agreed on the basic principles of democracy and capitalism. Consequently, all communist countries were excluded. The founding members took the position that such countries would damage GATT's efficiency and compromise the Agreement's intent.

The Clinton Administration critics further argue that the experience of the Cold War showed the world that we had a distinct polarization in global relations with democratic, capitalist nations on the one hand and authoritarian, communist dictatorships on the other. All of which solidified GATT as the pillar of the free world. Furthermore, within the genesis of GATT in 1947, the United States and its allies offered membership in GATT to countries that were intent on building a fair trading relationship with an alliance of democratic, capitalist nations.

References

Lighthizer, Robert, former deputy US Trade Representative in the Reagan administration and head of the international trade department of the Washington DC firm of Skadden, Arps, Slate, Meagher & Flom LLP, personal interview, 2010.

Knowlton, Brian, "Clinton Gives Strong Push to Admitting China to WTO," *The New York Times*, April 8, 1999.

Scott, Robert E., Thea Lee and John Schmitt, "Trading Away Good Jobs: An Examination of Employment and Wages in the US, 1979–94," Economics Policy Institute Briefing Paper, Washington, DC, October, 1997.

US Bureau of Labor Statistics (BLS) homepage: http://stats.bls.gov/. for changes in manufacturing employment.

US Census Bureau, US-China Trade, 2013, available at www.census.gov/foreign-trade/balance/c5700.html.

US Department of Commerce, Washington, DC, June 10, 2016.

World Trade Organization (WTO), Geneva, Switzerland, 1986–1994.

11 EU trade policies and trade balances with China in the 1990s

This chapter examines the international performance of the European Union within the context of the rise of China in the 1990s. This will give the reader an insightful overview of the formative years in the 1990s after the WTO Agreement took effect in 1995. More specifically, the chapter looks at the changes in specialization and market shares of the EU on external markets from 1990 to 2000. When it comes to trade and trade policies, the European Union is at the forefront of a multilateral trading system. The trade policies put in place by the EU dating back to 1993 demonstrated an increased interest in internal policy integration. Moreover, the 1993 trade policies show an expanding and complex network of free trade areas supported by a strong commitment and active participation in the creation of more liberal multilateral trade. The creation of the World Trade Organization (WTO) in 1995 provided the necessary framework to assist the EU in terms of future trade policies.

The very first report issued by the WTO Secretariat in July 1995 included the EU's trade policies established in 1993. At that time, the Single Market was finally completed and the Maastricht Treaty went into effect. Moreover by then, the EU had grown to 15 members. According to the report, the European Economic Area agreement took effect on January 1, 1994 along with continued negotiations on the Euro-Mediterranean Agreements. These accomplishments have enlarged a network of preferential trading partners where trade issues can be resolved by an independent body (WTO) away from the multilateral trading system.

The 1995 WTO report further stated that the essence of the EU's internal market process was the elimination of trade restrictions upheld by EU independent member nations. There were some exceptions to this rule, e.g. unified quotas for bananas, canned sardines and tuna plus certain steel supplies from the Commonwealth of Independent States (CIS) and a number of consumer products from China. Also in 1995, new environmental legislation was created putting constraints on production and trade, but the slight decrease in output was perfectly fine with the 15 EU members. The report claimed single market integration for pharmaceuticals had been delayed due to different member-state standards and the proposed EU steel industry reforms approved in early 1993 were abandoned in October 1994 (EC 1995).

It's important to note that in the early 1990s in the EU trade expanded very fast, but services were still less important in terms of overall EU GDP growth. At that time, the EU service sector, which usually fell short of manufactured goods in terms of revenues, had established a common framework of requirements for internal trade purposes. The General Agreement on Trade in Services (GATS) negotiations on financial services, maritime transport and basic telecommunications at that time set the stage for increased market access and robust growth in those sectors a few years later.

In terms of the Uruguay Round, at the time the European Union's commitments included extensive tariff reductions for manufacturers. However, it should also be noted that EU tariffs in a few sensitive sectors did not change appreciably and substantial increases in tariffs remained for textiles and clothing. In 1995 under the European Agreements, textiles and clothing imports from six EU countries were supposed to be fully liberalized on January 1, 1998.

As for agricultural products in the EU in 1995, market access involved high tariffs on meat, dairy products, cereals and tobacco. The WTO report further stated that regulatory disciplines on import-subsidized products to the EU should reduce the adverse effects on world markets in accordance with the WTO dispute settlements. However at the time, third country suppliers relied on tariff obligations to enter the EU markets with sensitive agricultural products such as sugar. In that kind of a situation, the third country exporter of sugar was forced to settle for less than domestic producers due to the pricing mechanisms for agricultural commodities.

Before the creation of the WTO, the EU was extremely aggressive in applying tough penalties through GATT in terms of import dumping into the EU by foreign manufacturers. After January 1995, the newly established WTO ushered in new batch of anti-dumping, countervailing and safeguard regulations relative to WTO provisions with some EU specific extensions. The WTO report further stated that the new WTO agreements defined the multilateral trade framework of the European Union in relation to EU external trade policies and the agreements also allowed for the process of further European integration and cooperation. In the report's conclusion was a comprehensive set of multilateral regulations with the appropriate disciplines under the authority of the WTO. Furthermore, the report ended with a reminder that if the agreements are respected by all of the WTO member-states, this will be a critical step in minimizing frictions between nations and it will also ensure an outward-looking focus so that the European Union and its trading partners can grow and prosper.

In 1994, the European Union economy grew by over 2.5 percent. Most of the EU economy was in recovery mode fighting the ramifications of the 1993 recession.

However, Denmark, the Netherlands, Ireland and the United Kingdom showed consistent growth in spite of the 1993 recession, which had little effect on their respective economies. The underlying stimulus for that growth was a stronger export market in combination with lower interest rates and greater profitability, which increased business confidence. Moreover, merchandise exports in January to August of 1994 grew by a robust 12 percent over the same period in 1993. Basically this was the result of wage moderation, strong productivity growth and the depreciation of some EU member-states' currencies.

Furthermore in 1994, a general pattern of sectoral change, deregulation, internal market integration and technical progress resulted in a rapid expansion in trade services. The EU trade services balance was constantly in a surplus, but it was a few years later that the whole notion of the West becoming a "service economy" was brought into question. The European Union, more so than the United States, realized in the mid-1990s that the whole idea of a service economy for hundreds of millions of people amounted to uncertainty at best.

A very good example is Germany in the 1990s to 2002. In terms of its economy, Germany has always had in place a strategic principle of openness or more specifically a free trade policy. In 2002, Germany's exports amounted to 35.5 percent of its GDP. Most of those exports, 42 percent, went into the euro area and 55 percent were sold to the 15 EU countries (as is today, not all EU member-states were part of the Eurozone); at the time, if the ten new members of the EU were included, that share would have been 64 percent. From the end of World War II, the percentage share of West German exports in its GDP increased steadily from 13.7 percent in 1950 to 18 percent in 1951 followed by 19 percent in 1960.

After the collapse of the Soviet Union, a united Germany posted a slight decline from its 1990 level of 25 percent. In 1993, the percentage share of German exports in its GDP declined to 22.8 percent before erasing that decline and rising again beyond its 1990 level the following year. In 2002, Germany's technology-based industry became the driving force for the bulk of that country's exports amounting to nearly 90 percent. A closer look shows that 59 percent of German exports in 2002 were derived from four industrial sectors: machine building, automobile, chemicals, and electro-technical products; only 10 percent of exports were services (Siebert 2005, 4–6).

In terms of Germany's GDP growth in the 1990s, the first year we have any data on the GDP growth rate of a reunited Germany is 1991. From 1991 to 2000, the annual growth rate for the reunited country stood at modest 1.3 percent, but this is a distortion because the higher growth rate of West Germany in 1990 and the united Germany in 1991 are not included in the data. If we consider the 1990 West German GDP as the base value, the annual GDP growth rate for the time period 1990 to 2000 would come in at around 3 percent per year, but this is also a distorted value. The addition of the East German economy to the German economy is interpreted as growth resulting in a growth rate that is misleading on the high side. However, if we include the West German growth rate in 1991 of 5.1 percent, the growth rate for the period 1990 to 2000 would be roughly 2 percent per year and that would be a number we could live with.

In terms of the institutional framework of the European Union, that was facilitated when the Treaty on European Union aka the Maastricht Treaty took effect on November 1, 1993 resulting in a new measurement to existing policies. The primary objectives of the Treaty were the creation of an economic and monetary union, the establishment of EU foreign policy, the development of common citizenship and a close alignment on justice and home affairs. The Treaty also enhanced the role of the European Parliament's decision-making process relative to all member-states of the EU. In 1994, the European Monetary Institute broke ground in preparation for the European System of Central Banks which was the catalyst for today's European Central Bank (ECB).

With the accession of Austria, Finland and Sweden into the EU on January 1, 1995, these three new member-states added an additional 7 percent to the EU GDP and 6 percent to the total population of the European Union. Their membership didn't create any institutional changes, but the Parliament, Council, Commission and the Court of Justice had to be enlarged to accommodate the 6 percent increase in EU population. From January 1, 1993, the accomplishment of the Single Market included a consolidation in a great many areas of an important stage of integration that substituted common policies of EU member-states for the national policies of each individual nation. This particular internal reform enhanced EU participation in the Uruguay Round. At that point, structural changes in traditional industries were inevitable. In some of the more basic sectors – such as coal, pharmaceuticals, financial services, telecommunications and aviation as well as in export-related policy areas – coordination had continued with virtually no interruptions; and new standards emerged for environmental protections depending on the sector. The EU's Uruguay Round included widespread tariff reduction for manufacturers reducing the average rate by roughly 38 percent to 3.7 percent in 2000 and the elimination of tariffs altogether for products like pharmaceuticals, steel, paper, furniture, toys, soaps and detergents. However, at the end of the Uruguay Round in some of the more "sensitive" sectors which included clothing and passenger cars, tariffs did not change appreciatively.

Under the WTO Agreement, market access commitments on agriculture in the EU involved the conversion of variable levies into tariff equivalents, which resulted in an overall reduction of 36 percent on all tariffs by July 1, 2001. Under the WTO Agreement on textiles and clothing, the EU began phasing out the quantitative restrictions written in the bilateral trade agreements among its member-states. Moreover, the WTO Agreement made it very clear that all restriction had to be eliminated by January 1, 2005. However each member-state participant had some leeway to determine the product mix at each stage of integration. It should also be noted that after the WTO Agreement took effect, the service sector lagged behind developments of goods traded within the EU integration. Legislation in core services areas had progressively established a common framework in terms of minimum requirements for internal trade. In some cases, the EU member-states initiated trade liberalization for certain service sectors, but in other cases, the European Commission resolved those issues.

Since the mid-1990s, there has been a foremost redistribution of market share between emerging and advanced economies and to a certain degree, among the advanced economies themselves. Given the intensity of this highly competitive trading environment, the EU has still managed to hold on to most of its world market share of 19.5 percent for general trade other than energy. With that said, the EU lost 1.3 percent over the period 1900 to 2000, but the market share losses are much greater for the other advanced economies, e.g. the United States and Japan whose world market share declined by 4.4 and 4.1 percentage points respectively in the same time frame.

The EU's key industries are the basic drivers behind the aforementioned percentage data and those industries are: chemicals, pharmaceuticals, automobiles and non-electrical machinery. In fact, the EU's trade balance for manufactured goods has improved significantly between 1990 and 2000 reaching a trade surplus in 2007 of 162 billion euros. However, the increase of 105 billion euros since 2000 helps offset the increase in the cost of energy in the EU which resulted in a trade deficit of 137 billion euros in the same time frame.

In the same time period, the emerging market economies have reinforced their position as the world's global exporters. China is, by far and away, the most remarkable on that subject. Since 1995, China has increased its overall EU market share by almost 100 percent reaching a 14.1 percent EU market share, which means that the United States was no longer the largest exporter into the European Union.

Moreover in the 1990s, the economic performance of the EU compared to the United States was a contrast in terms. The EU had outperformed the US in terms of "upmarket" manufactured exports. This was due primarily by the EU corporations' ability to create global demand for products that sell at premium prices thanks to the EU's ongoing concerted effort to continuously refine its European craftsmanship by producing the highest quality products while artfully promoting its luxury brands.

These upmarket brands accounted for one-third of global demand between 1990 and 2000, which equaled roughly 50 percent of EU exports. However, EU exports were not limited to luxury consumer goods only, but they also included a whole range of products, e.g. intermediary goods, machinery, transport equipment and so on. The European Union's ability to sell products at premium prices was the only way for the EU to maintain its extraordinary levels of social protection, employment and wages for its citizens especially in Western Europe.

From an economic perspective with 18.5 percent of the world market for high-tech products, the European Union became the principal exporter ahead of the US and Japan in the 1990s. However, the EU's performance in this export sector was somewhat disappointing considering that its market share for high-tech products was slightly lower than its overall export market share. On the surface, the EU would've done better with its high-tech exports given its level of development in that sector compared to its overall exports. This distortion could have been a warning signal from global importers raising concerns about the EU's future capacity to produce high-tech products on the cutting edge of quality and innovation – a subject covered extensively in Chapter 12.

Between 1990 and 2000, the EU's overall export performance was imbalanced and varied substantially among destination markets. At the time, the EU lost significant market share in some of the more aggressive emerging markets particularly in Asia. This statistic in itself created an alarming moment among the policymakers in the hierarchy of the European Union as well as the entire EU corporate community (EC 2016, 1). Moreover between 1990 and 2000 in the services sector, the EU was the leading exporter with 26.9 percent of the global market against 19.7 percent for the United States and 6.1 percent for Japan. Moreover in that same time frame, the EU expanded its share of world trade in most broad service categories except transport services in contrast with the downturn developments in the United States in that exact same time period for the exact same sector.

During the aforementioned time frame, the EU also became the world's largest investor in terms of foreign investments owning 33 percent of the world's investment equities. The EU also had a higher ratio of inward and outward investments compared to the United States and the other advanced economies which was an indication that between 1990 and 2000, the EU was comparatively more open to foreign investment and more willing to invest overseas than the other advanced economies including the United States. EU-China trade relations grew steadily in the 1990s. During this period, the structure of traded goods has also changed and an increasing bilateral trade imbalance evolved. This evokes some interesting thoughts. In terms of China's emergence on world markets in relation to the EU, there's no question that China's global aggressiveness has weakened the EU's comparative advantages in competing sectors. Between 1990 and 2000, EU trade with China became increasingly significant. By the end of that decade, Chinese imports ranked first among the EU's main trading partners.

However, in the same time period, China became one of the top five destinations for EU exports. In a global world, trade inflows and outflows change constantly; comparative advantages change and time and again bilateral trade imbalances appear and disappear. Interesting enough, the European Union's trade deficits with other emerging market economies were diminishing or in some cases were completely eliminated in concert with the uptick in trade deficits with China. Consequently, it's important to examine EU trade with China and compare those results with EU trade around the globe.

With the exception of energy, the development of EU bilateral trade with China in the 1990s shows that China was a net importer of natural resources. It should also be noted that EU's trade balance in that sector showed an increasing surplus, but in all other sectors the EU ran a trade deficit with China suggesting that the EU industrial trade structure changed faster than overall EU-China trade. Clearly, there was some sort of a structural adjustment which took place within the Chinese economy in terms of EU-China trade between 1990 and 2000, but that should be the subject of another book. Since the 1990s, Western exporters have always realized the future potential of China's agricultural food market. Naturally as the incomes rise for China's 1.3 billion people, demand for more, higher quality foods will also increase. With only 10 percent of Chinese farm ground that's fertile, there's no way China will ever solve its agricultural food demand even with its recent aggressive purchase of Syngenta in Switzerland. As mentioned earlier, Syngenta is a global agricultural chemical company that specializes in synthetic seeds for enhanced agricultural production. Prior to and after its entrée into the World Trade Organization (WTO), China made a major effort to open its markets for agricultural food products by lowering tariffs, reforming its currency and attempting to create a legal system that satisfies the global definition of a "rule of law". Following its accession into the WTO in 2001, China had to change and clarify its very unusual agricultural import policies.

This part of the chapter examines the EU agricultural food exports to China relative to China's agricultural trade reforms initiated at the onset of its accession into the WTO. China became a major destination for EU agricultural food products. In 2000, exactly one year prior to its accession into the WTO, the EU agricultural food exports to China topped $540 million, representing an increase of 60 percent compared to the EU agricultural food exports to China in 1990. Between 1990 and 2000, EU agricultural food exports to China grew at an average rate of 4.6 percent annually.

China's expanding middle class accounted for this substantial increase in EU agricultural food exports over the ten-year period. The agricultural food product mix remained fairly constant over the decade: barley, rapeseed, meat products, whey, milk powder, beer and wine. Combined, these seven food and alcohol staples accounted for roughly 50 percent of EU agricultural food exports to China in 2000. The breakdown by percentages of EU agricultural food products exported to China in 2000 went accordingly: barley 10.4 percent, rapeseed 8.6 percent, meat products 8.7 percent, whey 7.5 percent, milk powder 2.7 percent, wine 3.9 percent, beer 7.7 percent, beverages 2.7 percent, fish 13.2 percent, vegetable oil 4.1 percent and other agricultural food products 30.3 percent, totaling 584 million euros.

In spite of the surface success of EU agricultural food exports to China between 1990 and 2000, there are some product areas where export issues have come to the forefront such as rapeseed, cereals, dairy and meat products. With these agricultural food products, EU market penetration was obstructed due to China's agricultural policies, which fostered protectionism. China's agricultural protectionism included: unusually high tariffs and non-tariff barriers, e.g. price controls, discriminatory registration requirements and arbitrary sanitary standards. There were other issues that surfaced due to lack of transparency in the Chinese legal system, e.g. the cumbersome licensing and registration procedures. At the time, these specific problems created long delays for the entry of EU agricultural food products into the Chinese market.

Moreover, due to the vast potential of the Chinese agricultural market, the EU went to great lengths in encouraging China to engage in a more open and liberal agricultural policy. In that light, the EU was very supportive in promoting China's accession into the World Trade Organization (WTO). The EU also encouraged the bilateral EU-China Trade Agreement, which was signed in Beijing in May 2000.

This agreement in particular was supposed to mark a major step forward in EU-China trade relations. In 1999, the EU and China created an earlier EU-China Trade Agreement so the implementation of the combined trade agreements (1999 and 2000) literally smoothed the way for China's entrée into the WTO in December 2001. The EU took the position that the two agreements in effect would result in a reduction of tariffs, the elimination quantitative restrictions and the enhancement of Sanitary and Phytosanitary Agreements (abbreviated these agreements are called SPS which concerns the application of food safety and animal and plant health regulations).

Within the context of the WTO negotiations, the Chinese government agreed to constrain tariffs for all agricultural food imports, accept Tariff-Rate Quotas (TRQs) and reduce agricultural tariffs. According to WTO records, this action should have resulted in the constraint of all Chinese agricultural tariffs and all tariff reduction were to be implemented by 2004 – the end of the phase-in time frame for emerging market economies to initiate and comply with their respective Uruguay Round tariff reductions (WTO 2001).

In terms of the priority of EU agricultural food products, the EU was granted an additional tariff reduction on agricultural food products not covered in the two previous bilateral EU-China Trade Agreements. Moreover, the average tariff was slated to drop 31 percent in 1998 to 10.9 percent by January 2004 with even more dramatic reductions in tariffs for specific agricultural foods such as barley, butter, milk powder and oilseeds. EU barley and rapeseed oil were expected to gain the most in terms of tariff reductions on agricultural exports to China. The tariff reduction for EU barley was supposed to drop from 91 percent to 9 percent and for EU rapeseed oil was slated to drop from 85 percent to 9 percent by January 2004. The tariff reductions for meat and dairy products were also scheduled to decline significantly by the same date, e.g. meat products were supposed to drop from 32.5 percent to 15 percent and dairy products were slated to fall from 40 percent to 15 percent. Enhancements were also established on Tariff-Rate Quotas for wine: a decline from 65 percent to 14 percent; wheat gluten a reduction from 30 percent to 18 percent, and olives a decline from 25 percent to 10 percent (Niemi and Niemi 2002, 4).

In terms of non-tariff barriers by China in the WTO negotiations, the Chinese authorities included a major commitment to reduce non-tariff barriers to trade. For exporters into China, non-tariff barriers were always a very complicated, complex procedure, which represented the thrust of China's overall agricultural policy. Three very important non-tariff barriers were import licenses, import quotas and unfair competition with state-owned enterprises. The reader would do well to remember that most non-tariff barriers were implemented within China's overall agricultural policy for the sole purpose of protecting China's domestic agriculture in a concerted effort to uphold robust self-sufficiency in Chinese food grain production.

From 2000 through 2004, China's import quota quantities were slated to increase annually for major agricultural commodities, e.g. corn, wheat, rice, soybean oil and so on. In terms of the so-called "in-quota" tariff rate, the in-quota tariff rate was supposed to decrease significantly, e.g. 1 percent for grain and no more than 10 percent for grain products that are partially processed. Moreover, China agreed in principle to remove quotas on an assortment of oilseeds, oilseed products and oilseed by-products such as corn oil, peanut oil, cottonseed oil, sunflower oil and safflower oil. However after 2004, these import products were scheduled to have a 10 percent tariff. At the same time, China also agreed to enhance the import quota for rapeseed oil. With that said, the European Union was convinced that its oilseeds and oilseed export products to China would grow exponentially post 2004.

While future EU agricultural exports to China appeared to have the greatest potential, the Sino-EU Agreement on China's Accession to the WTO also contained a number of EU export products of significant importance to the bilateral EU-China trading relationship. The following is a brief overview of the most important EU export products into China. In terms of industrial goods, the EU focused on 150 specific products that ranged from building materials to gin. The tariffs fell on average from 18.6 percent to 10.6 percent. Tariffs on all spirits dropped to a level of 10 percent from a top of 65 percent. Tariffs on cosmetic products also declined to 10 percent from 30 percent. In terms of leather products, which account for almost 60 percent of total EU exports in this sector, China agreed to a tariff reduction from 25 percent down to 10 percent. China's textile tariffs were basically the same as textile imports to the EU. Tariffs on EU footwear exports to China were reduced from 25 percent to 10 percent.

As for EU marble/building stones (which by the way are very popular products sold in China), the tariffs were reduced from 25 percent to 10 percent. On ceramics, China agreed to reduce tariffs on 11 key ceramics products from 35 percent to a range between 10 percent and 15 percent. Tariffs on six particular glass products were reduced from 24.5 percent down to 5 percent. Of the 52 particular products in the all- important machinery and appliances sector, which accounts for 26 percent of total EU exports, tariffs were cut from a high of 35 percent to between 5 percent and 10 percent.

In terms of quotas on EU fertilizer exports (NPK), restrictions were lifted upon accession into the WTO. Furthermore, China agreed to liberalize the import monopolies on oil and fertilizer, providing an entry for private traders. Moreover, EU firms were able to buy raw silk directly from Chinese producers (China makes 70 percent of world total) liberalizing China's export monopoly on silk. Furthermore, the EU and China agreed to significant improvements for EU firms that manufacture motor vehicles in China, e.g. removal of joint-venture requirement, restrictions on class and models were lifted and substantial reduction in red tape.

In terms of services, the telecommunications sector was considerably enhanced. China opened its mobile phone market two years ahead of the proposed schedule. China provided seven new licenses for the insurance sector, five for EU life insurance companies and two for EU non-life insurance companies giving the EU a much larger insurance footprint in China. Moreover, China removed the 50-50 joint venture requirement for EU distribution centers in China.

As for the banking sector, EU financial institutions were allowed to provide credit for all motor vehicles rather than just for cars. Furthermore, China and the EU agreed to establish a regulatory dialogue on the development of the securities market in China. Infrastructure construction became open to EU firms operating in China mainly for dredging activities. Other agreements in the services sec-tor between the EU and China that were supposed to benefit the EU included: the tourism sector, construction, legal services, accountancy, architects, market research and "grandfathering". When the Chinese authorities first introduced the "reform and opening-up policy" 30 years ago, unlike the United States, the European Union and China had almost no trading activity. In 1989, the China-European Commission relations were frozen immediately after the Tiananmen Square Massacre. The European Commission imposed harsh sanctions on China that included an arms embargo. Approximately 18 months later, the EU and China began a progressive re-establishment of relations. In June 1992, the European Union and China launched a new bilateral "political" dialogue. In 1993, the European Commission opened an office in Hong Kong.

At that time, both China and the European Union had a very favorable opinion of one another with a sustained belief that there were a few points of significant tension inside the EU-China relationship. Those points were largely outnumbered by the positive aspects of cooperation involved in the EU-China relationship. However over time, concern had grown in Europe over the eco-nomic consequences of China's meteoric rise against the backdrop of China's internal political situation.

In 2006, the European Commission published an article entitled "A Communication on China" (EC 2006) plus a very much related policy paper on trade and investment with China and in China by EU companies, which outlined a number of important concerns. The European political message with respect to China reflected a sober uneasiness, which unfortunately replaced the earlier excitement about the long-term economic effects of China in Brussels. Nonetheless, the EU masked its uneasiness and continued to promote greater economic cooperation between the EU and China with the creation of the EU-China High Level Economic and Trade Dialogue.

From an historical perspective, the EU-China trading relationship got off to a very slow start at the beginning of the 1990s and really didn't take off until after China's accession into the WTO in December 2001. However, the EU has been running a structural trade deficit with China since 1997. At the time, the trade deficit in Chinese manufactured goods with the EU was 26 times greater than the EU trade surplus for services in China. The investment situation reveals a totally different picture. In that area, the EU was well ahead of China. In the early 1990s, the EU member-state companies made significant invest-ments in China. In that time period, EU investment in China far exceeded Chinese investment in the EU. The flow of EU investment has accelerated since the late 1990s, but the share of EU in total FDI in China has decreased in the last decade.

However, European investment in China is still clouded by overt barriers to trade and investment. Intellectual property rights (IPR) protection remains a problem for European businesses in China. Seven in ten European businesses operating in China say that they have been the victim of IPR violations. According to the European Commission, European manufacturers estimated that

IPR theft cost them 20 percent of their potential revenues in China. Almost 60 percent of all counterfeit goods seized at European borders came from China.

European services companies find it very difficult to break into the Chinese market. Since China's entry into the WTO in 2001, the Chinese government has granted 22,000 telecom licenses in China, but only 12 have gone to foreign companies. China maintains a very strict investment and ownership caps in many sectors such as banking, construction and telecommunications.

Foreign law firms in China are not allowed to employ Chinese lawyers and they are not permitted to participate in China's bar exams to gain Chinese qualifications. Also, the public procurement market in China remains very difficult for foreign operators as well as for foreign-owned companies in China to access. The following is yet another example of China's overt protectionism. In 1986, Mastercard issued China's first credit card. At the time of China's entry into the WTO foreign bank cards dominated in China, but shortly thereafter, the Chinese central bank created China UnionPay and then almost instantaneously China's central bank gave China UnionPay a de facto monopoly in terms of the handling of local currency payments between merchants and banks. According to the Nilson Report, "The setback might have been easier to take for foreign companies had the market not grown tenfold to $1.6 trillion" (*The Economist* Dec. 10, 2011). China's economy has grown faster than anyone would have ever thought, but unfortunately, its economic philosophy has not. Since China's entry into the WTO, it's moved further and further away from the organization's guiding principles. China's idea of modernizing its economy is to embrace: state industrial policies, state-owned enterprises and the protection of homegrown national technologies. More often than not, foreign companies operating in China feel that they're not in competition with competitors from the private sector, but rather they're in competition with the Chinese government. All total between China's central and local governments, the Chinese authorities own and operate over 100,000 different companies. By enforcing its own technological standards, China wants to create and promote its own state-owned enterprises, e.g. the 3G mobile phone. These types of interventions and shenanigans violate the spirit if not the letter of the WTO rules regarding free and fair trade. Both America and the EU have recently complained that China had failed to notify the WTO about its 200+ subsidy programs. Time and again, China continues to rack up dumping complaints in the West. By subsidizing its basic industries and selling those subsidized products in the West, it continues to create excess cash flow in dollars and euros which in turn finances its subsidies. And from that perspective the West in essence is financing its own economic demise.

References

The Economist, "China's Economy and the WTO," Hong Kong, December 10, 2011.

European Commission (EC), "European Union, Trade with China," Office of the Directorate-General for Trade, 1995.

European Commission (EC), "European Union, Trade with China," Office of the Directorate-General for Trade, 2006.

European Commission (EC), "EU-China Relations," Brussels, June 22, 2016.

Niemi, Jyrki and Ellen Huan-Niemi, "The Effects of China's Tariff Reductions on EU Agricultural Exports," Paper prepared for presentation at the 10th EAAE Congress, "Exploring Diversity in the European Agri-Food System," Zaragoza, Spain, August 18–31, 2002.

Siebert, Horst, *The German Economy*, Princeton, NJ: Princeton University Press, 2005.

World Trade Organization (WTO), "Report of the Working Party on the Accession of China," October 1, 2001.

12 US trade policies and trade balances with China from 2000

The US-China trade relationship has expanded significantly over the past 30 years. Total US-China trade has gone from $2 billion in 1979 to $599 billion in 2015. Currently, China is the United States' second-largest trading partner; the US' third- largest export market and China is the US' biggest source for imports. Moreover according to the Congressional Research Service (2016), sales of foreign affiliates of US corporations reached $365 billion in 2016.

There are a number of US multinational corporations who argue that participation in the Chinese market is critical for remaining globally competitive. For example between 2010 and 2014, General Motors sold more automobiles in China than it did in the United States. Over the last five years General Motors has made a substantial investment in manufacturing facilities in China. Interestingly, in 2009, the US government bailed out General Motors with $50 billion and when the US government sold its last remaining shares in 2013, it showed a loss of $11.2 billion according to the US Department of the Treasury (Beech April 30, 2014).

Moreover, China is one of the largest holders of US government debt. As of September 2017, China owned roughly $1.26 trillion in US treasury bonds which amounts to roughly 7 percent of the total US debt and that's sizable, but it's hardly the largest holder of US government bonds. The top holder by far is the United States citizens and United States entities such as state and local governments, pension funds, mutual funds and the Federal Reserve Bank which amounts to approximately 67.5 percent the vast majority of total US debt. Foreign nations only hold 32.5 percent of the total and the reader should keep in mind that 80 percent of the world's transactions are denominated in US dollars so it's only prudent for a foreign nation to have a large position in US treasury bonds which are denominated in US dollars.

In spite of the US-China commercial ties, the bilateral trading relationship has become increasingly complex and uneasy. The US-China trading relationship is often rife with anxiety and tension and here recently it has become headline news in the US 2016 presidential election.

Areas of deep concern for US policymakers and US corporations include: China's extremely poor record on intellectual property rights (IPR) enforcement; China's cyber economic espionage; Chinese government discrimination in its innovation policies; an uncertain record on implementing and adhering to WTO obligations; the widespread use of industrial policies to promote and protect industries favored by the Chinese government and that includes Chinese subsidies to state-owned enterprises and investment barriers for foreign corporations and controlling the value of the renminbi through monetary interventionist policies: currency manipulation (Morrison 2015, 2). There are a number of US policymakers who make the case that the above policies negatively impact the economic interests of the United States and they also claim that these policies have been a major contributor to US job losses.

Most recent developments

The seventh round of US-China Strategic and Economic Dialogue was held on June 7–9, 2016 in Beijing. The Dialogue was attended by US Treasury Secretary Jacob Lew and Chinese Vice Premier Wang Yang and the main topics included: exchange rate reforms, improvement of economic transparency, expansion of opportunities for US firms through consumption-led growth, expansion of renminbi trading and clearing capacity in the United States, the creation of a more open, resilient Chinese financial system, and US-China cooperation on global challenges. The United States suspected and later it was confirmed that China had implemented a hidden and discriminatory tax exemption favoring certain Chinese aircraft producers. On December 8, 2015, the US initiated a WTO dispute settlement case against China. At the end of 2017, the above-mentioned dispute settlement case outcome is still undecided.

The Joint Commission on Commerce and Trade (JCCT) is an expansive annual dialogue, usually held in late fall, that addresses commercial and trade issues between the United States and China. The dialogue is co-chaired on the US side by the Secretary of Commerce (currently Secretary Penny Pritzker) and the US Trade Representative (currently Ambassador Michael Froman) and chaired on the Chinese side by the Vice Premier responsible for trade and investment policy (currently Vice Premier Wang Yang). Given the scope of the commercial relationship, other agencies not under the direct jurisdiction of the chairs frequently participate such as the US Department of Agriculture (USDA) and the PRC Ministry of Industry and Technology.

Within the framework of the Joint Commission on Commerce and Trade, the United States and China held talks from November 21 to November 23, 2015. In terms of varieties of US soybeans and corn, China made a firm commitment to increase market access for new biotechnologies to enhance the above two US commodities in China. Furthermore, the US and China agreed to increase cooperation in overall biotechnology innovation and China also agreed to increase intellectual property rights (IPR) for certain US cheese products.

Both the US and China agreed to increase cooperation on food safety measures and expand protection of trade secrets. Moreover, the talks also included a statement from China that it would increase market access for US pharmaceutical products and medical devices. China also claimed that it would implement broad reforms to its anti-monopoly laws. China and the United States agreed to further discussions on China's overcapacity issues of its steel and aluminum industries. Moreover, China claimed that it would implement a semiconductor development plan according to market principles and it would not discriminate against foreign firms. Lastly, China further agreed to allow its banks to purchase information and communication technology (ICT) products according to their own requirements not the Chinese government.

President Obama hosted a state visit for President Xi Jinping in Washington DC in September 2015. The Chinese president visited both Washington DC and the state of Washington. While in Washington DC, the two sides reached mutual agreements on a number of issues, but none more important than cyber security. Both sides agreed that neither United States nor China will knowingly engage in conduct nor support cyber-enabled theft of intellectual property with the intention of providing competitive advantages to its respective domestic and foreign corporations and commercial sectors and this also includes trade secrets or other confidential business information (Mozur and Ewing 2016).

The two presidents also agreed that each country should set up a high-level dialogue mechanism between the two nations to address the whole issue of cybercrime and to improve bilateral communication when cyber-related issues occur. This also included the establishment of a hotline. Business deals were also announced during President Xi's visit. For openers, the Chinese president said that China had placed an order with Boeing Aircraft for 300 airplanes with a value of roughly $38 billion and he also announced a joint venture between Boeing and the Commercial Aircraft Corporation of China to build a completion and delivery center in China.

Furthermore, President Xi announced an agreement by Chinese agricultural distributors to purchase $5.3 billion worth of US soybeans. There were other business deal announcements that were made prior to President Xi's, e.g. Dell Inc. and a consortium of Chinese partners announced that they would invest $125 billion in China over the next five years. In that effort, Dell explained that the investment would unlock the demand for information technology products resulting in $175 billion in trade and would sustain 1 million jobs in China.

On September 16, 2015, a week before the Chinese president's visit, General Electric and China National Machinery Industry Corporation signed a Memorandum of Understanding on promoting African clean energy projects in Beijing. The two companies will join hands with the goal of doubling the population of Africans who have access to electricity mainly in the south of Africa's Sahara Desert. One day later, XpressWest announced a joint venture project with China Railway International (CRI) USA Co., Ltd to build a high-speed train line between Las Vegas, Nevada and Los Angeles, California. Ironically, on June 8, 2016 nine months after announcing that China would help build the high-speed rail line, XpressWest announced that the deal was off. The company said the decision to terminate the relationship with China Railway International was based primarily upon difficulties associated with timely performance and CRI's challenges in obtaining authority to proceed with required development activities. XpressWest indicated that the biggest challenge was a federal government requirement that high-speed trains must be manufactured in the United States to secure regulatory approval.

Moreover, US Trade Representative, Ambassador Michael Froman first became concerned on February 27, 2015 about a Chinese proposed banking regulation that would require high-tech companies to forfeit patented technologies and intellectual property to the Chinese authorities. Along the same lines, President Obama reportedly contacted President Xi on March 2, 2015 and supposedly raised concerns about certain aspects of a proposed Chinese anti-terror law that may oblige high technology companies to surrender encryption keys and install security backdoors in their systems in order to facilitate Chinese government surveillance. A backdoor is a method, often secret, of bypassing normal authentication in a computer system. Backdoors are often used for securing unauthorized remote access to a computer or obtaining access to plaintext in cryptographic systems. When the United States learned that China was using certain standards with respect to providing subsidies contingent on export performance, it initiated yet another dispute settlement case with the World Trade Organization on February 11, 2015.

On February 9, 2015 China's National Development and Reform Commission (NDRC) fined Qualcomm Incorporated $975 million for abusive patent licensing practices and imposed several remedies on the company. This decision is the most severe ever taken in China. According to Allen & Overy (2016), a law firm in China and Hong Kong, the decision is confirmation that China is resolute in its efforts to solve complex, anticompetitive activities. The case provides insight into the authorities' procedures and interpretation of the law and highlights the importance for companies of defending themselves in antitrust probes in China.

US trade with China

In January 1979, the United States and China re-established diplomatic relation and in July of that year both countries signed a bilateral trade agreement followed by a mutual most-favored-nation (MFN) status starting in 1980.[1] In 1979 after the implementation of China's economic reforms, the total amount of US-China trade was $2 billion (exports plus imports). China was ranked as the 23rd largest export market for the United States and China was ranked 45th largest source of imports to the United States. In contrast, US-China bilateral trade in 2015 amounted to $599 billion. China is currently the second largest trading partner after Canada and the third largest US export market and by far the largest source of US imports.

However, US policymakers continuously struggle with US trade deficits with China. The US trade deficit with China went from $10 billion in 1990 to a staggering $347 billion in 2016. Over the past several years, the US trade deficits with China have been substantially higher than with any other US trading partner provoking some in the economic community to make the argument

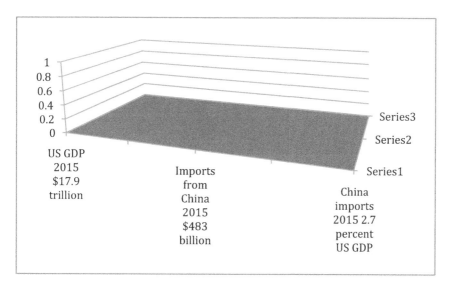

Figure 12.1 US 2015 GDP, China 2016 imports percentage of US GDP 2.7 percent

Source: Author with data from the Federal Reserve Bank of San Francisco, Bureau of Economic Analysis, Bureau of Labor Statistics and the Census Bureau

that the US-China trading relationship is unfair, unbalanced and harmful to the overall US economy.

Figure 12.1 shows that it's not the amount of goods imported from China that's the problem; it's the staggering trade deficit. A further breakdown of the 2015 GDP shows that roughly 85 percent of the US 2015 GDP was the by-product of US goods and services produced from US products. It also shows that approximately 6 percent of the US GDP was US manufactured using partly imported products. Less than 1 percent of US GDP was made in the US from parts imported from China. Final goods imported from other countries amounted to approximately 6+ percent of US GDP (Allen & Overy 2016). Some policy-makers attempt to make the case that due to the fact that China is often the final point of assembly for large export oriented multinational corporations the large trade deficit with China reflects more of a global supply chain. With that said, the US still needs more of a trade balance, not just with China, but also with all of its trading partners. On that very subject, research uncovered a 2009 joint study between the Organisation for Economic Co-operation and Development (OECD) and the WTO which claimed that the US trade deficit with China could be reduced by 25 percent if the bilateral trade flows were measured by the added value created in each country prior to the export of the final product.

In 2015, US exports to China amounted to $116 billion representing a decline from 2014 of roughly $7.7 billion. In 2014, US exports to China amounted to $123.7 billion. During the first six months of 2016, total US exports to China amounted to $51.2 billion. It would be a daunting task to try and estimate the US trade deficit with China for 2016. We can say that the largest month for Chinese imports to the United States is September when the retail outlets gear up for the upcoming holidays.

On the other hand, China was the second largest agricultural export market for the US in 2016 amounting to approximately $25 billion. With that said, China is also a significant market for US services exports which amounted to roughly $42 billion in 2016. In 2016, the top five US exports to China were oilseeds and grains; aircraft and parts; motor vehicles; waste and scrap; semiconductors and other electronic components. From 2005 to 2015, US exports to China increased by approximately 195 percent, which represents the largest growth rate of any of the US export top ten markets. US exports to China for the first six months of 2016 fell by roughly 9.9 percent from 2015 – a poignant indication that as of this writing China's economy is slowing.

China claims that its overall trade policy is intended to increase the opening of its economy to the outside world and to simultaneously introduce foreign technology and know-how and promote economic development that is "mutually beneficial" while developing foreign trade. China's Ministry of Commerce (MOFCOM) is responsible for the design and implementation of the institutional framework for China's trade policies. The MOFCOM works through a consortium of other Chinese ministries, which primarily include the National Development and Reform Commission (NDRC), Ministry of Finance, Agriculture, Transportation and Land and Resources, the National Bureau of Energy, and the Ministry of Industry and Information Technology.

Table 12.1 Total US goods exports to China, 2008–2015

US Billion							
					$120.0 B	$120.7 B	$113.4 B
			$102.2 B	$108.7 B			
		$89.7 B					
$68.4 B	$68.4 B						
2008	2009	2010	2011	2012	2013	2014	2015

Source: Author with data from the US Census Bureau

Top US Goods Export Markets, 2015		*Top US Goods Exports to China, 2015*	
1. Canada	$251 billion	Transportation Equipment	$26 billion
2. Mexico	$228 billion	Computers & Electronics	$17 billion
3. China	$113 billion	Agricultural Products	$15 billion
4. Japan	$59 billion	Chemicals	$13 billion
5. United Kingdom	$49 billion	Machinery	$9 billion

Following China's accession into the WTO in 2001, it was only logical to think that US exports to China would increase dramatically due to reduced tariffs and increased market access. A closer examination of US-China trade data from 2000 to 2015 revealed the following US-China trade patterns: it was true; the US expectation that its exports to China would increase dramatically was highlighted by the fact that US exports to China in that 15-year period quintupled in value, but as dramatic as that increase was, it was dwarfed by the surge in Chinese imports into the United States. The consequence was an ever-expanding US trade deficit with China.

The next trading pattern to surface was underscored by the dramatic rise in the levels of non-manufactured goods exported by US producers to China. These non-manufactured goods included: agricultural products, raw materials and mined natural resource products. Interesting enough in this particular pattern, we actually saw a US trade surplus with China for non-manufactured goods.

The third US-China trading pattern between 2000 and 2015 was a significant increase in imports of manufactured goods from China to the US. This occurred in concert with the significant downturn in US manufactured goods exported to China between 2000 and 2015 as a share of total US exports.

The fourth or final trading pattern to surface was the overall steady climb up the value chain for Chinese imports into the US, e.g. especially in the high-tech sector: computers and consumer electronics. However, the reader should also note that in this category China often serves as an assembly and export platform for multinational corporations. These corporations have components of their products manufactured elsewhere in the world and shipped to China for final assembly. Unfortunately, this kind of economic activity may not have any transparency and it may not be reflected in trade statistics. If China were a force for democracy, rule of law, and responsible governance on the global stage, these patterns would be of lesser concern for the United States. To be fair in an effort to contribute to global peace, China has undertaken some action in terms of anti-piracy patrols, peacekeeping operations, humanitarian assistance and disaster relief efforts, but at the same time, China's willingness to empower corrupt elites in other countries undermines good governance and human rights. Meanwhile, Beijing continues to undermine the autonomy of Hong Kong and use incentives and intimidation to draw Taiwan closer to the Mainland (MOFCOM 2016).

Unfortunately, the expected reforms that were supposed to take place when President Xi came into power have obviously not come to fruition. This conclusion is supported by his government's activities which include resorting to old economic advantages such as government subsidies for favored industries, currency manipulation, and overinvestment in fixed manufacturing assets of China's state-owned enterprises resulting in overcapacity and constant and excessive intervention in the global financial system. The Chinese authorities continue to violate WTO rules in a national effort to avoid short-term domestic unemployment and retain popular support. Other major concerns by the global economic community include: China's very aggressive military buildup in the South China Sea and its recent intensive crackdown on dissidents and journalists. Needless to say, this is a very significant concern by the other Asian countries and the result is increased doubts about China's "real" intentions now that China is major player on the global stage.

In spite of a 7 percent annualized growth rate for the first six months of 2015, that year the Chinese economy suffered some very significant downturns plus it was subjected to a number of mismanaged government interventions which took its toll on the intricate workings of China's overall economy. The Chinese authorities have acknowledged that China needs to develop a model that emphasizes a much stronger consumer economy, but that is not going to be easy. For the past three decades China's economy was driven by high levels of investment in export-oriented manufacturing capacity and infrastructure.

In addressing this structural imbalance, President Xi presented a sweeping economic reform agenda in 2013 at the Third Plenary Session of the 18th Chinese Communist Party Central Committee. However in 2015, the Chinese government's response to definite signs of economic weakness and a sharp reduction in global exports resulted in rolling back some reforms and resorting to its old stimulus measures to prop up GDP growth targets. In an effort to take control of a tanking stock market, the Chinese government intervened with increased rules on short selling and selling periods and at the same time, the government devalued the renminbi in an attempt to increase Chinese exports by making them cheaper.

By mid-June 2015 and after a swift climb in the first half of 2015, the Shanghai Stock Exchange stock values declined by almost $4 trillion. Given the stock market's importance as an economic indicator, the Chinese authorities responded in a very heavy handed manner: the government ordered brokerage houses to buy shares; it forbid large shareholders to sell their shares; the Chinese authorities sent in the police to root out "malicious" sellers; the Chinese government literally ordered state-owned enterprises and pension funds to immediately invest in the stock market and it halted trading in many companies. Moreover, the government also censored any negative information and it arrested journalists for focusing on bad news and it put out a general warning to all of its citizens about spreading "rumors" about the stock market massacre.

From the US' perspective, the US-China bilateral relationship continues to be troubled about Beijing's blatant failure to uphold its WTO commitments and its unfair treatment of US companies investing in or exporting to China. As we discussed earlier, the US trade deficit with China is a growing concern for US policymakers and it continues to sour the US-China bilateral trade agreement. In August 2014 in a surprise move, the Chinese government once again devalued the renminbi and of course that set off a flurry of concern by a number of US policymakers that this was another attempt by the Chinese authorities to increase its exports by making them cheaper through currency manipulation.

China's most recent devaluation came at a time when China had an all-out effort to promote a much greater international role for the renminbi which included making the renminbi one of the reserve currencies authorized by the International Monetary Fund (IMF). China wants its currency to be internationalized so that the renminbi becomes denominated in global transactions, but China has made it a practice to limit its currency's convertibility and it also limits the renminbi's exposure to global currency markets.

All of these Chinese interventions whether they are in its stock market or its currency valuation come at the expense of China's credibility in the global economy. As of this writing there are any number of global policymakers who question China's ability to successfully manage its economy. In terms of China's intervention into its stock market slide in 2015 that effort still failed to really stop the sell-off and stabilize the economy, but the worst of it was that it undermined public confidence in China's ability to manage a fair and orderly market.

Moreover, China moved the renminbi to a managed float roughly ten years ago, but the Chinese government continues to intervene in the foreign exchange markets. In an effort to place its renminbi into the IMF's Special Drawing Rights (SDR) basket of reserve currencies, the Chinese authorities prevented its currency from depreciating in the first six months of 2015. However, on August 11 the People's Bank of China devalued the renminbi sending a clear signal to the global economic community that China's economic slowdown was becoming more and more deep-rooted.

The US government's efforts to reduce systemic tension within the US-China bilateral trading relationship through constructive bilateral dialogue have produced very little results. With that said, some progress on mutual environmental and financial issues was accomplished within the framework of the latest 2015 Strategic and Economic Dialogue, but unfortunately, the dialogue came to a halt in addressing fundamental strategic and economic issues, e.g. anti-corruption cooperation, cybersecurity, and the ongoing investment barriers for foreign corporations in most industries operating in China. When President Xi visited the United States in September 2015, he and President Obama discussed several issues of primary concern including cyber espionage by Chinese actors, but nothing of any real substance ever materialized. China continued to press its case by denying any involvement in commercial cyber theft along with its half-hearted commitments to work together and enhance cooperation on issues of climate change.

China repeatedly comes under extreme US criticism on its inability to adhere to WTO principles. In the most recent confrontation (February 2016), the Office of the US Trade Representative faulted China over its ever-expanding program that provides export subsidies that the World Trade Organization considers illegal to businesses in seven critical industries: advanced materials and metals, textiles, specialty chemicals, light industry, hardware and building materials, medical products and agriculture. Moreover, in 2015–2016 China launched two new development banks: the Asian Infrastructure Bank and the New Development Bank in response to the very established World Bank. A closer look at the business models of these two banks reveals a secondary and a primary reason for China's establishment of the two development banks: from a secondary perspective, these two banks will increase China's economy by creating export opportunities for its companies and from a primary perspective, in terms of the mission of both banks, it's readily apparent that the new banks will serve as a catalyst to extend China's role in the global economic order of their liking.

Foreign investment conditions in China

According to the OECD, China maintains the most restrictive foreign investment regime among all the OECD and G20 countries. In addition to over 1,000 rules and regulatory documents related to foreign direct investment (FDI) and issued by the Chinese central government, the US Department of State claims that local governments and local legislatures also enact their own restrictive rules and regulations on foreign investments within their jurisdictions. The Chinese government engages in a very sophisticated system of identifying inbound FDI that will help facilitate specific industrial policy goals which are, for the most part, designed to strengthen the development of domestic industries and the creation of national economic treasures by identifying different industries as desirable for or restricted from foreign investment within the context of China's joint venture regime. All total, Chinese laws, regulations and rules pertinent to foreign investment combined with the ongoing government favoritism for state-owned enterprises in competition with private sector foreign corporations create a complex, opaque and adverse business environment for foreign investors.

Due to the never-ending stream of strenuous laws, regulations and rules in China, foreign investment interest in China is waning to the point of deterioration. With that said, most American firms operating in China still consider it a profitable market, but on the whole, they're much less optimistic about increasing future foreign direct investment. In sectors where China's blatant favoritism towards domestic competition is interwoven into its industrial policies, it should come as no surprise that these are the exact same sectors where foreign corporations feel the least welcome.

Western corporations operating in China continue to cite the same problems over and over again: the lack of market access in certain sectors and market access conditions in terms of the transfer of technology and/or know-how. China employs a Foreign Investment Catalogue, which specifies its national-level market access restrictions. This quandary is exacerbated even further by local governments who frequently employ regional or industry-specific catalogues. In 2016, China released an updated version of its Foreign Investment Catalogue, which reduced the number of sectors where foreign investment is encouraged. In these sectors, foreign investment is either severely restricted or prohibited altogether. These are industries that the Chinese government has historically nurtured wishing to create its next "national champion" such as automobiles and health care.

With a legal system that does the personal bidding of the Chinese Communist Party combined with very convoluted, complex national rule-making procedures,

US corporations operating in China have virtually no legal recourse to protect their rights or to resolve corporate disputes. Moreover, it's almost impossible to estimate the complete impact of China's investment barriers on US foreign direct investment flows in China; it's very difficult to quantify an unknown quantity except to say that it would be very large. Market access is just part of the problem for US companies operating in China. Foreign corporations constantly voice grave concerns about discretionary, opaque legal and regulatory interpretation and or inconsistent enforcement on the part of Chinese law enforcement and the Chinese judicial system in general. Furthermore in recent years, a broad range of range of new regulatory decisions seems to have disproportionally focused on foreign corporations currently operating in China.

In 2013 and 2014, the Chinese authorities increased enforcement of China's Anti-Monopoly Law (AML) and in so doing, China singled out very high profile foreign multinational corporations, e.g. General Electric, Procter & Gamble, IBM and so on. The US Chamber of Commerce makes the case that Chinese regulatory and enforcement agencies have used the law to facilitate industrial policy objectives. The Chamber further claims that the Chinese authorities use the threat of investigations against foreign firms to control price and supply of goods to benefit Chinese market participants. US corporations in China continuously make the case that Chinese market enforcement activities include non-market factors which include Chinese industrial policy. These companies further claim that Chinese market enforcement lacks due process and regulatory transparency; and the entire Chinese enforcement system relies on legal language that is more than ambiguous and open to a broad selection of discretionary interpretations. A very good case in point occurred in September 2015. A total of 26 transactions were either rejected or conditionally approved by China's Ministry of Commerce (MOFCOM). This particular ministry reviews proposed mergers and acquisitions for effects involved in unfair competition. All of the proposed 26 transactions involved foreign corporations. Along the same lines, the National Development and Reform Commission (NDRC), which is China's price-related AML enforcement agency disproportionately enforced the anti-monopoly law against foreign corporations in a blatant effort to achieve industrial policy objectives. None of the NDRC's enforcement activities had anything to do with the protection of competition. At this point, US corporations operating in China are extremely concerned about intellectual property rights (IPR). They claim the Chinese authorities use the threat of AML investigations in a concerted effort to reduce licensing fees of certain foreign technologies to Chinese companies. This results in a competitive advantage for China's domestic corporations in both domestic and global markets. Under a Chinese 2015 law, the State Administration for Industry and Commerce can literally force foreign corporations operating in China to license their patents to domestic corporations under unfavorable and/or unfair conditions.

Moreover, there is absolutely no transparency in the above-mentioned law. Overall, it lacks the specific and objective criteria normally required in IP licensing and consequently, foreign corporations are unable to predict reliably whether a refusal to grant a license to a domestic corporation would constitute a violation of China's Anti-Monopoly Law (AML). Furthermore in 2015, the Chinese authorities issued a statement claiming that the Chinese government will enact new legislation for foreign investment no earlier than January 2016, but as of this writing, only a rough draft has materialized. These new revisions to China's Foreign Investment Law are designed specifically to boost its service sector. The new revisions are expected to be submitted to the National People's Congress in November 2016.

After taking a look at the rough draft, it appears that this is just another fabricated attempt at putting on the appearance of initiating foreign investment reforms in its service sector and high-tech manufacturing sector. At this point in time, both China's service sector and its high-tech manufacturing sector are in need of Western technology. These new so-called foreign investment reforms are more of the same: a facade combined with a national agenda that facilitates China's latest industrial policy. Nothing productive will take place in China for US corporations until China resolves its core problems pertinent to: the rule of law, intellectual property rights, international patent rights, international copyrights, human rights and the establishment of a fair and orderly stock market. China's brand of capitalism is nothing more than communism combined with Western technology.

Note

1 The United States (USCMFN 1980) suspended China's MFN status in 1951, which cut off most bilateral trade. China's MFN status was conditionally restored in 1980 under the provisions set forth under Title IV of the 1974 Trade Act, as amended (including the Jackson-Vanik freedom-of-emigration provisions). China's MFN status (which was redesigned under US trade law as "normal trade relations" status or NTR was renewed on an annual basis until January 2002 when permanent NTR was extended to China after it joined the WTO in December 2001.

References

Allen & Overy, "China's New Restrictions on Outbound Investments and Remittance," New York, NY, December 30, 2016.

Beech, Eric, "US government says it lost $11.2 billion on GM bailout," Reuters News Service, April 30, 2014.

Congressional Research Service 2016 (CRS).

Ministry of Finance and Commerce (MOFCOM), the People's Republic of China, "Report to Congress of the US-China Economic and Security Review Commission," 2016.

Morrison, Wayne M., "China-US Trade Issues," Congressional Research Service, December 15, 2015.

Mozur, Paul and Jack Ewing, "Rush of Chinese Investment in Europe's High-Tech Firms Is Raising Eyebrows," *The New York Times*, September 16, 2016.

OECD/WTO Trade in Value-Added (TIVA) Database: China, available at www.oecd.org/sti/ind/TiVA%20China.pdf.

Office of the United States Trade Representative (USTR), Executive Office of the President, 2014.
US Bureau of Economic Analysis (USBEA), "International Transactions," 2016.
The US-China Business Council, "Joint Commission on Commerce and Trade (JCCT)," April 19, 2016.
US-China Strategic Economic Dialogue 2016.
World Trade Organization (WTO), Geneva, Switzerland, 2015.

13 EU trade policies and trade balances with China from 2000

Having established official diplomatic relations in 1975, the European Union and China have created two of the three largest economies in the world in 2016. Over the years, the EU and China have tried to forge a deep and comprehensive partnership, but there have been times when that has become strained. Under the banner of the annual EU-China Summit, the EU and China have engaged in over 60 substantive and sectoral dialogues. Moreover in 2013, the EU-China 2020 Agenda for Cooperation was adopted. This particular agenda is the highest-level joint document of the EU-China relationship. It is basically a broad-based effort for bilateral cooperation in the areas of peace, prosperity, sustainable development and people-to-people exchanges.

On June 22, 2016 the High Representative of China and the European Commission adopted the Joint Communication on elements for a new EU strategy on China. This strategy ambitiously outlines how both the EU and China can take advantage of these economic openings in order to provide and promote the long-term economic benefits for citizens of both countries. A lot has changed for both the EU and China since the establishment of diplomatic relations in the mid-1970s. China's transformation from an economy that struggled to feed its people to a major industrial powerhouse is unprecedented in the annals of economic history. This transformation not only changed the country internally, but also it propelled China to a major player on the international economic stage.

Today, the EU and China are major trading partners. Trade in goods and services between the EU and China averages over 1.5 billion euros per day. In 2016, EU exports to China totaled 170 billion euros and China imports to the EU amounted to over 350 billion euros, creating an EU trade deficit with China of roughly 180 billion euros. While that number is not as large as the US trade deficit with China of $367 billion for 2016, it would be fair to claim that the EU is a very good customer of China.

Figure 13.1 shows that China's imports to the EU were much larger than EU exports to China. In fact, EU exports to China never reached a value of over 100 billion euros until around 2010. Figure 13.1 emphasizes the first half of 2016 because that was the point where the value of EU exports to China reached over 150 billion euros, but within the same time frame the gap between EU exports to

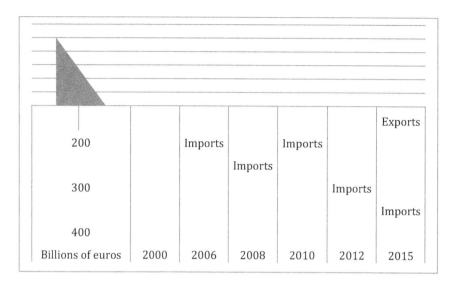

| Billions of euros | 2000 | 2006 | 2008 | 2010 | 2012 | 2015 |

Figure 13.1 EU trade deficits with China, 2000–2016
Source: Author

China and Chinese imports to the EU had widened considerably. The EU works together with China on key issues of mutual interest through their annual High-Level Economic and Trade Dialogue. In this setting, the EU and China discuss in elaborate detail their mutual interest in the key issues of investment, services, procurement and intellectual property rights. Another area of acute interest for the EU is the actual progress completed in China's announced economic reform program. The EU is particularly interested in those reforms that will enhance and facilitate more of a free market in the Chinese marketplace, e.g. a level playing field. The same issues exist with China for the EU that are equally problematic for the United States: capacity developments within its basic industries, government policies and support measures in overcapacity sectors such as steel. The High-Level Economic and Trade Dialogue is calling for a global forum on steel which will analyze in depth the international steel industry's global restructuring. At least this effort would give China the opportunity to admit that it has an overcapacity problem within its steel industry.

In terms of foreign direct invest (FDI) to China the European Union is in the top five countries that provide foreign investment to China. In 2014, the EU accounted for approximately 16 percent of all foreign investment into China. That percentage is a paltry 4.5 percent of the total EU FDI outflows. Consequently, there's room for much more, but given China's problematic and opaque laws, regulations and rules, it's doubtful that will happen. On the other hand, China's investment into the EU has grown dramatically over the last decade. In 2014, Chinese FDI outflows to the European Union totaled over 12.1 billion. And in

2016, China's total FDI outflows to the EU represented 19 percent of all FDI in the EU making the EU one of the most important destinations for Chinese FDI. As of this writing, negotiations are underway for the Comprehensive Agreement on Investment between the EU and China, which is supposed to improve protection of investments, market access and the overall investment climate for EU investors in China and Chinese investors in the EU.

As for the 17th annual EU-China Summit, both the EU and China expressed a very strong interest in each country's major investment initiatives, mainly the Investment Plan for Europe and China's "One Belt, One Road" initiative. In 2016, the EU and China agreed on an increase in connectivity between the EU and Asia. To that end, both countries established the EU-China Connectivity Platform, which promotes increased cooperation in infrastructure financing, logistics and an increase in maritime and rail links across the Eurasian continent.

On the surface, both the EU and China claim that strengthening innovation and research cooperation plays a big part in the EU-China economic relationship. Along those lines, the EU and China have drawn-out plans to ensure reciprocal access to each other's research and innovation funding programs. This effort in particular will be underscored in the development of co-funding mechanisms and primary initiatives relative to the EU's Horizon 2020. The idea behind Horizons 2020 is to promote long-term joint research and innovation partnerships with various nations in strategic areas of common interest. Horizon 2020 is the biggest EU research and innovation program ever with nearly 80 billion euros of funding available over a seven-year period (2014–2020). This amount is in addition to the private investment this money will attract. Horizon 2020 promises more breakthroughs, discoveries and world firsts by taking great ideas from the lab to the market. Seen as a means to drive economic growth and create jobs, Horizon 2020 has the political backing of Europe's leaders and members of the European Parliament. They agreed that research is an investment in the EU's future and consequently they put it at the heart of the EU's blueprint for smart, sustainable economic growth, which will create jobs.

The European Union has made a major commitment to promote human rights around the globe and it constantly articulates worries over the human rights issues in China. In a concerted effort to promote human rights and foster the rule of law in a civil society, the EU and its nation-states intend to work with China to explain the national benefits accrued in the promotion of human rights and the establishment of the rule of law. To that end, the EU-China Human Rights Dialogue is held on an annual basis. The Dialogue is attended by high-ranking officials of both the EU and China.

As discussed earlier, the EU and China are very large trading partners and along those lines, they both have a vested interest in each other's market. Even after the 2008 financial crisis, the EU remained a very large market for Chinese manufactured goods, but the EU corporations operating in China have to do better in terms of the goods they sell and the services they supply. In terms of China's trading relationship with the EU, the EU is the perfect counterbalance to the US market. With that said, it certainly would not be an exaggeration to make the argument that China's stellar economic rise since it first entered the World Trade Organization in 2001would have been severely stunted if not for its lopsided trading relationships with the European Union and the United States which provided China with over $500 billion in free cash flow in 2015.

According to the European Commission, in 2015 total trade between the EU and China amounted to almost 521 billion euros: Chinese imports to the EU amounted to roughly 350 billion euros and EU exports to China totaled 170 billion euros which gives us an US-China import-export ratio of over 2 to 1. In other words, for every 1 euro of goods and services exported to China from the EU, the EU buys 2 euros of goods and services imported from China.

The following datasets were provided by the European Commission, the office of the Directorate-General for Trade in conjunction with SITC (Standard International Trade Classification) and the HS (Harmonized System). In terms of Chinese imports to the EU in 2015, the product mix consists of agricultural products (WTO Agreement on Agriculture) with a market value of 5.1 billion euros; fishery products with a market value of 1.6 billion euros and industrial products with a market value of 343.6 billion euros; total Chinese imports into the European Union in 2015 amounted to 350.4 billion euros. In terms of EU exports to China in 2015, the product mix consists of agricultural products (WTO Agreement on Agriculture) with a market value of 10.3 billion; fishery products with a market value of 422 million euros and industrial products with a market value of 159.6 billion euros; total EU exports into China in 2015 amounted to 170.3 billion euros.

The SITC (Standard International Trade Classification) product groups for Chinese imports into the EU for 2016 were: Primary Products with a market value of 10.7 billion euros representing 3 percent of the total; Manufacturers with a market value of 338.4 billion euros representing 96.6 percent of the total; Other Products with a market value of 635 million euros representing 0.2 percent of the total and other with a market value of 732 million euros representing 0.2 percent of the total. The Standard International Trade Classification (SITC) is a classification of goods used to classify the exports and imports of a country to enable comparing different countries and years. The classification system is maintained by the United Nations. Currently, the SITC classification is at revision four, which was promulgated in 2006. The SITC is recommended only for analytical purposes. Trade statistics are recommended to be collected and compiled in the Harmonized System (HS).

The SITC product groups for EU exports into China for 2015 were: Primary Products with a market value of 22.2 billion representing 13.1 percent of the total; Manufacturers with a market value of 136.1 billion euros representing 79.9 percent of the total; Other Products with a market value of 10.3 billion representing 6.1 percent of the total and other with a market value of roughly 1.6 billion euros representing 0.9 percent of the total. In terms of the Harmonized Commodity Description and Coding System or also known as the Harmonized System (HS) of tariff nomenclature is an internationally standardized system of names and numbers to classify traded products. It came into effect in 1988 and has since been developed and maintained by the World Custom Organization (WCO) an independent intergovernmental organization based in Brussels, Belgium with over 200 member countries.

The top five HS sections with product numbers for imports from China into the EU for 2015 were: machinery and appliances XVI with a market value of 169.6 billion euros representing 48.4 percent of the total; textiles and textile articles XI with a market value of 39.6 billion euros representing 11.3 percent of the total; miscellaneous manufactured articles XX with a market value of 32.3 billion euros representing 9.2 percent of the total; base metals and articles thereof with a market value of 23.4 billion euros representing 6.7 percent of the total and products of the chemical or allied industries VI with a market value of 14.7 billion representing 4.2 percent of the total.

The top five HS sections with product numbers for exports from the EU into China were: machinery and appliances XVI with a market value of 50.7 billion euros representing 29.8 percent of the total; transport equipment XVII with a market value of 38.1 billion euros representing 22.4 percent of the total; products of the chemical or allied industries VI with a market value of 16.7 billion euros representing 9.9 percent of the total; base metals and articles thereof XV with a market value of 10.5 billion euros representing 6.2 percent of the total and optical and photographic instruments, etc. XVIII with a market value of 10.3 billion representing 6.1 percent of the total.

The top five SITC sections with product numbers for imports from China into the EU for 2015 were: machinery and transport equipment (7) with a market value of 175.6 billion euros representing 50.1 percent of the total; miscellaneous manufactured articles (8) with a market value of 103.7 billion representing 29.6 percent of the total; manufactured goods classified chiefly by material (6) with a market value of 43.3 billion euros representing 12.9 percent of the total; chemicals and related products (5) with a market value of 16.2 billion representing 4.6 percent of the total and food and live animals (0) with a market value of 4.6 billion euros representing 1.3 percent of the total.

The top five SITC sections with product numbers for exports from the EU into China for 2015 were: machinery and transport equipment (7) with a market value of 89.3 billion euros representing 52.4 percent of the total; chemicals and related products (5) with a market value of 21.1 billion euros representing 12.4 percent of the total; miscellaneous manufactured articles (8) with a market value of 14.8 billion euros representing 8.7 percent of the total; manufactured goods classified chiefly by material (6) with a market value of 13.3 billion euros representing 7.9 percent of the total and commodities and transactions (9) with a market value of 10.3 billion euros representing 6.1 percent of the total.

Total goods: EU-China trade flows and balance 2005–2016

Beginning in 2005, imports from China into the European Union amounted to 161.0 billion euros and exports from the EU to China totaled 51.7 billion euros creating a 109.2 billion euros EU trade deficit with China. In 2006, imports from China to the EU amounted to 195.8 billion euros representing a 21.6 percent increase over 2005. Exports from the EU to China totaled 63.6 billion euros representing a 23.1 percent increase over 2005 creating a 132.1 billion euros EU trade deficit with China. In 2007, imports from China to the EU amounted to 233.8 billion euros representing 19.4 percent increase over 2006. Exports from the EU to China totaled 71.8 billion euros representing 12.8 percent increase over 2006 creating a 162.0 billion trade EU trade deficit with China.

In 2008, imports from China into the EU amounted to 249.1 billion euros representing a 6.5 percent increase over 2007. Exports from the EU to China totaled 78.3 billion euros representing a 9 percent increase over 2007 creating a 170.8 billion euros EU trade deficit with China. In 2009, imports from China to the EU amounted to 215.2 billion representing a decrease of 13.6 percent over 2008. Exports from the EU to China totaled 82.4 billion euros representing a 5.3 percent increase over 2008 creating 132.8 billion euros EU trade deficit with China. In 2010, imports from China to the EU amounted to 283.9 billion euros representing a staggering increase of 31.9 percent over 2009. Exports from the EU to China totaled 113.4 billion euros representing a whopping 37.7 percent increase over 2009 creating a 170.4 billion euros EU trade deficit with China.

In 2011, imports from China to the EU amounted to 295.0 billion euros representing a 3.9 percent increase over 2010. Exports from the EU to China totaled 136.4 billion euros representing a 20.2 percent increase over 2010 creating 158.6 billion euros EU trade deficit with China. In 2012, imports from China to the EU amounted to 292.1 billion euros representing a decrease of 1 percent over 2011. Exports from the EU to China totaled 144.2 billion euros representing a 5.7 percent increase over 2011 creating a 147.9 billion euros EU trade deficit with China. In 2013, imports from China to the EU amounted to 280.1 billion euros representing a 4.1 percent decrease over 2012 and exports from the EU to China totaled 148.1 billion euros representing a 2.7 percent increase over 2012 creating 131.9 billion euros EU trade deficit with China. In 2014, imports from China to the EU amounted to 302.1 billion euros representing a 7.9 percent increase over 2013. Exports from the EU to China totaled 164.6 billion euros representing a 11.1 percent increase over 2013 creating a 137.5 EU trade deficit with China. In 2015, imports from China to the EU amounted to 350.4 billion euros representing a 16 percent increase over 2014. Exports from the EU to China totaled 170.3 billion euros representing a 3.5 percent increase over 2014 creating a 180.0 billion euros EU trade deficit with China.

Earlier in this chapter, the difference between the Standard International Trade Classification (SITC) and the Harmonized System (HS) were explained. The reasons behind this are analysis and statistical examination. Not only is it important to realize the monetary value of the imports and exports traded between the European Union and China, but also, it's equally important for us to know which products account for the import and export trade between the EU and China. This provides a better understanding of the product production climate of each relative to the employment trends in specific industries in both the EU and China.

Trade flows by STIC section 2015–2016

In 2015–2016, food and live animals (0) imports from China to the EU amounted to 4.6 billion euros representing 1.3 percent of the total and food and live animals (0) exports from the EU to China amounted to 6.3 billion euros representing 3.7 percent of the total. Beverages and tobacco (1) imports from China to the EU amounted to 134 million euros representing 0 percent of the total and beverages and tobacco (1) exports from the EU to China totaled 1.7 billion euros representing 1 percent of the total. Crude materials, inedible, except fuels (2) imports from China to the EU amounted 2.8 billion euros representing 0.8 percent of the total and crude materials, inedible, except fuels (2) exports from the EU to China totaled 9.5 billion euros representing 5.6 percent of the total. Also in 2015–2016, mineral fuels, lubricants and related materials (3) imports from China to the EU amounted to 410 million euros representing 0.1 percent of the total and mineral fuels, lubricants and related materials (3) exports from the EU to China totaled 1.9 billion euros representing 1.2 percent of the total. Animal and vegetable oils, fats and waxes (4) imports from China to the EU amounted to 94 million euros representing 0 percent of the total and animal and vegetable oils, fats and waxes (4) exports from the EU to China totaled 271 million euros representing 0.2 percent of the total. Chemical and related products (5) imports from China to the EU amounted to 16.2 billion euros representing 4.6 percent of the total and chemical and related products (5) exports from the EU to China totaled 21.1 billion euros representing 12.4 percent of the total.

Moreover in 2015–2016, manufactured goods classified chiefly by material (6) imports from China to the EU amounted to 45.3 billion euros representing 12.9 percent of the total and manufactured goods chiefly by material (6) exports from the EU to China totaled 13.3 billion euros representing 7.9 percent of the total. Machinery and transport equipment (7) imports from China to the EU amounted to 175.6 billion euros representing 50.1 percent of the total and machinery and transport equipment (7) exports from the EU to China totaled 89.3 billion euros representing 52.4 percent of the total.

Furthermore in 2015–2016, miscellaneous and manufactured articles (8) imports from China to the EU amounted to 103.7 billion euros representing 29.6 percent of the total and miscellaneous and manufactured articles (8) exports from the EU to China totaled 14.8 billion euros representing 8.7 percent of the total. Commodities and transactions (9) imports from China to the EU amounted to 581 million representing 0.2 percent of the total and commodities and transactions (9) exports from the EU to China totaled 10.3 billion euros representing 6.1 percent of the total. Other imports from China to the EU amounted to 732 million euros representing 0.2 percent of the total. Other exports from the EU to China totaled 1.6 billion euros representing 0.9 percent of the total. The total imports from China to the EU amounted to 350.4 billion euros for 2015 and total exports from the EU to China totaled 170.3 billion euros. The total amount of EU-China trade for 2015 was 520.7 billion euros and that number was basically divided into four product groups: Primary Products and Manufactured Products are by far and away the largest. The other two groups are Other Products and Other. Other Products and Other are basically a "catch-all" for products and services that aren't classified.

The Primary Products groups amounts to 3 percent of the total on the EU imports side and 13.1 of the total on the EU exports side. Manufactured Products group amounts to a staggering 96.6 percent of the total on the EU imports side and 79.9 percent of the total on the EU exports side. Other Products group amounts to 0.2 percent of the total on the EU imports side and 6.1 percent of the total on the EU exports side. The Other group amounts to 0.2 percent of the total on the EU imports side and 0.9 percent of the total on the EU exports side.

The Primary Products group includes: agricultural products, food including fish, raw materials, fuels and mining products, ores and other minerals, petroleum and petroleum products and non-ferrous metals. The Manufactured Products group includes: iron and steel, chemicals, pharmaceuticals, other semi-manufactured products, machinery and transport equipment, office and telecommunication equipment, integrated circuits and electronic components, transport equipment, automobiles, automotive products, other machinery, power generating machinery, non-electrical machinery, electrical machinery, textiles, clothing, and other manufactured products which includes scientific and controlling instruments.

The Other Products group and the Other group are extremely small compared to the Primary Products group and the Manufactured Products group and as previously mentioned these two groups are more of a "catch all" for products that are produced on a very small scale. Consequently, they fall off the radar and don't have a Standard International Trade Classification.

Trade flows by SITC section 2012–2014

At this point, we need a brief historical perspective of the EU-China trade. If we go back three years to 2012, we'll have a much better understanding of the dramatic growth that took place in the EU-China trade. In 2012, the total imports from China to the EU amounted to 292.1 billion euros and total exports from the EU to China totaled 144.2 billion euros. The total amount of EU-China trade for 2012 was 436.3 billion euros.

In 2012, food and live animals (0) imports from China to the EU had a monetary value of 4.1 billion euros and exports from the EU to China in this classification amounted to 2.8 billion euros. Beverages and tobacco (1) imports from China to the EU amounted to 160 million euros and exports from the EU to China in this classification totaled 1.5 billion. Crude materials, inedible except fuels (2) imports from China to the EU totaled 2.8 billion euros and exports from the EU to China in this classification amounted to 9.8 billion euros.

Also in 2012, mineral fuels, lubricants and related materials (3) imports from China to the EU had a monetary value of 315 million euros and exports from the

EU to China in this classification totaled 1.9 billion euros. Animal and vegetable oils, fats and waxes (4) imports from China to the EU amounted to 74 million euros and exports from the EU to China in this classification had a monetary value of 182 million euros. Chemicals and related products (5) imports from China to the EU totaled 13.0 billion euros and exports from the EU to China in this classification amounted to 16.8 billion euros. Moreover in 2012, manufactured goods chiefly by material (6) imports from China to the EU had a monetary value of 36.1 billion euros and exports from the EU to China in this classification amounted to 13.7 billion euros. Machinery and transport equipment (7) imports from China to the EU totaled 146.1 billion and exports from the EU to China in this classification amounted to 84.4 billion euros. Furthermore in 2012, miscellaneous and manufactured articles (8) imports from China to the EU had a monetary value of 87.9 billion euros and exports from the EU to China in this classification amounted to 11.0 billion euros. Commodities and transactions (9) imports from China to the EU totaled 753 million and exports from the EU to China in this classification had a monetary value of 1.1 billion euros. Other products imports from China to the EU amounted to 427 million and exports from the EU to China in this unclassified product mix had a monetary value of 619 million euros.

In 2013, the total imports from China to the EU amounted to 260.1 billion euros and total exports from the EU to China totaled 148.1 billion euros. The total amount of EU-China trade for 2013 was 436.3 billion euros. In 2013, food and live animals (0) imports from China to the EU had a monetary value of 4.2 billion euros and exports from the EU to China in this classification amounted to 3.6 billion euros. Beverages and tobacco (1) imports from China to the EU amounted to 140 million euros and exports from the EU to China in this classification totaled 1.3 billion. Crude materials, inedible except fuels (2) imports from China to the EU totaled 2.6 billion euros and exports from the EU to China in this classification amounted to 9.6 billion euros.

Also in 2013, mineral fuels, lubricants and related materials (3) imports from China to the EU had a monetary value of 217 million euros and exports from the EU to China in this classification totaled 2.0 billion euros. Animal and vegetable oils, fats and waxes (4) imports from China to the EU amounted to 72 million euros and exports from the EU to China in this classification had a monetary value of 498 million euros. Chemicals and related products (5) imports from China to the EU totaled 13.1 billion euros and exports from the EU to China in this classification amounted to 17.3 billion euros. Moreover in 2013, manufactured goods chiefly by material (6) imports from China to the EU had a monetary value of 35.1 billion euros and exports from the EU to China in this classification amounted to 14.0 billion euros. Machinery and transport equipment (7) imports from China to the EU totaled 139.2 billion euros and exports from the EU to China in this classification amounted to 85.4 billion euros.

Furthermore in 2013, miscellaneous and manufactured articles (8) imports from China to the EU had a monetary value of 84.3 billion and exports from the EU to China in this classification amounted to 12.1 billion. Commodities and transactions (9) imports from China to the EU totaled 558 million and exports from the EU to China in this classification had a monetary value of 1.3 billion euros. Other products imports from China to the EU amounted to 466 million euros and exports from the EU to China in this unclassified product mix had a monetary value of 763 million euros.

In 2014, the total imports from China to the EU amounted to 302.1 billion euros and total exports from the EU to China totaled 164.6 billion euros. The total amount of EU-China trade for 2014 was 466.7 billion euros. In 2014, food and live animals (0) imports from China to the EU had a monetary value of 4.2 billion euros and exports from the EU to China in this classification amounted to 4.3 billion euros. Beverages and tobacco (1) imports from China to the EU amounted to 171 million euros and exports from the EU to China in this classification totaled 1.3 billion. Crude materials, inedible except fuels (2) imports from China to the EU totaled 2.7 billion euros and exports from the EU to China in this classification amounted to 8.9 billion euros.

Also in 2014, mineral fuels, lubricants and related materials (3) imports from China to the EU had a monetary value of 182 million euros and exports from the EU to China in this classification totaled 2.1 billion euros. Animal and vegetable oils, fats and waxes (4) imports from China to the EU amounted to 75 million euros and exports from the EU to China in this classification had a monetary value of 186 million euros. Chemicals and related products (5) imports from China to the EU totaled 14.3 billion euros and exports from the EU to China in this classification amounted to 18.8 billion euros. Moreover in 2014, manufactured goods chiefly by material (6) imports from China to the EU had a monetary value of 40.3 billion euros and exports from the EU to China in this classification amounted to 13.9 billion euros. Machinery and transport equipment (7) imports from China to the EU totaled 146.5 billion and exports from the EU to China in this classification amounted to 95.8 billion euros. Furthermore in 2014, miscellaneous and manufactured articles (8) imports from China to the EU had a monetary value of 95.3 billion euros and exports from the EU to China in this classification amounted to 13.1 billion euros. Commodities and transactions (9) imports from China to the EU totaled 648 million euros and exports from the EU to China in this classification had a monetary value of 5.0 billion euros. Other products imports from China to the EU amounted to 627 million euros and exports from the EU to China in this unclassified product mix had a monetary value of 915 million euros.

The top five HS sections with product numbers for imports from China into the EU for 2012 were: machinery and appliances XVI with a market value of 139.1 billion euros; textiles and textile articles XI with a market value of 35.5 billion euros; miscellaneous manufactured articles XX with a market value of 25.6 billion euros; base metals and articles thereof XV with a market value of 17.7 billion euros and products of the chemical or allied industries VI with a market value of 11.9 billion. The top five HS sections with product numbers for imports from China into the EU for 2013 were: machinery and appliances XVI with a market value of 133.3 billion euros; textiles and textile articles XI with a market value of 34.4 billion euros; miscellaneous manufactured articles XX with a market value of 24.1 billion euros; base metals and articles thereof XV with a market value of 17.2 billion euros and products of the chemical or allied industries VI with a market value of 12.0 billion euros.

The top five HS sections with product numbers for imports from China into the EU for 2014 were: machinery and appliances XVI with a market value of 140.7 billion euros; textiles and textile articles XI with a market value of 37.0 billion euros; miscellaneous manufactured articles XX with a market value of 27.6 billion euros; base metals and articles thereof XV with a market value of 20.4 billion euros and products of the chemical or allied industries VI with a market value of 12.9 billion euros. The top five HS sections with product numbers for exports from the EU into China for 2012 were: machinery and appliances XVI with a market value of 48.5 billion euros; transport equipment XVII with a market value of 35.3 billion euros; products of the chemical or allied industries VI with a market value of 13.2 billion euros; base metals and articles thereof XV with a market value of 12.2 billion euros and optical and photographic instruments, XVIII with a market value of 8.0 billion.

The top five HS sections with product numbers for exports from the EU into China for 2013 were: machinery and appliances XVI with a market value of 48.9 billion euros; transport equipment XVII with a market value of 35.7 billion euros; products of the chemical or allied industries VI with a market value of 13.6 billion euros; base metals and articles thereof XV with a market value of 11.7 billion euros and optical and photographic instruments, XVIII with a market value of 8.6 billion. The top five HS sections with product numbers for exports from the EU into China for 2014 were: machinery and appliances XVI with a market value of 52.2 billion euros; transport equipment XVII with a market value of 43.2 billion euros; products of the chemical or allied industries VI with a market value of 14.7 billion euros; base metals and articles thereof XV with a market value of 10.9 billion euros and optical and photographic instruments, XVIII with a market value of 9.3 billion euros.

The EU top trading partners 2015–2016

In terms of imports into the European Union, the EU's top trading partners for 2015 were: China (1) with imports of 350.4 billion euros; USA (2) with imports of 248.9 billion euros; Russia (3) with imports of 135.5 billion euros; Switzerland (4) with imports of 102.3 billion euros; Norway (5) with imports of 74.2 billion euros; Turkey (6) with imports of 61.6 billion euros; Japan (7) with imports of 59.7 billion euros; South Korea (8) with imports of 42.3 billion euros and India (9) with imports of 39.4 billion euros. In terms of exports from the European Union, the EU's top trading partners for 2015 were: USA (1) with exports totaling 371.3 billion euros; China (2) with exports totaling 170.3 billion euros; Switzerland (3) with exports totaling 150.8 billion euros; Turkey (4) with exports totaling 79.1 billion euros; Russia (5) with exports totaling 73.9 billion euros; Japan (6) with exports totaling 56.5 billion euros; Norway (7) with exports totaling

48.8 billion euros; United Arab Emirates (8) with exports totaling 48.5 billion euros and South Korea (9) with exports totaling 47.8 billion euros.

The previously mentioned data on trade between the EU and China shows that China has a competitive advantage in manufactured products over the European Union and there's no one on the European Commission that would say otherwise. However, the European Union's problem with China is not based on the argument that China can manufacture certain products cheaper than the EU. The EU would like to reach an investment agreement with China that will benefit both the EU and China.

The current negotiations taking place between the EU and China with respect to the proposed EU-China Investment Treaty have been tense. Time and again, the EU has stressed in its talks with China that it wants a comprehensive EU-China investment agreement that will benefit both the EU and China by ensuring that the markets are open to investment in both directions. The EU takes the position that the agreement will also provide a simpler, secure predictable legal framework to investors over the long term. One of the EU's priorities in the negotiations is to remove the barriers for EU investors in the Chinese market.

All total, there have been ten rounds of EU-China bilateral investment treaty negotiations between the EU and China since 2013 when the proposition was announced by China's Premier Li Keqiang and the presidents of the European Council and the European Commission. Supposedly on August 28, 2016, China's legislature began its very first reading of the proposed draft amendment that would rewrite the four laws regarding foreign investment in China. As of this writing, there has been no response from the Chinese legislature. Apart from all the other obstacles involved in the EU-China negotiations, overcapacity in China's basic industries is also at the forefront of the EU's negotiating agenda. In "Elements for a New EU Strategy on China," published in June 2016 before the 18th EU-China Summit, the European Union advised China to create a more determined, quantifiable and transparent restructuring plan to decrease overcapacity (HRUFASP 2016). According to a recent press release from president of the European Commission Jean-Claude Juncker, China and the EU have formed a working group specifically to monitor China's steel export volume in a concerted effort to solve China's overcapacity issues. However, the Chinese government is confident that the working group will come to the conclusion that the Chinese authorities have nothing to do with the export process of steel and iron. Furthermore, the Chinese officials claim that this will be readily apparent after the group examines current production costs and operations of China's steel industry.

Chinese officials always respond either by denying that an overcapacity problem even exists or with the same kind of aforementioned rhetoric where they claim China's steel industry cut excess steel capacity by a specific number of tons, but for whatever reason, these cuts are inconsistent with China's steel production. Moreover, there are some officials in the Chinese government who will come right out and make the argument that there is no absolute overcapacity, but rather a structural capacity insufficiency.

References

Annual EU-China Summit 2016. http://ec.europa.eu/research/innovation-union/index_en.cfm.

European Commission (EC), "EU-China Relations," available at http://eeas.europa.eu/factsheets/news/eu-china_factsheet_en.htm, Brussels, June 22, 2016.

European Commission (EC), "European Union, Trade with China," Office of the Directorate-General for Trade, 2016.

High-Level Economic & Trade Dialogue, Brussels, October 24, 2013.

High Representative of the Union for Foreign Affairs and Security Policy (HRUFASP), "Elements for a New EU Strategy on China," Joint Communication to the European Parliament and the Council, European Commission, Brussels, June 30, 2016.

Institute of International Finance (IIF) website, Washington, DC, available at www.iif.com.

Part V
Conclusions

14 Conclusions

In June 2016, the EU launched a third case against China's restrictions on the export of raw materials essential for European industries. Following the successful legal actions in 2012 and 2014 on similar measures, this time the EU is focusing on restrictions concerning graphite, cobalt, lead, chromium, magnesia, talcum, tantalum, tin, antimony and indium. The EU legal action underscores the export restrictions China imposes on the raw minerals listed above for companies outside of China. The complaint makes the case that China imposes excessive export duties and very restrictive export quotas that limit access to these raw materials for foreign corporations. "The complaint further states that these measures have resulted in a distorted market that favors Chinese industries at the expense of EU corporations and EU consumers" (EC Press Release 2016).

This allegation is a direct violation of the general rules of the World Trade Organization (WTO) and it's also in direct violation of China's specific commitments upon its accession into the WTO. Inadvertently in this case, the first steps in a WTO dispute settlement between the European Union and China are coincidentally parallel with a similar complaint by the United States against China in the exact same time frame. The US filed its complaint against China on July 13, 2016 and the EU filed its complaint against China on July 19, 2016. Both allege the exact same WTO violations. The WTO has 60 days to produce a satisfactory solution for both the European Union and the United States. If not, the EU and the US can ask the WTO to establish an independent panel to evaluate and rule on the compatibility of China's self-imposed restrictions in accordance with the rules of the WTO. In the original US complaint, the US alleged issues over export restrictions on select raw materials used in industrial manufacturing: antimony, cobalt, copper, graphite, lead, magnesia, talc, tantalum and tin. These raw materials are used in the aerospace, automotive, electronics and chemical industries among others to a lesser degree.

The original US complaint also cites Chinese specifically cited export duties for the above-mentioned raw materials, but on July 19, 2016, the US further claimed that it was expanding the above raw materials list to include export duties on chromium in concert with export quotas on antimony, indium, magnesia, talc and tin. Coincidentally, the EU is alleging the exact same export restrictions on the exact same list of raw materials. The EU took the situation a step further when Brussels cited a 2013 document that listed the above-mentioned as critical raw materials whose value for industry and the environment have made them very important for the EU economy (ICTSD 2016). According to EU statistics, China is the world's largest producer of graphite. In terms of copper, China produces over 10 percent of the world's supply. At this point, the US and the EU will use the WTO as a conduit to consult with China in an effort to find a satisfactory solution within the 60-day bridge.

Within their original complaints, both the EU and the US have focused the terms associated with China's original accession into the WTO in 2001. Although the General Agreement on Tariffs and Trade (GATT) does not explicitly prevent WTO member-states from imposing export duties, China's accession protocol specifically requires it to remove all taxes and other charges applied to exports, unless they are specifically provided for in an annex to the protocol or are charges in conformity with the GATT provision on these conditions (GATT 1994). In its original July 13, 2016 complaint, the United States alleges that China has not eliminated export duties on these specific raw materials. Therefore, China is in direct violation of its WTO accession terms. Furthermore, the US makes the argument that these export duties which range anywhere from 5 percent to 20 percent *ad valorem* are applied and administered through various and assorted government instruments including China's domestic customs and trade laws. In its July 19, 2016 complaint, the US made the case that China's quantitative restrictions on these raw materials not only violate the terms of its WTO accession commitments on trading rights, but they're also in violation of Article XI:1 of the GATT 1994 which stipulates that WTO member-states cannot impose "prohibitions or restrictions other than duties, taxes or other charges whether made effective through quotas, import or export licenses or other measures" on any imports or exports (WTO 2016). In its follow-up complaint, the United States also cited GATT Article X:3 in conjunction with China's original WTO accession protocol. GATT Article X mainly deals with the publication and administration of trade regulations, which stipulates that all trade measures of member-states should be published and therefore transparent. The US follow-up complaint further argues that China's export policies relative to the stated raw materials were put in place "in a manner that is not uniform, impartial or reasonable".

On a similar note in its own complaint, the European Union also cited China's WTO accession commitments along with other WTO rules. For whatever reason as of this writing, the US consultation requests with the WTO and China are available to the general public, but the EU's requests were not available to the public, which is an indication that this is more of a clerical procedural issue than anything else. In its rough draft, the EU has also raised concerns about the Chinese administration and allocation of China's export quotas.

Michael Froman, the United States Trade Representative publicly stated that the alleged export duties are a direct attempt by China to "game the system". In so doing, this would give Chinese manufacturers a significant competitive advantage by making the raw materials much more expensive for downstream

US manufacturers that rely on China's WTO accession commitments. China's alleged export duties result in lower sales prices for domestic Chinese manufacturers. China's official response to the US' claim came from officials at China's Ministry of Commerce (MOFCOM) who are making the argument that China's export restrictions are part of overall measures to strengthen environmental protection in accordance with WTO rules. Furthermore, the same officials also claim that these restrictions are particularly beneficial due to "daily worsening pressure on resources and the environment" (Lawder 2016).

In previous similar disputes with China by the West, the WTO's Appellate Body ruled that Chinese export restrictions on raw materials and rare earths were not in accordance with its international trade obligations. Consequently, China was not permitted to invoke the "general exceptions" clause pursuant to Article XX of the GATT 1994 in order to justify its export duties breaching its WTO accession commitments. Article XX of GATT 1994 summarizes specific justifications that WTO member-states may employ specific measures that usually violate WTO global trade rules in order to respond to global public policy goals such as protecting specific natural resources that may have a limited duration in terms of supply. The Article further emphasizes that such actions must not be put in place as trade restrictions and these actions must not be arbitrary in terms of discrimination among WTO member-states.

The WTO disputes against China on February 1, 2012 and September 10, 2014 were filed by the United States and the European Union. Moreover, both dispute filings by the US and the EU were for the exact same violation: the United States and the European Union requested consultations with China under the dispute settlement system concerning China's restrictions on exports of various forms of rare earths, tungsten and molybdenum. The only difference between the two filings is that they were filed 32 months apart. Even after the WTO Appellate Body ruled against China in the 2014 dispute settlement case, two years later (July 26, 2016) and China continues to produce the exact same violations. This is a pattern and unfortunately it comes at the expense of US and EU manufacturing corporations. The real problem going forward is China's export duties. Export duties are a general or a product specific tax on goods or services that become payable to the host country (China) when the goods leave the country or when the services are delivered to non-residents.

China's export restriction policies artificially drive up Chinese export prices which in turn increase world prices resulting in serious disadvantages for foreign corporations. These restrictions also act as a catalyst for lower domestic prices for raw materials in China. However, the domestic prices are artificial in nature which result in increased domestic supplies giving China's domestic manufacturers a distinct competitive advantage. Some economists claim that this unfair advantage puts pressure on foreign corporations to relocate their manufacturing operations along with their respective technologies to China. Cheaper manufacturing costs tend to be the incentive for a foreign corporation to relocate its operations to China. Time and again, China has attempted to make the argument that its export restrictions on rare earths are part of its overall conservation policy, "but the WTO's position has traditionally been that export restrictions cannot be imposed to conserve exhaustible natural resources if the domestic production or consumption of the same raw materials is not also restricted for the same purpose" (WTO 2016).

In 2012 and 2014, China lost a number of WTO disputes to the West mainly the European Union and the United States for the same repeatable violations. At this point, the EU and the US have joined together in a major lawsuit against Beijing for unfairly favoring domestic Chinese corporations. On July 13, 2016, the Western Bloc filed yet another complaint with the WTO seeking formal consultations with China on export restrictions on the 11 raw materials previously mentioned at the beginning of this chapter. Consultations are the first step in WTO dispute settlement procedures and by now China should have the so-called WTO consultations memorized.

In order to match the complaint made by the European Union, the United States expanded its WTO challenge that was originally filed a week before against China's export duties on nine raw materials to match the EU complaint. The Office of the US Trade Representative added chromium and indium to its list of materials that was previously filed. Moreover, the US trade office stated that the United States will challenge Chinese export duties on all 11 raw materials which now include: antimony, chromium, cobalt, copper, graphite, indium, lead, magnesia, talc, tantalum and tin. Furthermore, the US trade office also announced that it will challenge China's quota restrictions on the following five raw materials: antimony, indium, magnesia, talc and tin. In a separate press release, the European Union announced that the 11 previously mentioned minerals and metals are among the top 20 raw materials that are extremely critical for the overall EU economy. It should also be noted that China is the world's largest producer of most of the top 20 raw materials, which are imperative for the EU economy. In their respective complaints filed with the WTO, the US and the EU also made the case that China's export duties on all of the previously mentioned raw materials range anywhere between 5 and 20 percent.

In a joint conference call with US Trade Representative Michael Froman and EU Trade Commissioner Cecilia Malmström to the WTO and China's Ministry of Commerce, the two trade officials made it abundantly clear that China's export restrictions enable to China to unfairly influence global market prices for aforementioned raw materials. Trade Commissioner Malmström made the case that China's export restrictions are very damaging to the long-term competitiveness of EU industries. Malmström further stated that the EU would "not sit on our hands seeing our producers and consumer being hit by unfair trade practices and we hope that this joint US-EU action will motivate China to reconsider its current policy" (Blenkinsop and Martina 2016).

A big part of the reasoning behind the US-EU push to get China into the WTO was the need for a steady stream of raw materials and this is exactly what China agreed to in its WTO accession. The EU and the US can buy these raw materials elsewhere on a piecemeal basis, but it was their understanding that a steady stream of all 11 raw materials from one country would be much more efficient and economical. Unfortunately, China's Ministry of Commerce rejected the US-EU challenge. The Ministry claimed that its export restrictions were in accordance with WTO rules, which are intended to protect the environment. Later in a statement posted online, the Ministry said, "China regrets the US-EU requests for consultations and will appropriately handle it according to WTO dispute resolution procedures" (Blenkinsop and Martina 2016).

The EU-US export restrictions challenge comes at a time when both countries have to make a decision about China's market economy status which would lower trade barriers for Chinese imports across all sectors. In the conference call, both Malmström and Froman claimed that the WTO export restrictions challenge was a completely separate issue from any upcoming discussions about granting China market economy status. Obviously both trade officials feel that China is skirting the issue by using the environment as an excuse. China's export restrictions distort the markets and favor Chinese corporations at the direct expense of EU and US corporations and their customers. Beijing could very easily initiate other measures in its so-called effort to support the environment that would not affect and distort global trade and at the same time it would comply with its WTO accession protocol.

According to the EU-US complaints, total China exports in these raw materials are valued at $1.3 billion per year of which the EU and the US receive roughly one-sixth each. The complaints further state that removal of the export restrictions could increase Chinese raw material exports to the EU and the US by roughly 9 percent and that percentage could be even greater if other measures were removed. The formal consultations between the EU and China will be in conjunction with consultations between the US and China. Unfortunately, the EU-US challenges on raw material export restrictions are nothing new.

It should also be noted that these latest challenges by the US and the EU follow a string of successful legal actions in terms of China's export restrictions on rare earths and other raw materials including bauxite and zinc. The formal consultations take place over a 60-day period and if for any reason there is no resolution, the United States and the European Union can petition the WTO to create a dispute settlement panel. The reader should also remember that rulings from the World Trade Organization can take up to three years. However in the past, China has always complied with WTO rulings concerning its exports on rare earths and/or raw materials.

Trade deficits and the manufacturing sectors of the West

The trade deficits of the West (US and EU) with China are mainly derived from the import of manufactured goods. In the United States in the 1990s, manufacturing jobs held steady at about 17 million jobs, but between 2000 and 2014 manufacturing payroll employment declined by 5.7 million jobs. In the European Union within the same time frame, over 3.8 million jobs have been lost in the EU manufacturing sector. These are very large declines and some of it may be the result of the Great Recession, but this is six years after the fact.

In terms of the US economy, the last achieved balance of trade with China in the manufacturing sector occurred in the early 1980s. The US trade deficit with China in the mid-2000s in its manufacturing sector was equal in value to approximately 50 percent of the manufacturing value added. Today that number hovers around 40 percent and it's approximately the same for the EU. However, both the EU and the US have trade surpluses with China in their respective service sectors. Moreover, the US trade deficit with China in its manufacturing sector alone was roughly $460 billion in 2012 which was greater than the total current account balance of $440 billion in 2012. In all fairness in terms of its trading relationship with China, the EU has more of a balanced relationship. The EU runs a good-sized trade deficit with China, but it's around half of the US trade deficit with China (2015 180 billion euros).

According to Pierce and Schott (2012), statistics argue that the US rising trade deficit with China is the primary reason for the steep decline in manufacturing value and employment following 2000. They link the steep reduction in US manufacturing employment to the permanent normalization of US-China trade relations, which took place in 2000. Furthermore, they also claim that "industries where the threat of tariff hikes experience greater employment loss due to suppressed job creation, exaggerated job destruction and a substitution away from low-skill workers" (quoted from the abstract). Moreover, Autor, Dorn, and Hanson (2013) calculate that between 1991 and 2007, Chinese competition resulted in a 25 percent decline in US manufacturing employment during that specific time frame and they also estimated that during the 2000s Chinese competition in the US markets resulted in a 40 percent decline in US manufacturing employment.

It's also noteworthy to remember that there were some US officials especially in the Congressional Budget Office who tried to make the argument that a growing trade deficit was associated with a growing domestic economy and they isolated the period from 1985 to 2007. They further claimed that the growing trade deficit with China in that time frame was more of a response to changing domestic economic conditions that pushed aggregate demand beyond United States' production capacity. The so-called excess domestic demand was then satisfied by importing more and exporting less. After the 2008 financial crisis, this particular mindset disappeared and today (2016) no one in the US government mentions this ludicrous economic scenario.

In terms of Chinese trade to the West, there are basically two components involved in China's trade: normal trade and processing trade. Processing trade takes place when goods are shipped into China duty-free for assembly by Chinese manufacturers and once the assembly is completed; the manufactured product is re-exported. China's processing trade amounts to roughly half of China's total export trade and it's an integral part of a large production network of companies operating in Asia. These are firms who have been exporting manufactured goods to the West for years, but now they've moved their assembly work to China.

According to Wayne Morrison (2012) of the US Congressional Research Service, exports to the West from the Pacific Rim countries including China account for a constant share of manufactured exports to the West since 1990, but China's share of that trade went from 8 percent in 1990 to 55 percent in 2012. Exports from these countries go all over the globe, but the EU and the US receive the largest percentage of these manufactured exports. In terms of the US manufacturing sector, China's processing trade and the evolution of the Asian production network are of particular importance to the understanding of the shrinking US manufacturing sector. Many American corporations have changed their corporate structure away from manufacturing and their primary focus is on research, product design and marketing. For example, the US trade deficit in the computer and electronics industry has gone from 14 percent of the gross industry output in 1998 to roughly 60 percent in 2015 and that particular industry accounted for approximately 40 percent of all imports from China in 2015. A very good case in point is Apple Inc. It has no large production facilities in the United States. Apple prefers to contract that out to companies in Taiwan and South Korea like Foxconn who assemble the products in China.

At the same time, Apple controls the key elements in the value chain. Consequently, Apple is able to extract the lion's share of the profit. Unfortunately for the US manufacturing sector, similar networks have become commonplace in the electronics and computer industries. Conversely, a company like the giant toy-maker Mattel has closed virtually all of its manufacturing facilities in the United States but continues to operate large manufacturing facilities throughout Asia.

Most of the analyses on US trade deficits with China focus on the value of the import side of the accounts. However, when the value of imports is measured against the recipient country's GDP, the magnitude of the US trade deficit with China is approximately the same as the European Union, but the EU exports more goods and services to China than the United States so it receives a much bigger offset. In 2015, the imports from China to the US amounted to 2.7 percent of GDP and for the EU that number was 2.6 percent. The differences in trade are on the export side of the accounts. In 2015, US exports to China totaled 0.8 percent of US GDP, but the EU exports to China came in at 1.2 percent of EU GDP. In terms of the size of the US GDP as well as the size of the EU GDP, that is a very big difference resulting in a very large trade imbalance for the United States.

Exports from China to the United States were 20 percent of China's total exports in 2015, which is approximately the same as the US share of global GDP, but that number was down from 29 percent in 2001, the year of China's accession into the WTO. China runs a large trade surplus with the United States, but a big percentage of its exports to the US come from its processing sector where the margins are much smaller and the value-added benefits to China are limited.

In a 2013 study written by Lawrence Edwards and Robert Lawrence of the Peterson Institute of International Economics, the two researchers found that the trade deficit with China has a large jobs component and if that trade deficit were eliminated, US manufacturing employment would increase by approximately 25 percent. They further assert that during the boom years, Americans in general were not that concerned with trade deficits, but going forward from an employment perspective, the United States cannot afford ongoing trade deficits of 3 percent and more of GDP.

The future of EU and US manufacturing

From an historical perspective on average, manufacturing employment declines by roughly 0.3 percent per year. In the US, the Congressional Budget Office estimates the civilian employment will total 159 million workers by 2023. Consequently, if the historical trend in manufacturing employment continues to decline by 0.3 percent per year, the implied level of manufacturing employment would drop to 10 million workers which is roughly 2 million jobs less than manufacturing employment today. This is only an estimate and it's not written in stone. There continues to be dialogue from US manufacturers about the different avenues that can be taken domestically to re-shore the US manufacturing sector through better technologies and efficient market forces in order to return manufacturing jobs back to the United States. Within that context, the US needs to also develop the right set of government policies to help facilitate this effort. The manufacturing sector of any economy is far too important to the economic health of a nation. For all intents and purposes, it is the lifeblood of the country. Both the EU and the US have very large populations and it's completely foolhardy to think that a combined population of over 830 million people can survive as a service economy as if combined they were both the size of Switzerland. Manufacturing is what separated the West from the rest of the world through our respective industrial revolutions. With the exception of Japan, Asia never had an industrial revolution until the end of World War II. Moreover, in World War II, the US manufacturing sector had as much to do with winning the war as the US military.

Manufacturing has characteristics that make it very significant. First, the Americans as well as the Europeans live and work in a global economy. By that very nature, they exchange products they produce for products they consume and they wish to do so without an ongoing decline in the products they produce for trade. Manufacturers represent a very large portion of tradable products, but more importantly, these same manufacturers represent industries where the West could potentially run a trade surplus. With that said, the West needs to reverse its current mindset and become a better exporter and that means more exports of manufactured products.

Historically, manufacturing was, for the most part, identified and supported by ongoing research and development. In fact, it represented the launching pad for new and better technologies, but with more specialized biotechnologies and high-technologies found in the pharmaceutical and consumer electronics industries, the balance of the manufacturing sectors in the West have become increasingly separate from research and development. In the United States, of the manufacturing industries that still remain, most have become increasingly capital intensive, but in spite of that plus increasing labor costs, the US can still prosper in basic manufacturing industries such as export machinery production where it does very well.

The manufacturing industries found in the West still provide good jobs with good wages for workers who may lack advanced education. In the US since 2000, the loss of over six million manufacturing jobs has had devastating repercussions on millions of families, and scores of cities and communities at large, but this is not an answer; it's an excuse. The US as well as the EU needs to demonstrate a resolve and do a better job in exports. With that said, there's a lot of controversy about how this should be accomplished. Some economists in the West want the EU-US manufacturing sectors to receive special treatment such as special tax rates and/or special subsidies and then there's the other side who does not agree with any kind of special treatment. If Chinese competition played by the same rules, no special treatment would be acceptable, but unfortunately, that's not the case. In order to offset inexpensive labor found in the emerging economies, the future of manufacturing in the West will be determined by the advancements of technologies in manufacturing. These technologies will influence the structure of manufacturing in future years.

Emerging technologies in manufacturing include: industrial robots and automation; advanced design; additive manufacturing; internet direct interconnections between sensor and machines; materials science and biotechnology; and energy productions. With these new technologies, the West will be able to increase output and efficiency in a number of manufacturing sectors, but exactly how many new manufacturing jobs would be created is an unknown. With that said, it's a foregone conclusion that the West will be able to compete head-on with China. Consequently, new jobs in Western manufacturing will definitely increase, but the exact amount of jobs that will be created can't be determined until everything is in place. Within the last five years, tremendous advances have been made in the technology of industrial robots and automation. An industrial robot can perform tasks today that could only have been done by humans yesterday. Early in the evolution of the industrial robot was the issue of dexterity, but technology has overcome that problem. While industrial robots have been used in several industries for heavy lifting, dangerous operations, and repetitive, precise movements (painting and welding in the auto industry for example), they have been priced well out of range for more regular "human" tasks. That could change soon with the development of robots that have the capability to work safely alongside humans. For example, a robot priced at $20,000 can now sense a human in the path of its arms and stop movement. It can be "reprogrammed" for new tasks by a human operator who physically manipulates its arms to move, bend, lift or drop in the desired way.

However, robotics is a double-edged sword for manufacturing employment. In terms of output, advanced robotics could reduce manufacturing employment up to a specific level, but simultaneously, the labor cost differential enjoyed by China's manufacturers would be greatly reduced or even eliminated. This would give the West a distinct competitive advantage and it would re-shore manufacturing production to the United States and the European Union.

Additive manufacturing is technically a range of technologies, but at this point in its evolution, its most important contribution is three-dimensional printing.

The functionality of 3D printing enables the technologist to create objects from very small particles. Primarily, 3D printing thus far has been used to create prototypes or objects that otherwise would be impossible to build using a machine tool. In the future, these companies will use the web to sell designs instead of selling products directly. At that point, the customer can either contract out the 3D printing services or if they have the know-how, they can print it themselves. Additive manufacturing will cut development time and costs, increase flexibility, eliminate tooling costs, reduce material waste and simplify production runs.

In terms of advanced design, this is a function of computer power and software advances which enhances a company's ability to produce digital prototypes and perform much more initial testing before the creation of a physical prototype. According to the McKinsey Global Institute, this specific technology will result in a reduction in research and development costs as well as a reduction in time to the market by 20 to 50 percent (McKinsey Global Institute 2017).

Internet direct interconnections is a fascinating technology that underscores how low-cost sensors can lead to any number of direct interconnections over the internet among different machines and different locations. This technology enhances the connection of machines in an effort to improve monitoring of production processes from a remote location. This allows the operators to give instructions to one set of equipment based on the activity taking place in another set of equipment. Based on sensor readings from all the network equipment, the process designer will be able to create a system that will automatically make the necessary adjustments while applying the optimum algorithms for increased efficiency. In terms of materials science and biotechnology, these particular technologies have experienced major breakthroughs over the last few years, but because these technologies are highly sophisticated, the timeline for actual utilization is not clear. The application of technology to carbon nanotubes and graphene facilitates the creation of high-performance transistors and durable, light composite cells. In terms of biotechnology, nano-enabled technologies pave the way for a more rapid diagnosis of illnesses by health care professionals. Moreover, nano-enabled technologies will also detect contamination particles; provide glucose monitoring as well as many other biotechnical applications. However, biotechnology advances require an inordinate time horizon and enormous investment before they assimilate into the economic mainstream.

The trade deficit with China and the macroeconomic factors

From a macroeconomic perspective, trade deficits with China put US and EU manufacturers at distinct disadvantage. Trade deficits distort capital flows and the foreign exchange value of the euro and the US dollar. The following statement is more germane to the US than the EU. In the US particularly, the economy has undergone an unusual confluence of economic factors. These economic factors encouraged American consumption. Consequently, the American people have, for the most part, consumed well beyond their means, financed by an ongoing sale of assets to foreigners in exchange for an unusually large net inflow of imports from

China. Since 2013, American consumption expenditures and investments in residential homes have made up a smaller share of US GDP resulting in a 5 percent gap in US GDP. Unfortunately since then, the United States has made very little progress in filling the previously mentioned 5 percent gap in GDP accounting for the anemic GDP growth rates for the last three years. From a historical perspective, the US trade deficits with China have been supported by an anemic savings rate compared to domestic foreign investment. Moreover, subpar levels of national savings have pushed up the value of the US dollar exchange rate resulting in more expensive US exports making US products less competitive in the Chinese marketplace. In terms of the ridiculously high US trade deficit with China, it should also be noted that in any trading partnership low exports are equally problematic as high imports. In an ideal trading partnership, imports would equal exports, but there's rarely a perfect trading partnership in today's global economy.

Wall Street constantly complains that the US corporate tax rate is too high and supposedly that reduces the US competitive advantage on the global stage. Nominally, the US corporate tax rate is 39 percent and from a numerical perspective, that would be one of the highest in the world. However, research shows that the average US corporation pays roughly 12 percent in federal income taxes after deductions which is competitive with most other advanced economies. With that said in January 2018, President Trump and the US Congress approved a tax bill that lowers the maximum corporate nominal tax rate from 35 percent to 20 percent, but the unfortunately the bill's intricate details have not been released as of this writing.

Western exports are vital for the long-term prospects of the EU and US economies, but stimulating Western exports will not be that easy to achieve. There has to be an internal driving force that will rebuild the domestic supply chain and remove the incentives that domestic corporations have by relocating their manufacturing facilities abroad especially in the United States.

Trade deficits equal a reduction in GDP

At the risk of being redundant as discussed in Chapter 1, Gross Domestic Product (GDP) is the total monetary value of all finished goods and services produced within a country's borders in a specific time period. Normally, GDP is calculated on an annual basis. It includes all of the private and public consumption, government outlays, investments and *exports minus imports* or GDP = C + G + I + (exports-imports) negative exports equal a trade deficit. Consequently, when the US and the EU import finished goods that result in trade deficits, they are in essence exporting part of their national economies (*trade deficits = a reduction in GDP*). However, this would not be the case if China's imports to the US and the EU equaled the US and EU exports to China, but the above equation underscores the reality of the one-sided, asymmetrical trading relationships between China and the United States and China and the European Union.

Reviving manufacturing in the West especially in the United States will require eliminating trade deficits with China. Since China's entrée into the

World Trade Organization in 2001 millions of jobs have been shipped overseas. The West needs to put an end to China's currency manipulation, which is the primary driver of China's massive export business. Ending China's currency manipulation would be an extremely effective tool to support job creation in the manufacturing sector. According to the Economic Policy Institute, currency manipulation can be eliminated simply by making it illegal for China and other currency manipulators to purchase US Treasury bills, notes or bonds (Scott et al. 2013, 20). The EPI estimates that ending currency manipulation would lead to the creation of 2.2 million to 4.7 million new jobs in the United States alone.

Both the United States and the European Union need to devise some sort of penalty program in concert with the WTO or even without the WTO for China's blatant dumping violations. Whatever the WTO is doing in these cases is just not working. In March 2016, Tata Steel of India announced that it plans to sell its steel manufacturing plant in the United Kingdom putting 15,000 jobs in jeopardy. The UK steel industry cited unfair competition from China as the primary driver behind the proposed sale. Steel imports into the UK from the rest of the EU cost on average 897 euros per ton, but steel imports from China into the UK are priced 583 euros per ton. That is an unusually large price differential amounting to roughly 35 percent less than the EU steel manufacturers' price. The margins are not that great in the steel industry and the only way Chinese steel can sell at that price is through government subsidies. China subsidizes its steel industry and then it turns around and dumps Chinese steel in the West.

Figure 14.1 shows that UK steel production since China was allowed entry into the WTO in 2001 has been decimated, resulting in the loss of thousands of

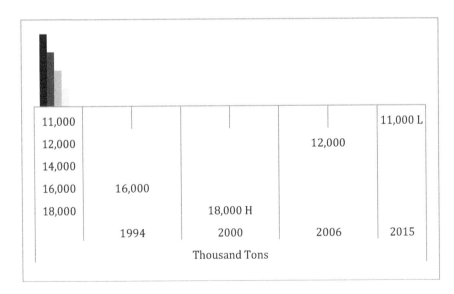

Figure 14.1 Steel production in the United Kingdom, 1994–2015

Source: Author with data from ISSB

good UK jobs. UK steel production went from a high of over 18 million metric tons in 2000 to somewhere around 11 million tons in 2015 or a decline of almost 40 percent. That's not what the global economy is supposed to be about. When a country's imports exceed its exports, the country incurs a trade deficit. The overall combined trade deficit of the EU and the US with China was nearly $550 billion in 2015. When China sells its products in the West, it receives either US dollars or euros resulting in free cash flow for the Chinese government.

In the trading relationship between the China and the United States, the above statement applies more to China's ownership position of US Treasury debt instruments (bills, bonds and notes) and large purchases of US real estate. In the past, Chinese companies have purchased equities (stocks) in various US publicly traded corporations, but rarely are they able to take a majority position.

However in the EU-China trading relationship, Chinese government companies have been very successful in their purchase of large chemical and high-tech companies. There are two very recent examples: the purchase of the agrichemical giant Syngenta Corporation of Switzerland for a staggering $37 billion. Syngenta is the largest deal ever put together by a Chinese government corporation. Another very good case in point is German high-tech company Aixtron Corporation. On September 16, 2016 the *New York Times* ran an interesting article on Aixtron. Apparently after one of Aixtron's customers canceled a very large order which unfortunately caused the shares of Aixtron to drop precipitously. Within a few months with Aixtron stock still in decline, a Chinese investor agreed to buy the company (Mozur and Ewing 2016). Financial filings and public statements indicate a web of relationships between the customer that canceled the order, the buyer and the Chinese government. The connections underscore the opaque lines between the Chinese companies who are participating in the very aggressive purchases of EU high-tech firms and the Chinese government's long-term industrial policy. According to Sebastian Heilmann president of the Mercator Institute for China Studies, a think-tank based in Berlin, "The Aixtron case makes it very clear: it is not a regular investment at work here. Instead, we see governmental-program capital working behind the scenes" (Mozur and Ewing 2016). The Chinese authorities have made their intentions abundantly clear: they intend to use state funds to acquire technological capabilities overseas and relocate them to mainland China. A series of Chinese high-tech company purchases over the past three years have underscored that strategy.

Unfortunately for the West, this has become the norm rather than the exception. This author could write another 300 pages highlighting similar Chinese acquisitions, but the point of this book is to underscore the inordinate trade deficits that China runs with the West. Trade deficits equal free cash flow and free cash flow helps China's aggressive acquisition strategy. Whenever the EU and the US purchase Chinese imports that result in trade deficits, the European Union and the United States are actually exporting their national economies: *exports minus imports* or GDP = C + G + I + (exports-imports) negative exports equal a trade deficit and trade deficits equal a reduction in a nation's GDP.

References

Autor, David H., David Dorn and Gordon H. Hanson, "The China Syndrome: Local Labor Market Effects of Import Competition in the United States," *American Economic Review* 103 (6): 2121–2168, 2013.

Blenkinsop, Philip and Michael Martina, "EU launches WTO challenge to Chinese raw material duties," Reuters, July 19, 2016, available at www.reuters.com/article/us-china-eu-trade/eu-launches-wto-challenge-to-chinese-raw-material-duties-idUSKCN0ZZ11Q.

Edwards, Lawrence and Robert Z. Lawrence, "Rising Tide: Is Growth in the Emerging Economies Good for the United States?" Peterson Institute of International Economics, Washington, DC, February 2013.

European Commission (EC Press Release), "EU takes legal action against export restrictions on Chinese raw materials," Brussels, July 19, 2016.

General Agreement on Tariffs and Trade (GATT), Article XI:1, 1994.

International Centre for Trade and Sustainable Development (ICTSD), "US, EU file WTO Challenges Against Chinese Export Restrictions on Raw Materials," Geneva, Switzerland, July 21, 2016.

Lawder, David, "U.S. challenges China raw material export duties in trade enforcement push," *Reuters*, July 13, 2016, available at www.reuters.com/article/us-usa-china-trade-idUSKCN0ZT1LT.

McKinsey Global Institute, "Jobs Lost, Jobs Gained: Workforce Transitions in a Time of Automation," December 2017, available at www.mckinsey.com/~/media/McKinsey/Global%20Themes/Future%20of%20Organizations/What%20the%20future%20of%20work%20will%20mean%20for%20jobs%20skills%20and%20wages/MGI-Jobs-Lost-Jobs-Gained-Report-December-6-2017.ashx.

Morrison, Wayne M., "China-US Trade Issues," US Congressional Research Service report, RL33536, 2012.

Mozur, Paul and Jack Ewing, "Rush of Chinese Investment in Europe's High-Tech Firms Is Raising Eyebrows," *The New York Times*, September 16, 2016.

Pierce, Justin R. and Peter K. Schott, "The Surprisingly Swift Decline of US Manufacturing Employment," NBER Working Paper 18655, December 2012.

Scott, Robert E., Helene Jorgensen and Doug Hall, "Reducing US trade deficits will generate a manufacturing-based recovery," Economic Policy Institute, Washington DC, February 7, 2013.

US WTO, Follow-up Settlement Complaint of July 19 against China (WTO), 2016.

US-China Policy Foundation, "US-EU Trade Complaints against China with WTO," Washington, DC, July 26, 2016.

World Trade Organization (WTO), "Disciplines on Export Prohibitions and Restrictions," Key GATT Disciplines, Geneva, Switzerland, 2016.

Index

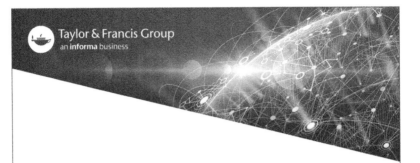

For Product Safety Concerns and Information please contact our EU
representative GPSR@taylorandfrancis.com Taylor & Francis Verlag GmbH,
Kaufingerstraße 24, 80331 München, Germany

Printed and bound by CPI Group (UK) Ltd, Croydon, CR0 4YY
01/05/2025
01858434-0002